Return to an Address of the Honourable the House
dated 14th July 2004
for the

Review of Intelligence
on
Weapons of Mass Destruction

Report of a Committee
of
Privy Counsellors

Chairman:

The Rt Hon The Lord Butler of Brockwell KG GCB CVO

Ordered by the House of Commons to be printed 14th July 2004

HC 898   London: The Stationery Office   **£22.50**

© **Parliamentary copyright 2004**

The text of this Report may be reproduced in whole or in part free of charge in any format or media without requiring specific permission. This is subject to the material not being used in a derogatory manner or in a misleading context. Where the material is being republished or copied to others, the source of the material must be identified and the copyright status acknowledged.

Any enquiries relating to the copyright in this report should be addressed to Her Majesty's Stationery Office, Licensing Division, St Clements House, 2–16 Colegate, Norwich NR3 1BQ. Fax: 01603 723000 or e-mail: licensing@cabinet-office.x.gsi.gov.uk

MEMBERS OF THE COMMITTEE

The Rt Hon The Lord Butler of Brockwell KG GCB CVO
    (Chairman)

The Rt Hon Sir John Chilcot GCB

The Rt Hon Field Marshal The Lord Inge KG GCB DL

The Rt Hon Michael Mates MP

The Rt Hon Ann Taylor MP

TABLE OF CONTENTS

TERMINOLOGY

1. We use the following terms in this report:

Munitions	Projectiles, bombs, warheads or dispensing systems.
Weapons	Munitions and their delivery systems.
Chemical/BiologicalAgent	The non-explosive fill for chemical/biological munitions.
Programme	Means that people and resources are being allocated under a management structure for either the research and development of a WMD capability or the production of munitions. It does not necessarily mean that WMD munitions have been produced, as only when the capability has been developed can weapons be produced.
Capability	Means that a country has the technical knowledge, the production facilities and the necessary raw materials to:

    a) produce chemical and/or biological agents and weaponise them; and/or

    b) produce a nuclear device and weaponise it.

Having a WMD capability means that chemical, biological and/or nuclear munitions could be produced if required. It does not mean that they have been produced.

GLOSSARY

Ababil-100	Solid-propellant short-range (c. 150 km) Iraqi ballistic missile
Aflatoxin	A fungal toxin used as a BW agent
Al Abbas	900-km-range Iraqi development of the Scud B (see below) missile; not taken beyond the development stage
Al Hussein	650-km-range Iraqi development of the Scud B (see below) missile; several hundreds were fired during the Iran/Iraq war and the first Gulf war
Al Qaida	Literally translated, it means 'The Base'. Founded by Usama bin Laden, it is now a loose network of Islamist extremist groups
Al Samoud	Iraqi development of Soviet SA2 surface-to-air missile as a short-range surface-to-surface missile (150 km range, but Al Samoud 2 was being developed to attain significantly longer range)
Ansar al Islam	Literally, Supporters of Islam: an Islamist extremist group based in northern Iraq
Anthrax	A disease caused by the bacterium Bacillus Anthracis: used as a BW agent
BCW	See CBW
Botulinum toxin	A toxin used as a BW agent
BTWC	Biological and Toxin Weapons Convention
BW	Biological Weapons (or Biological Warfare)
CB	Chemical and Biological
CBR	Chemical, Biological and Radiological
CBRN	Chemical, Biological, Radiological and Nuclear
CBW	Chemical and Biological Weapons (sometimes "BCW")
Centrifuge	A piece of equipment containing a rotating device used to separate solid or liquid particles of different densities by spinning them at high speed in a tube.

	Many hundreds or thousands of centrifuges are connected in 'cascades' to enrich uranium
CIA	Central Intelligence Agency, US
CIG	Current Intelligence Group, UK
Clostridium perfringens	A BW agent
CPC	Counter Proliferation Committee (UK)
CPIC	Counter Proliferation Implementation Committee (UK)
CW	Chemical Weapons (or Chemical Warfare)
CWC	Chemical Weapons Convention
Cyclosarin	A CW nerve agent (sometimes referred to as GF)
Desert Fox	US and UK air campaign against key military targets in Iraq in December 1998, shortly after UNSCOM inspectors had left the country
Desert Storm	The military operation undertaken by the allied coalition in 1991 to liberate Kuwait from Iraqi occupation
DIA	Defense Intelligence Agency, US
DIS	Defence Intelligence Staff, UK
DTI	Department of Trade and Industry (UK)
ECO	Export Control Organisation, part of the Department of Trade and Industry (UK)
EMIS	Electromagnetic Isotope Separation (one of several routes to uranium enrichment)
EU3	Informal name for the UK, France and Germany in the context of their 2003 demarche to Iran
FCO	Foreign and Commonwealth Office, UK
Fissile material	Material (eg, uranium) capable of undergoing nuclear fission
G7 (or G8)	The group of seven (or eight, including Russia) leading industrial countries: the US, UK, Canada, France, Germany, Italy and Japan
GCHQ	Government Communications Headquarters, UK
Ghauri	Pakistani medium-range ballistic missile (1,300 km range) based on North Korean No-Dong technology)
HEU	Highly Enriched Uranium
Humint	Human intelligence
IAEA	International Atomic Energy Agency
ICBM	Inter-continental Ballistic Missile
Imint	Imagery intelligence
ISC	Intelligence and Security Committee, UK
ISG	Iraq Survey Group
JIC	Joint Intelligence Committee, UK
Jihad	The usual translation 'holy war' is misleading; 'exertion' or 'struggle' is more accurate: "A general injunction to strive in the way of God" (Albert Hourani: A History of the Arab Peoples, Faber and Faber, 1992)
JTAC	Joint Terrorism Analysis Centre, UK
KAZ	Kurdish Autonomous Zone (of Iraq)

Key Judgement	In a paper produced by the JIC (see above), one of several judgements extracted from the main body of the text and listed on the front page of the paper
Liaison	Term used to indicate a collaborative relationship between the intelligence services of different countries, as in 'liaison service' or 'liaison source'
Masint	Measurement and Signature Intelligence
MOD	Ministry of Defence, UK
MTCR	Missile Technology Control Regime
NBC	Nuclear, Biological and Chemical (often used in describing defensive equipment, as in "NBC suits")
No-Dong	Western name for the North Korean Medium-Range Ballistic Missile (MRBM), with a range of 1,300 km
NPT	The Treaty on the Non-Proliferation of Nuclear Weapons
OPCW	Organisation for the Prohibition of Chemical Weapons
OSE	Official Committee on Strategic Exports (UK)
P5	The five permanent members of the UN Security Council (the US, the Russian Federation, China, the UK and France)
R&D	Research and Development
REU	Restricted Enforcement Unit, part of the Department of Trade and Industry, UK
Ricin	A toxin used as a BW agent, derived from the castor bean
Sarin	A CW nerve agent (sometimes referred to as GB)
SCR	Security Council Resolution (of the United Nations)
Scud	Western designation for a family of short-range ballistic missiles, originally of Soviet design but subsequently adapted and upgraded by North Korea
Scud B	Short-range ballistic missile, with a range of 300 km
Scud C	Short-range ballistic missile, with a range of 500 km
Scud D	Short-range ballistic missile, with a range of 800 km
Shahab	Family of Iranian ballistic missiles (literally, meteor or shooting star)
Sigint	Signals intelligence
SIS	Secret Intelligence Service, UK
Soman	A CW nerve agent
SSO	Special Security Organisation, Iraq
Tabun	A CW nerve agent (sometimes referred to as GA)
Taopo Dong 1	Western name for a North Korean medium-range ballistic missile, with a range of 2,000 + km
Taepo-Dong 2	Western name for a North Korean inter-continental ballistic missile (ICBM) with an assessed range of up to 15,000 km (under development)
UBL	Usama bin Laden (see also Al Qaida)
UF6	Uranium hexafluoride (a compound used in the process of enriching uranium which may be used for a nuclear bomb)
UN	United Nations
UNMOVIC	United Nations Monitoring, Verification and Inspection Commission, set up by UNSCR 1284 of 17 December 1999 as a replacement for UNSCOM (see

	below)
UNSCOM	United Nations Special Commission, set up by UNSCR 687 of 3 April 1991 "to carry out immediate on-site inspection of Iraq's biological, chemical and missile capabilities"
UNSCR	United Nations Security Council Resolution
VX	One of the most toxic CW nerve agents
WMD	Weapons of Mass Destruction (see Introduction for a description of the difficulties of using this term)
Yellowcake	Uranium ore concentrate

INTRODUCTION

OUR TERMS OF REFERENCE

1.   On 3 February 2004, the Foreign and Commonwealth Secretary announced in the House of Commons:

> *My right hon. Friend the Prime Minister has decided to establish a committee to review intelligence on weapons of mass destruction. This committee will be composed of Privy Counsellors. It will have the following terms of reference: to investigate the intelligence coverage available in respect of WMD programmes in countries of concern and on the global trade in WMD, taking into account what is now known about these programmes; as part of this work, to investigate the accuracy of intelligence on Iraqi WMD up to March 2003, and to examine any discrepancies between the intelligence gathered, evaluated and used by the Government before the conflict, and between that intelligence and what has been discovered by the Iraq survey group since the end of the conflict; and to make recommendations to the Prime Minister for the future on the gathering, evaluation and use of intelligence on WMD, in the light of the difficulties of operating in countries of concern.*

> *My right hon. Friend the Prime Minister has asked the committee to report before the summer recess. The committee will follow the precedent in terms of procedures of the Franks committee. It will have access to all intelligence reports and assessments and other relevant Government papers, and will be able to call witnesses to give oral evidence in private. The committee will work closely with the US inquiry and the Iraq survey group.*

> *The committee will submit its final conclusions to my right hon. Friend the Prime Minister in a form for publication, along with any classified recommendations and material. The Government will, of course, co-operate fully with the committee.*

OUR WORK

2.   The Committee met for the first time on Thursday 5 February and four of us were sworn in as Members of the Privy Council on Wednesday 11 February. Mrs Taylor was already a Privy Counsellor.

3.   In view of the very tight timetable for our Review, it was essential to make a rapid start. We are therefore especially grateful for the speed with which the Security and Intelligence Co-ordinator, Sir David Omand, supplied us with accommodation and an excellent team of support staff in the Cabinet Office. We are also grateful to the Intelligence and Security Committee and their staff for enabling us to use the Committee's room in the Cabinet Office for our hearings, and for the forbearance and co-operation they extended to us.

4.   Since 5 February, we have met 36 times. We have visited Washington, where we met the co-Chairs of the President's Commission on the Intelligence Capabilities of the United States Regarding Weapons of Mass Destruction, Governor Charles S. Robb and Judge

Laurence H. Silberman and members of their Commission; General Brent Scowcroft, Chairman of the President's Foreign Intelligence Advisory Board; and senior members of the Administration and the Congress, including Senator Pat Roberts and Senator John Rockefeller, Chairman and Ranking Member of the Senate Intelligence Committee; Congressman Porter Goss and Congresswoman Jane Harman, Chairman and Ranking Member of the House Intelligence Committee; Dr Condoleezza Rice, National Security Adviser; General Colin Powell and Mr Richard Armitage, State Department; Mr George Tenet, Director, and staff of the Central Intelligence Agency; and Vice Admiral Lowell Jacoby and staff of the Defense Intelligence Agency. We are grateful to Sir David Manning, HM Ambassador at Washington, and his team for making the arrangements for this visit. We also visited Baghdad and we express our particular appreciation to Major General Keith Dayton, Brigadier Graeme Morrison and Mr Charles Duelfer and their staffs for being willing to receive and brief us at a very difficult and busy time, and to staff of the Ministry of Defence and the Royal Air Force for organising the visit and arranging our safe journey there and back. We also had useful discussions with representatives of a number of other countries.

5.   The tight timetable for our Report has caused some difficulties for us. The main one is that the Iraq Survey Group, with whose findings our terms of reference require us to compare the intelligence received by the British Government, have not yet produced any publicly available report. They produced an interim report in September 2003 and a Status Report in March 2004. We have had access to these. We were very grateful to General Dayton and Mr Duelfer for also briefing us about their progress. We have undertaken not to anticipate their findings but, on the basis of the information they gave us, we believe that our conclusions are not inconsistent with what they have discovered so far. The much longer timetable given to the US Presidential Commission has had the result that, while we had useful initial discussions with them, we have not been able to fulfil the Foreign Secretary's statement that we would work closely with them.

6.   On the other hand, we were greatly helped by the evidence given to Lord Hutton's Inquiry, by the report of the House of Commons Foreign Affairs Committee on "*The Decision to go to War in Iraq*" (HC 813) and above all by the report of the Intelligence and Security Committee entitled "*Iraqi Weapons of Mass Destruction—Intelligence and Assessments*" (Cm 5972). We should like to express particular thanks to the Intelligence and Security Committee for giving us access to the classified evidence which underlay their report. This saved us much spadework.

7.   It may be asked what further we could add by going over such heavily traversed ground. One answer is perhaps that, as in the search for weapons in Iraq, one can never do too much digging. But others are that we have had the considerable advantage of the further passage of time which has allowed us to consider the evidence that has emerged since the war on Iraqi nuclear, biological, chemical and ballistic missile programmes and the results of post-war validation by the Secret Intelligence Service of their relevant human intelligence sources. More importantly, we have had much wider access to the Government's intelligence and policy papers. Even so, we do not pretend that ours can be the last word on every aspect of the issues we cover.

OUR APPROACH

8. Our approach has been to start with the intelligence assessments of the Joint Intelligence Committee (JIC) and then to get from the intelligence agencies a full list of the underlying intelligence, both accepted and rejected, which was available to inform those assessments. We have then compared that intelligence with the JIC's assessments and considered whether it appears to have been properly evaluated. In the other direction, we, like the Franks Committee, have obtained from Government departments those policy papers which their Permanent Secretaries have certified as containing all the material relevant to our Review, to allow us to establish the use which was made of the intelligence. Finally, where outcomes are known, we have compared the prior intelligence and the assessments made of it with those outcomes.

9. We have received 68 written submissions from members of the public and have taken oral evidence from 47 witnesses, some of whom gave evidence more than once. Except where witnesses asked for their identity to be protected, we list our witnesses at Annex A.

10. We have focussed on the intelligence available to the British Government and the use made of it by our Government. Although that inevitably has led us to areas of UK/US co-operation, we have deliberately not commented in this Report on the actions of the US intelligence agencies, ground that is being covered by the Presidential Commission.

11. We have been conscious of the Foreign Secretary's statement that our report should be submitted to the Prime Minister in a form fit for publication. We have also been conscious of the overriding need not to prejudice continuing or future intelligence operations or to endanger sources and have shaped our report accordingly. We are confident that what is published here gives Parliament and the public a fair representation of our conclusions and views.

12. In furtherance of this, we have exceptionally included in our Report extensive quotations from assessments of the Joint Intelligence Committee. We have ensured that in all cases our quoting these will not have implications for national security. The Government has made clear that our action in doing so will not be accepted as a precedent for putting those assessments into the public domain in the future.

DEFINITIONS AND USAGE

13. The Intelligence and Security Committee started their report with definitions of the terminology they used. We repeat their definitions in our 'Terminology and Glossary' and have tried to follow them. But we believe that there are problems with the term 'weapons of mass destruction' and with the shorthand 'chemical and biological weapons' (CBW) and 'chemical, biological, radiological and nuclear' (CBRN) weapons.

'WMD'

14. There is a considerable and long-standing academic debate about the proper interpretation of the phrase 'weapons of mass destruction'. We have some sympathy with the view that, whatever its origin, the phrase and its accompanying abbreviation is now

used so variously as to confuse rather than enlighten readers. Rather than adding to this debate and this confusion, we have in our Report chosen to spell out what we mean in full. In cases where it is used by others, most notably in JIC assessments, we have had in mind in interpreting those assessments the definition at paragraphs 8 and 9 of United Nations Security Council Resolution 687 of 3 April 1991, which defined the systems which Iraq was required to abandon:

> *Nuclear weapons or nuclear-weapons-usable material or any sub-systems or components or any research, development, support or manufacturing facilities relating to* [nuclear weapons].

> *Chemical and biological weapons and all stocks of agents and all related sub-systems and components and all research, development, support and manufacturing facilities.*

> *Ballistic missiles with a range greater than 150 kilometres and related major parts, and repair and production facilities.*

'CBW'

15.   The abbreviation 'CBW' (often expressed as 'BCW') occurs regularly both in intelligence reporting and in related analysis and assessment. At a certain level of generality, 'CBW' can be a useful term to embody the concept of chemical and biological warfare. Thus, for example, in the face of a 'CBW' attack the tempo of military operations is significantly impeded by soldiers having to don cumbersome clothing whether facing chemical weapons or biological weapons. But for detailed technical intelligence assessments, the distinction is important. Chemical weapons and biological weapons involve very different technologies, and are usually developed by different people at different facilities. Delivery requirements, and hence doctrine, training, storage and handling, are different, as are the troops involved. One of our witnesses said that any report in which the terms 'CW' and 'BW' were interwoven or combined through the use of the single acronym 'CBW':

> *. . . always makes me slightly suspicious.*

16.   We agree that such use is confusing. Thus, although the term may have some value in some contexts, we have sought to avoid it altogether, although it does feature in some of the extracts from JIC assessments which we have taken in to our Report.

'CBRN'

17.   As well as nuclear, biological and chemical weapons, JIC assessments and intelligence reports, especially those on terrorism, also consider radiological weapons, which employ conventional, typically high-explosive means to distribute radioactive material. As a result, our Report includes where relevant the phrase 'chemical, biological, radiological and nuclear weapons', and its abbreviation 'CBRN'.

OUR THANKS

18.   Notwithstanding our short timetable, a massive amount of paper has been relevant to our Review. Sorting out and providing these papers has been a huge task for the intelligence

agencies and departments at a time when they have also had their vital day-to-day work to undertake. As noted above, we have relied on certificates from Permanent Secretaries that all papers relevant to our interpretation of our terms of reference have been supplied to us. While we have on some occasions been critical of the slow rate at which these have been supplied and by the coverage of those originally offered, we are now reasonably confident that we have obtained the papers relevant to our work. We are grateful to all those who have had the task of identifying them and providing them. We have also been greatly helped by the fact that the intelligence community co-operated in providing a co-ordinated service so that we did not receive separate streams of papers from each agency which we would subsequently have had to relate to each other.

19.   We would like to express our particular thanks to Mr Daniel Thornton and his team who were our link with the Government for the supply of intelligence material, departmental papers and other evidence. The documents they provided and the other evidence have of course all come to rest on the desks of our Secretary, Mr Bruce Mann, and his team, Mr Michael Ryder, Mr Peter Freeman, Mr Nigel Pearce, Mr Patrick Sprunt, Ms Carol Hook, Ms Judith Freeman and an additional team of transcribers. They have been indefatigable and we cannot find words to praise their skill and commitment adequately. We thank and commend them above all.

CHAPTER 1

THE NATURE AND USE OF INTELLIGENCE

"Much of the intelligence that we receive in war is contradictory, even more of it is plain wrong, and most of it is fairly dubious. What one can require of an officer, under these circumstances, is a certain degree of discrimination, which can only be gained from knowledge of men and affairs and from good judgement. The law of probability must be his guide."

[Clausewitz, On War, Vol I, Bk I, Ch VI]

1.1 INTRODUCTION

20. In view of the subject matter of our Review, and of what we have found in the course of it, we think that it may be helpful to the general reader to describe the nature of intelligence; the successive processes of validation, analysis and assessment which are necessary for using it properly; its limitations; and the risks which nevertheless remain.

21. Governmental decisions and actions, at home and abroad, are based on many types of information. Most is openly available or compiled, much is published, and some is consciously provided by individuals, organisations or other governments in confidence. A great deal of such information may be accurate, or accurate enough in its own terms. But equally much is at best uninformed, while some is positively intended to mislead. To supplement their knowledge in areas of concern where information is for one reason or another inadequate, governments turn to secret sources. Information acquired against the wishes and (generally) without the knowledge of its originators or possessors is processed by collation with other material, validation, analysis and assessment and finally disseminated as 'intelligence'. To emphasise the point, the term 'secret intelligence' is often used (as, for instance, enshrined in the title of the Secret Intelligence Service), but in this Review we shall use the simple word 'intelligence'.

22. The protective security barriers which intelligence collectors have to penetrate are usually formidable, and particularly so in the case of programmes which are the subject of this Review. Nuclear, biological and chemical programmes are amongst the ultimate state secrets, controlled by layers of security protection going beyond those applied to conventional weapons. Those of the greatest concern to governments are usually embedded within a strong apparatus of state control. Few of the many people who are necessarily involved in such programmes have a view of more than their own immediate working environment, and very few have comprehensive knowledge of the arrangements for the control, storage, release and use of the resulting weapons. At every stage from initial research and development to deployed forces, nuclear, biological and chemical weapons and their delivery systems are treated as being of particular sensitivity, often to the extent of the establishment of special command and control arrangements in parallel with, but separate from, normal state or military channels.

1.2 COLLECTION

23. The UK has three intelligence and security agencies ('the agencies') responsible for the collection of intelligence[1]: the Secret Intelligence Service (SIS), the Security Service and Government Communications Headquarters (GCHQ). The Defence Intelligence Staff (DIS), part of the Ministry of Defence (MOD), also manages some intelligence collection, notably that of imagery, but its main function is all-source analysis and assessment and the production of collated results, primarily to serve MOD requirements.

24. There is a panoply of collection techniques to acquire intelligence which do not exactly correspond to inter-departmental organisational boundaries. The three main ones are signals intelligence (the product of interception, generally abbreviated to 'Sigint'); information from human sources such as classical espionage agents (which is conveniently described, by extension from the previous category, as 'Humint'): and photography, or more generally imagery ('Imint'). Signals intelligence and human intelligence are of widespread and general applicability. They can produce intelligence on any topic (for example, the intentions, plans, negotiations, activities and achievements of people involved in the development, acquisition, deployment and use of unconventional weapons), since ultimately the data they acquire stem from the human beings involved. Imagery is more confined to the study of objects (buildings, aircraft, roads, topography), though modern techniques have extended its abilities (for example, infra-red photography can in some circumstances show where an object was, even though it may have gone by the time the photograph is taken).

25. There are also other, more specialised intelligence techniques, some of particular relevance to this Review[2]. For example, the development of nuclear explosives inevitably involves highly-radioactive materials, radiation from which may be detected. Leakage from facilities concerned with the development of chemical and biological agents, and deposits in testing areas, can provide characteristic indicators. Missile testing may involve the generation of considerable heat, which can be detected, and missiles may be tracked by radar.

26. In the case of the weapons covered by this Review, there is additionally another category of information which is frequently mentioned by the Joint Intelligence Committee (JIC) in its assessments. International inspection and enforcement bodies have been established, on a permanent basis (e.g. the International Atomic Energy Agency), or temporary basis (e.g. the United Nations Special Commission), to ensure compliance with international treaties or United Nations resolutions[3]. Some of the findings and reports of these bodies are published on an official basis to United Nations members and are of considerable importance. In Iraq between 1991 and 1998, in many ways they surpassed anything that national intelligence agencies could do, but since their work is carried out on behalf of the United Nations it can hardly be considered 'intelligence' by the definitions to which we are working. Data obtained in the course of work on export licensing can also be important.

---

[1] They also have other functions not relevant here.

[2] The term 'Masint' (Measurement and Signature Intelligence) has been coined for at least some of these techniques, though they lack the unifying themes which characterise Sigint and Humint.

[3] Such bodies often also have a wider operational role in the implementation of treaties or Security Council Resolutions.

1.3 VALIDATION

27.   Intelligence, though it may not differ in type or, often, reliability from other forms of information used by governments, operates in a field of particular difficulty. By definition the data it is trying to provide have been deliberately concealed. Before the actual content of an intelligence report can be considered, the validity of the process which has led to its production must be confirmed. For imagery and signals intelligence this is not usually an issue, although even here the danger of deception must be considered. But for human intelligence the validation process is vital.

28.   Human intelligence reports are usually available only at second-hand (for example, when the original informant talks to a case officer[4] who interprets – often literally – his words to construct an intelligence report), and maybe third- or fourth-hand (the original informant talks to a friend, who more or less indirectly talks to a case officer). Documentary or other physical evidence is often more compelling than the best oral report[5], and has the advantage of being more accessible to specialised examination, but is usually more difficult to acquire. Conventional oral reporting can be difficult enough if all in the chain understand the subject under discussion. When the topic is unfamiliar to one or more of the people involved, as can be the case when details of (say) nuclear weapons design are at issue, there is always the chance of misunderstanding. There is in such cases a considerable load on the case officer to be familiar with the subject-matter and sufficiently expert in explaining it. It need only be added that often those involved in providing intelligence may for one reason or another have deliberately mis-represented (or at least concealed) their true identities, their country of origin or their employment to their interlocutors[6], to show how great is the need for careful evaluation of the validity of any information which eventually arrives.

29.   The validation of a reporting chain requires both care and time, and can generally only be conducted by the agency responsible for collection. The process is informed by the operational side of the agency, but must include a separate auditing element, which can consider cases objectively and quite apart from their apparent intelligence value. Has the informant been properly quoted, all the way along the chain? Does he have credible access to the facts he claims to know? Does he have the right knowledge to understand what he claims to be reporting? Could he be under opposition control, or be being fed information? Is he fabricating? Can the *bona fides,* activities, movements or locations attributed to those involved in acquiring or transmitting a report be checked? Do we understand the motivations of those involved, their private agenda[7], and hence the way in which their reports may be influenced by a desire to please or impress? How powerful is a wish for (in particular) financial reward? What, if any, distorting effect might such factors exert? Is there – at any stage – a deliberate intention to deceive? Generally speaking, the extent and depth of validation required will depend on the

---

[4] An official responsible for handling and receiving reports from human intelligence sources.

[5] Such evidence is no more immune to deception or fabrication than is oral testimony, though of a different type.

[6] The ultimate in such deceptions is the classic 'double agent', who is infiltrated into an espionage network to discover, misinform, expose or pervert it.

[7] We have been assured that SIS has for half a century been viscerally wary of emigre organisations. We return to this below in the context of Iraq.

counter-intelligence sophistication of the target, although the complexity of the operational situation will affect the possibility of confusion, misrepresentation or deception.

1.4 ANALYSIS

30.   The validation process will often have involved consideration of the coherence and consistency of intelligence being provided by an informant, as one of the ways in which that source's reliability can be tested. But at the next stage, analysis, the factual material inside the intelligence report is examined in its own right. This stage may not be required where the material is self-explanatory, or it may be readily subsumed into assessment and conducted by the same people. But much intelligence is fragmentary or specialised and needs at least a conscious analytic stage. Analysis assembles individual intelligence reports into meaningful strands, whether weapons programmes, military operations or diplomatic policies. Intelligence reports take on meaning as they are put into context. Analysis is also the process required to convert complex technical evidence into descriptions of real-world objects or events.

31.   The department which receives the largest quantity of intelligence is the MOD, where analysis is carried out by the DIS[8] whose reports are distributed not only internally in the MOD but also to other relevant departments. Although the DIS is a component of the MOD, funded from the Defence Account and managed in accordance with defence priorities, it is a vital component of and contributor to the national intelligence machinery, and its priorities and work programme are linked with those of the Cabinet Office.

32.   Analysis can be conducted only by people expert in the subject matter – a severe limitation when the topic is as specialised as biological warfare or uranium enrichment, or the internal dynamics of terrorist cells or networks. A special danger here can be the failure to recognise just what particular expertise is required. The British intelligence assessment of the German V-2 rocket during the Second World War was hindered by the involvement of the main British rocket expert, who opined that the object visible on test-stands could not possibly be a rocket. The unrecognised problem was that he was an expert only on *solid powder* rockets, of the type that the UK had developed for short-range artillery. It was true that a solid firework of the size of the V-2 was, with the technology then available, impracticable. But the Germans had developed *liquid-propellant* rocket engines, with the combustion chamber fed by powerful turbo-pumps. On that subject, there were no British experts.

1.5 ASSESSMENT

33.   Assessment may be conducted separately from analysis or as an almost parallel process in the mind of the analyst. Intelligence reports often do not immediately fit into an established pattern, or extend a picture in the expected way. Assessment has to make choices, but in so doing runs the risk of selection that reinforces earlier conclusions. The risk is that uneven standards of proof may be applied; reports that fit the previous model

---

[8] The DIS also has other management and intelligence collection responsibilities.

are readily accepted, while contrary reports have to reach a higher threshold. This is not only perfectly understandable, it is the way perception normally operates. But in the intelligence world in which data are scanty, may be deliberately intended to confuse and may sometimes be more inadequate than can be appreciated, normal rules do not apply.

34. In the UK, assessment is usually explicitly described as 'all-source'. Given the imperfections of intelligence, it is vital that every scrap of evidence be examined, from the most secret sources through confidential diplomatic reports to openly published data. Intelligence cannot be checked too often. Corroboration is always important but seldom simple, particularly in the case of intelligence on 'hard targets'[9] such as nuclear, biological or chemical weapons programmes or proliferation networks. The simple fact of having apparently coincident reports from multiple types of intelligence sources is not in itself enough. Although reports from different sources may say the same thing, they may not necessarily *confirm* one another. Is a human intelligence report that a factory has been put into operation confirmed by imagery showing trucks moving around it? Or are both merely based on the same thing – observation of physical external activity? Reporting of different but mutually consistent activities can be complementary. This can build up knowledge to produce a picture which is more than the simple sum of the parts. But it may be false, if there is no link between the pieces other than the attractiveness of the resulting picture. Complementary information is not necessarily confirmatory information.

35. Multiple sources may conflict, and common sense has to be used in evaluation. A dozen captured soldiers may have provided mutually consistent and supportive reports about the availability of chemical weapons to their neighbouring battalion. But if these were flatly contradicted by a single report from a senior member of that battalion, which should be believed?

36. It is incorrect to say, as some commentators have done, that 'single source' intelligence is always suspect. A single photograph showing missiles on launchers, supporting a division deployed in the field, trumps any number of agent reports that missiles are not part of a division's order of battle. During the Second World War, innumerable Allied command decisions were taken on the basis of intelligence reports from a single type of source (signals intelligence, providing decrypts of high-level German and Japanese military plans and orders), and quite often (e.g. re-routing convoys in the middle of the Atlantic) important decisions had to be taken on the basis of a single report. As before, common sense and experience are the key.

37. Assessment must always be aware that there may be a deeper level of reality at which apparently independent sources have a common origin. Multiple sources may have been marshalled in a deception campaign, as the Allies did in Operation Fortitude before D-Day to mislead the German High Command about the location of the landings. Although deception on so grand a scale is rare, the chance of being deceived is in inverse proportion to the number of independent sources – which, for 'hard targets', are few.

---

[9] In a sense, almost all intelligence is conducted against 'hard targets'. If the information were readily available, it would not be necessary to call on intelligence resources to acquire it. But within the hierarchy of intelligence activities it is inevitable, given the protection afforded to nuclear, biological and chemical weapons programmes, that they are among the hardest targets.

38. Many of the manifestations of nuclear, biological or chemical weapons programmes can have innocuous, or at least non-proscribed, explanations – the 'dual-use' problem. Nuclear developments can be for peaceful purposes. Technologies for the production of chemical and biological agents seldom diverge from those employed in normal civilian chemical or bio-chemical industries. And, in the case of missile development, some procurement and development activities may be permissible.

39. Thus, the recipients of intelligence have normally to make decisions on the basis of the balance of probabilities. That requires, first, the most effective deployment of all possible sources and, secondly, the most objective assessment possible, as unaffected as may be by motives and pressures which may distort judgement.

40. In the UK, central intelligence assessment is the responsibility of the Assessments Staff. This comprises some 30 senior and middle-ranking officials on secondment from other departments, within the Cabinet Office, together with secretarial and administrative support.

1.6 THE JOINT INTELLIGENCE COMMITTEE

41. The agencies and the DIS are brought together with important policy departments in the JIC[10]. The JIC was established in 1936 as a sub-committee of the Committee of Imperial Defence. During the Second World War, it comprised the heads of the agencies and the three Services' Directors of Intelligence, under the chairmanship of a senior member of the Foreign Office and was joined by other relevant departments such as the Ministry of Economic Warfare, responsible for the Special Operations Executive.

42. The JIC has evolved since 1945. It became part of the Cabinet Office rather than of the Chiefs of Staff organisation in 1957. To the original membership of the JIC (intelligence producers, with users from MOD and the FCO) were added the Intelligence Co-ordinator when that post was established in 1968, the Treasury (1968), the Department of Trade and Industry (1997) and the Home Office (2000). Other departments attend when papers of relevance to them are taken. Representatives of the Australian, Canadian and United States intelligence communities also attend as appropriate. In 1993, the post of Chairman of the JIC and that of the Head of the Cabinet Office's Defence and Overseas Secretariat[11] were combined, the two posts remaining so until 1999. From 1992 to 2002, the chairmanship was combined with the post of Intelligence Co-ordinator. A new post of Security and Intelligence Co-ordinator was created in 2002, taking on the responsibilities of the previous Intelligence Co-ordinator together with wider responsibilities in the field of counter-terrorism and crisis management. The holder became a member of the JIC.

---

[10] For a fuller description see *National Intelligence Machinery*, HMSO 2001, which puts the JIC into context within the structures of Parliamentary and Cabinet government.
[11] From 1984 to the end of 1993 the Chairman of the JIC was also the Prime Minister's Foreign Policy Adviser. This title was revived in September 2001 and assumed by the Head of the Defence and Overseas Secretariat.

43. The JIC's main function[12], on which its regular weekly meetings are centred, is to provide:

Ministers and senior officials with co-ordinated intelligence assessments on a range of issues of immediate and long-term importance to national interests, primarily in the fields of security, defence and foreign affairs.

The Assessments Staff are central to this role, and the Chief of the Assessments Staff is a member of the JIC in his own right. With the assistance of other departments, the Assessments Staff draft the JIC assessments, which are usually debated at Current Intelligence Groups (CIGs) including experts in the subject before being submitted to the JIC. The JIC can itself ask the Assessments Staff to draft an assessment, but the process is usually triggered by a request from a policy department. The forward programme of assessments to be produced is issued three times a year, but is revised and, when necessary, overridden by matters of more immediate concern. The JIC thus brings together in regular meetings the most senior people responsible for intelligence collection, for intelligence assessment and for the use of intelligence in the main departments for which it is collected, in order to construct and issue assessments on the subjects of greatest current concern. The process is robust, and the assessments that result are respected and used at all levels of government.

44. Intelligence is disseminated at various levels and in different forms. The agencies send reports direct to users in departments and military commands; these reports are used by civil and military officials in their daily business, and some of them are selected and brought to Ministers' attention. The JIC's co-ordinated intelligence assessments, formally agreed at their weekly meetings, are sent to Ministers and senior officials. In addition the JIC produces Intelligence Updates and Immediate Assessments whenever required, which are sent to a standard distribution throughout government.

45. A feature of JIC assessments is that they contain single statements of position; unlike the practice in the US, there are no minority reports or noted dissents. When the intelligence is unclear or otherwise inadequate and the JIC at the end of its debate is still uncertain, it may report alternative interpretations of the facts before it such as they are; but in such cases all the membership agrees that the interpretations they are proposing are viable alternatives. The JIC does not (and this is borne out by our examination of several hundred JIC assessments in the course of our Review) characterise such alternatives as championed by individual members who disagree with colleagues' points of view. While the JIC has at times been criticised for its choice of language and the subtlety of the linguistic nuances and caveats it applies[13], it has responded that when the intelligence is ambiguous it should not be artificially simplified.

46. In the sometimes lengthy line that leads to the production of the JIC's output, all the components of the system – from collection through analysis and assessment to a well-briefed and educated readership – must function successfully. Problems can arise if the

---

[12] The JIC also has other responsibilities, for the establishment of intelligence collection priorities and monitoring of agency performance.

[13] We have been told that some readers believe that important distinctions are intended between such phrases as "intelligence indicates . . .", "intelligence demonstrates . . ." and "intelligence shows . . .", or between "we assess that . . .", "we judge that . . ." and "we believe that . . .". We have also been told that there is in reality no established glossary, and that drafters and JIC members actually employ their natural language.

JIC has to make bricks without (enough) straw. Collection agencies may produce too little intelligence, or too much intelligence about the wrong subjects, or the right intelligence but too late to be of value. Although assessments generated under such circumstances may have proper caveats, with attention drawn to important gaps in knowledge and with the dubious steps in an argument clearly identified, they may reach misleading conclusions. Or – which is equally destructive of their purpose – even if they are correct they may be mistrusted. In either case, the reputation of the JIC product is at risk, and the Committee has on occasion refused to issue drafted papers which it has felt are not sufficiently supported by new intelligence or add nothing to the information already publicly available.

1.7 THE LIMITATIONS OF INTELLIGENCE

47. Intelligence merely provides techniques for improving the basis of knowledge. As with other techniques, it can be a dangerous tool if its limitations are not recognised by those who seek to use it.

48. The intelligence processes described above (validation, analysis, assessment) are designed to transform the raw material of intelligence so that it can be assimilated in the same way as other information provided to decision-makers at all levels of government. Validation should remove information which is unreliable (including reporting which has been deliberately inserted to mislead). Analysis should assemble fragmentary intelligence into coherent meaningful accounts. Assessment should put intelligence into a sensible real-world context and identify how it can affect policy-making. But there are limitations, some inherent and some practical on the scope of intelligence, which have to be recognised by its ultimate recipients if it is to be used wisely.

49. The most important limitation on intelligence is its incompleteness. Much ingenuity and effort is spent on making secret information difficult to acquire and hard to analyse. Although the intelligence process may overcome such barriers, intelligence seldom acquires the full story. In fact, it is often, when first acquired, sporadic and patchy, and even after analysis may still be at best inferential.

50. The very way that intelligence is presented can contribute to this misperception. The necessary protective security procedures with which intelligence is handled can reinforce a mystique of omniscience. Intelligence is not only – like many other sources – incomplete, it can be incomplete in undetectable ways. There is always pressure, at the assessment stage if not before, to create an internally consistent and intellectually satisfying picture. When intelligence becomes the dominant, or even the only, source of government information, it can become very difficult for the assessment process to establish a context and to recognise that there may be gaps in that picture.

51. A hidden limitation of intelligence is its inability to transform a mystery into a secret. In principle, intelligence can be expected to uncover secrets. The enemy's order of battle may not be known, but it is knowable. The enemy's intentions may not be known, but they too are knowable. But mysteries are essentially unknowable: what a leader truly believes, or what his reaction would be in certain circumstances, cannot be known, but can only be

judged. JIC judgements have to cover both secrets and mysteries. Judgement must still be informed by the best available information, which often means a contribution from intelligence. But it cannot import certainty.

52. These limitations are best offset by ensuring that the ultimate users of intelligence, the decision-makers at all levels, properly understand its strengths and limitations and have the opportunity to acquire experience in handling it. It is not easy to do this while preserving the security of sensitive sources and methods. But unless intelligence is properly handled at this final stage, all preceding effort and expenditure is wasted.

1.8 RISKS TO GOOD ASSESSMENT

53. It is a well-known phenomenon within intelligence communities that memory of past failures can cause over-estimation next time around. It is equally possible to be misled by past success. For 45 years of Cold War, the intelligence community's major task was to assess the intentions and capabilities of the Soviet Union and its satellite states[14]. As the details which had been sought became more accessible, first through *glasnost'* and explicit exchanges of data under international agreements and then fairly readily through open sources after the dissolution of the Soviet empire, most of the intelligence community's conclusions were vindicated – at least in the areas in which it had spent the largest part of its efforts, the Soviet bloc's military equipment, capabilities and order of battle.

54. But it is risky to transfer one model to cases where that model will only partially apply. Against dictatorships, dependent upon personal or tribal loyalties and insensitive to international politics, an approach that worked well for a highly-structured, relatively cohesive state target is not necessarily applicable even though many aspects of the work may appear to be identical. The targets which the UK intelligence community needs to study most carefully today are those that structurally and culturally look least like the Government and society it serves. We return to this when we consider terrorism, at Chapter 3.

55. Risks in intelligence assessment will arise if this limitation is not readily recognised. There may be no choice but to apply the same intelligence processes, methods and resources to one target as were developed for and applied to others. But it is important to recognise that the resulting intelligence may need to be analysed and assessed in different ways.

56. A further risk is that of 'mirror-imaging' – the belief that can permeate some intelligence analysts that the practices and values of their own cultures are universal. The more diffuse range of security challenges of the 21st century means that it will not be possible to accumulate the breadth and depth of understanding which intelligence collectors, analysts and users built up over the years about the single subject of the Soviet Union. But the more alien the target, the more important is the ability of intelligence analysts to appreciate that their own assumptions do not necessarily apply everywhere. The motives

---

[14] The intelligence community did, of course, have many other tasks during this period ranging from the consequences of the withdrawal from empire through the many facets of the conflicts and confrontations in the Middle East to the Falklands War.

and methods of non-state organisations built on a special interest (whether criminal, religious or political) can be particularly hard for members of a stable society to assess.

57.   There is also the risk of 'group think' – the development of a 'prevailing wisdom'. Well-developed imagination at all stages of the intelligence process is required to overcome preconceptions. There is a case for encouraging it by providing for structured challenge, with established methods and procedures, often described as a 'Devil's advocate' or a 'red teaming' approach. This may also assist in countering another danger: when problems are many and diverse, on any one of them the number of experts can be dangerously small, and individual, possibly idiosyncratic, views may pass unchallenged.

58.   One final point should be mentioned here, to which we return in our Conclusions. The assessment process must be informed by an understanding of policy-makers' requirements for information, but must avoid being so captured by policy objectives that it reports the world as policy-makers would wish it to be rather than as it is. The JIC is part (and an important part) of the UK's governmental machinery or it is nothing; but to have any value its product must be objective. The JIC has always been very conscious of this.

1.9 THE USE OF INTELLIGENCE

59.   In addition to the use of intelligence to inform government policy, which we describe in Chapters 2 and 3, there are important applications in the enforcement of compliance with national law or international treaties and other obligations, in warning of untoward events, in the support of military and law enforcement operations, and in long-term planning for future national security capabilities. The British Government's machinery for the areas covered by our Review is described at Chapter 4.

CHAPTER 2

COUNTRIES OF CONCERN OTHER THAN IRAQ AND GLOBAL TRADE

2.1 INTRODUCTION

60.   Our terms of reference require us:

> *To investigate the intelligence coverage available on WMD programmes of countries of concern and on global trade in WMD, taking into account what is now known about these programmes.*

61.   We do so in this Chapter. This has allowed us to form an overall judgement of the UK's performance in obtaining intelligence on the nuclear, biological, chemical and ballistic missile programmes of a wide range of states and on sources of proliferation, whether by states or by trading networks. Given its significance for the activities of some states, we open this Chapter with the AQ Khan network.

62.   Many of these countries remain of concern. Sensitive intelligence operations and diplomatic activity are continuing. So the information we include in this Report must necessarily be limited. But in some cases declarations by the countries concerned, and statements by the International Atomic Energy Agency (IAEA) and other bodies about the results of their activities, have made it possible to judge the work of the intelligence agencies against what is now known. (Indeed, the extent and accuracy of the knowledge gained by the intelligence agencies were in some cases significant factors in persuading the states concerned to abandon their covert programmes.) Although our Review has gone more broadly, we have deliberately chosen to report only on those cases where information about the extent of states' programmes or of illicit trading activity is now publicly available, so that comparison can be made with the judgements in prior intelligence assessments without damage to continuing operations.

63.   We draw out broad Conclusions at the end of this Chapter.

2.2 AQ KHAN

INTRODUCTION

64.   AQ Khan directed Pakistan's nuclear programme for 25 years and is known as the 'father of the Pakistani nuclear bomb'. After studying in Europe, Khan worked for a company involved with the construction of an enrichment facility in the Netherlands. In 1976, he obtained Dutch and German designs for uranium centrifuges and took them to Pakistan. Based on these designs, Khan built a uranium enrichment facility at Khan Research Laboratories, where he successfully produced enough highly enriched uranium for Pakistan to test its first nuclear device in 1998. Khan subsequently exploited the supply network he developed to support the Pakistani programme in order to sell nuclear

technologies to countries of concern. In this Section of our Report, we describe the significant help his activities gave to the nuclear programmes of several countries of concern, particularly Libya, and actions taken by the British Government in conjunction with others to close down Khan's network.

WHAT WAS KNOWN

65. During the 1990s, there were intermittent clues from intelligence that AQ Khan was discussing the sale of nuclear technology to countries of concern. By early 2000, intelligence revealed that these were not isolated incidents. It became clear that Khan was at the centre of an international proliferation network.

66. By April 2000, the Joint Intelligence Committee (JIC) was noting that there was an evolving, and as yet incomplete, picture of the supply of uranium enrichment equipment to at least one customer in the Middle East, thought to be Libya, and evidence linking this activity to Khan. By September 2000, it was pointing out that the network was expanding to mass-produce components for large-scale centrifuge cascades.

67. During 2001, the JIC continued to track AQ Khan's activities. An assessment in March 2002 pulled together all the strands of intelligence on AQ Khan then available. The conclusions showed the wide spread of Khan's network and that he had moved his base outside Pakistan and was now controlling it through his associates in Dubai. At the same time, intelligence showed that he had now established his own production facilities, in Malaysia. He was being helped in his activities by a network of associates and suppliers, including BSA Tahir (a Sri Lankan businessman operating out of Dubai).

68. By July 2002, the JIC had concluded that AQ Khan's network was central to all aspects of the Libyan nuclear weapons programme. Since Khan had access to nuclear weapon designs and had been involved in the development of Pakistani missiles, the Government feared that he might not only pass on the technology for enriching uranium but that he might also enable his customers to build nuclear warheads for missiles. As intelligence continued to build up, the JIC assessed that this was the first case of a private enterprise offering a complete range of services to enable a customer to acquire highly enriched uranium for nuclear weapons.

69. Intelligence also identified further individuals in the supply chain, and more intelligence was also becoming available on finance and transportation methods, including details of banks in a number of countries and the names of the shipping companies involved. Khan was also continuing to develop his business through his overseas facilities. By January 2003, the JIC was becoming particularly concerned at the progress Libya might be able to make as a result of the assistance it had received from the network.

70. Action to close down the network had until this stage been deferred to allow the intelligence agencies to continue their operations to gather further information on the full extent of the network. This was important to gain a better understanding of the nuclear programmes of other countries which Khan was supplying. But Khan's activities had now reached the point where it would be dangerous to allow them to go on.

71. At the tactical level, action was taken to interdict supplies of components moving from Khan's manufacturing facility in Malaysia to Libya. The various stages in this supply chain had been tracked through intelligence reports. In October 2003, the *BBC China,* a German-registered ship carrying centrifuge parts, was diverted to Italy as part of a carefully-planned intelligence operation in co-operation with the Italian and German authorities. On the basis of the material found on board the *BBC China,* in November 2003 the UK and US Governments approached the Malaysian authorities to investigate a Malaysian company run by BSA Tahir. According to the official Malaysian police report:

> *His* [Tahir's] *involvement . . . started in 1994/1995. That year the* [Pakistani nuclear expert] *had asked B S A Tahir to send two containers of used centrifuge units from Pakistan to Iran. B S A Tahir organised the transshipment of the two containers from Dubai to Iran using a merchant ship owned by a company in Iran. B S A Tahir said the payment for the two containers of centrifuge units, amounting to about US$3 million, was paid in UAE Dirham currency by the Iranians. The cash was brought in two briefcases.*

72. At the strategic level, action was taken in co-operation with President Musharraf of Pakistan to stop Khan from continuing his activities. Khan subsequently appeared on national television on 4 February 2004 to:

> *. . . offer my deepest regrets and unqualified apologies to a traumatised nation . . .*

and admitted that an investigation by the Pakistani government:

> *. . . has established that many of the reported activities did occur, and that these were inevitably initiated at my behest.*

VALIDATION

73. Key individuals in the network have provided verification of the intelligence (for example, as indicated by the press release issued on 20 February 2004 by the Inspector-General of the Royal Malaysian Police after an investigation into BSA Tahir's activities). The discovery of centrifuge parts on the *BBC China* bore out the intelligence on the supply chain. Libyan co-operation following Colonel Qadhafi's decision to abandon his nuclear weapons programme has produced firm evidence that the intelligence on AQ Khan's support for this programme was accurate.

CONCLUSIONS

74. The uncovering and dismantlement of this network is a remarkable tribute to the work of the intelligence agencies. As we looked at the reasons behind this success, several key points became apparent. First, a team of experts worked together over a period of years, overcoming setbacks and patiently piecing together the parts of the jigsaw. Although an element of luck was important in providing a breakthrough, this was not a flash in the pan. It was the result of a clear strategy, meticulously implemented, which included the identification of key members of the network and sustained work against their business activities. Secondly, there was close co-operation between UK and US agencies, with

both sides working to the same agenda. But most importantly of all, there was strong integration in the UK between all the agencies. A decision was taken early on that at working level all information, however sensitive, would be shared.

75. There was also a high degree of co-operation between the agencies and policy-makers in departments. This enabled swift and effective action to be taken at the right time. The action was intelligence-led. The agencies uncovered the activities of the network. The development of policy and action to close it down followed: by interdicting shipments; seeking co-operation from the Pakistani authorities; taking action with the recipients of AQ Khan's products, most notably Libya; and by encouraging legal action, where possible, against members of the network.

2.3 LIBYA

INTRODUCTION

76. On 19 December 2003, in a public statement, the Libyan Government said that:

> . . . Libya has taken the initiative and has instigated among the countries of the world, especially the Middle East, Africa, and the Third World, the abandonment of WMD programmes . . .

77. Colonel Qadhafi's dramatic change of policy should be viewed in the wider context of his decision in the late 1990s to move towards rapprochement with the West through, among other things, an attempt to resolve the Lockerbie issue. Much of Colonel Qadhafi's motivation for this rapprochement was economic. He recognised that he needed western, and especially US, investment in Libya's economy. The UK was important to him because it offered the best route to the US.

78. It is a matter of judgement how far the 'Iraq factor' was decisive in Colonel Qadhafi's policy change, but it seems likely that coalition action in Iraq in 2003 accelerated a process that was already under way. Nevertheless, between the late 1990s and 2003, Colonel Qadhafi may well have thought that he could achieve rapprochement with the West while retaining nuclear, chemical and ballistic missile programmes. If so, it took some time for him to recognise the incompatibility between these two objectives.

WHAT WAS KNOWN

79. The principal JIC assessments on Libya between 1998 and 2003 paint a picture of steady progress in its nuclear and ballistic missile programmes. At first the JIC was not too concerned, judging that these programmes were not making any significant headway. But by mid-2000 the JIC was picking up signs of increased activity. By 2003, when the AQ Khan network was much better understood, Libya had been identified both as a prime customer and as one already in receipt of nuclear-related materiel. This was disturbing enough in itself, but was even more so when combined with knowledge of Libya's long-range ballistic missile aspirations. The JIC felt confident enough to conclude that Colonel Qadhafi was actively pursuing the acquisition and development of *"weapons of mass destruction"*.

80. The various strands of intelligence on Libya's nuclear programme were precise, detailed and collectively strong. The intelligence on the AQ Khan network was extremely important, but it was backed up by other multi-agency reporting. Likewise, different strands of reporting combined to fill out the picture of Libyan ballistic missile and chemical weapons programmes. Most of the JIC's assessments were later borne out by validation of Libya's declarations of its nuclear, chemical and ballistic missile holdings and capabilities.

USE OF THE INTELLIGENCE

81. One use of intelligence in the Libyan case has been to stimulate interceptions of goods destined for Libya's programmes. This has involved activity by HM Customs and Excise, co-operation with European partners and actions by other Governments.

82. A particularly notable example is that of the interception of the *BBC China* referred to above. The discoveries made enabled the UK and US Governments to confront Libyan officials with this evidence of their nuclear-related procurement at a time when Libya was still considering whether to proceed to full admission of its programmes.

VALIDATION

83. Since Libyan Foreign Minister Shalgam's public statement, also on 19 December 2003, on his country's decision to eliminate:

> *. . . the materials, equipments and programmes which lead to the production of internationally proscribed weapons . . .*

and

> *. . . to restrict itself to missiles with a range in line with the standards agreed in the MTCR* [Missile Technology Control Regime] *. . .*

much progress has been made in validating Libya's declarations of its holdings of nuclear and chemical materiel, ballistic missiles and associated facilities. The inspection process for validation has been carried out by the relevant international organisations and by UK and US experts working closely with the Libyans. This in turn has helped to confirm the validity of many of the original intelligence concerns. The same intelligence that uncovered the Libyan programmes was helpful to the inspectors for another reason: it demonstrated to the Libyans how much was known about their programmes and helped to persuade them to be fully co-operative. As the 2003–04 Annual Report of the Intelligence and Security Committee[1] said in June 2004:

> *The detailed intelligence on Libya and its procurement activities, collected by the UK and USA from all sources over a significant period of time, enabled the UK and USA to demonstrate to the Libyan authorities that they knew about their WMD programmes. Consequently, when the inspectors went to Libya the Libyan authorities, while they tried, were not able to hide their programmes and full disclosure was eventually achieved.*

---

[1] Cm 6240. June 2004.

CONCLUSIONS

84.   Where intelligence is good it can create its own positive momentum. Successful interdictions, having been proved to be based on sound intelligence, increase confidence in the reliability of reporting from the sources. They will also often uncover new leads (from documents and questioning of those involved) that help to fill out an intelligence picture. This was a major intelligence success.

2.4 IRAN

INTRODUCTION

85.   Iran was attacked by Iraq at the beginning of the Iran/Iraq War in 1980, and suffered enormous casualties. Ballistic missiles were used by both sides in battlefield confrontations. Iran had considerably the worse of the strategic-level exchanges in the 'War of the Cities' in the final months of the war in 1988. It also suffered seriously from the Iraqi use of chemical warfare munitions on the battlefield, notably during the capture of the Fao Peninsula in early 1988.

86.   During the Iran/Iraq war, Iran launched a chemical weapons programme and invested heavily to develop its ballistic missile capabilities. It now has a substantial and advanced indigenous ballistic missile industry. It has also been pursuing for many years a wide range of nuclear fuel cycle activities, which it claims are for entirely peaceful purposes but which could enable it to produce fissile material for nuclear weapons.

87.   Despite Iran's recent engagement with the IAEA, the UK remains concerned by the potential dangers inherent in the combination of Iran's ballistic missile capabilities and its nuclear fuel cycle activities.

WHAT WAS KNOWN

88.   It is clear to us that, for the British Government, the greatest concern has been the development by Iran of a capacity to produce fissile material (which could be used to make a nuclear weapon); and ballistic missiles.

89.   Iran acquired the Scud B missile from Syria (produced in the Soviet Union) and from North Korea (indigenously produced). After the Iran/Iraq war, North Korea sold to Iran production technology for first the Scud B and then the Scud C missile (an upgraded North Korean design with a range of 500km), as well as a number of complete missiles of both types.

90.   In the mid-1990s, Iran bought a few examples of the then latest North Korean missile, known to the West as the No Dong 1 and with a range of some 1300km. Iran has since developed its own version of the No Dong 1, called the Shahab 3. The Shahab 3 brings within range the capitals and most of the territories of the states of the Near and Middle East; the Caucasus; Pakistan; most of Central Asia and Turkey; and part of India. Iran is now considering systems beyond the Shahab-3. Some of these longer-range systems are represented as space launchers rather than as ballistic missiles.

91. Iran's nuclear fuel cycle activities have developed slowly over more than two decades, but in recent years it has become apparent that it is developing facilities that will enable it to enrich uranium indigenously on a significant scale. Iran has announced or the IAEA has reported that Iran:

    a.   Intends to mine indigenous uranium deposits near Yazd and to produce yellowcake from the ore.

    b.   Has constructed a large uranium conversion facility at Esfahan that is in the process of being commissioned and will be able to convert yellowcake into uranium hexafluoride (the feed material required for gas centrifuges).

    c.   Has constructed a large, underground facility at Natanz to house a Pilot Fuel Enrichment Plant and a full-scale Fuel Enrichment Plant, both using gas centrifuge technology.

    d.   Has indigenous facilities to manufacture centrifuge components.

    e.   Has engaged in work on both the P-1 gas centrifuge (work which led to the actual enrichment of uranium, an activity it did not declare to the IAEA at the time) and on the P-2 gas centrifuge, about which, important information as the IAEA has recently said, has in some cases been incomplete, and continues to lack necessary clarity.

    f.   Has had help with its gas centrifuge programme from a number of foreign sources. In particular, having reviewed the original P-2 technical drawings which Iran says it received from foreign intermediaries, the IAEA's experts concluded that the origin of the drawings was the same as that of the drawings provided to Libya[2].

92. The IAEA has also reported that Iran:

    a.   Has plans to produce a Heavy Water Research Reactor.

    b.   Has largely completed a Heavy Water Production Plant to provide the heavy water it will require.

    c.   Has plans for a Fuel Manufacturing Plant.

    d.   Has experimented in the past with plutonium separation, without declaring it at the time to the IAEA.

The IAEA has also raised concerns about work on laser enrichment and polonium-210.

VALIDATION

93. France, Germany and the UK (sometimes known as the 'EU3') have worked together to support the IAEA on its activities. Intelligence supplements what the UK knows from the IAEA, and policy formulation and execution has made full use of both sets of information. Separately, since the National Council of Resistance of Iran publicised previously secret

---

[2] That is, by AQ Khan.

facilities in August 2002 (the enrichment facility at Natanz and the Heavy Water Production Plant at Arak), the IAEA has sought to obtain a better understanding of all Iran's past and current nuclear activities. It has also called on Iran to accept additional safeguards obligations and urged it, as a confidence-building measure, to suspend some of its activities.

94.   As regards the chemical weapons programme launched during the Iran/Iraq War, Iran has subsequently signed and ratified the Chemical Weapons Convention (in 1993 and 1997 respectively). Although Iran did not meet the declaration timetable specified by the Convention, it did later declare two former chemical weapons production facilities. The Organisation for the Prohibition of Chemical Weapons has since verified that this production capability has been eliminated.

CONCLUSIONS

95.   As with other cases we have reviewed, we have observed in the case of Iran that British policy is to promote the effective use of international processes. Hence Britain, with France and Germany, played an important role in October 2003 in persuading Iran to respond to the IAEA Board of Governors' calls on Iran to make a full declaration about its past and current activities, to commit itself to signing an Additional Protocol (and to apply its provisions while moving to ratification), and to suspend all enrichment-related and any reprocessing activities.

96.   There are also clearly outstanding issues about Iran's activities. Iran has signed an Additional Protocol to its Safeguards Agreement and is making additional declarations to the IAEA as a result, but has still not ratified it. Furthermore, negotiations with Iran over the scope and verification of the activities to be suspended have been difficult. Most recently, Iran has decided to resume manufacturing of components and assembly of centrifuge machines under IAEA supervision, having earlier decided voluntarily to suspend them.

2.5 NORTH KOREA

INTRODUCTION

97.   We have focused mainly on the threat that North Korea poses as a proliferator. However, to put North Korean exports in context, we have kept in mind that North Korea itself could pose a nuclear threat not just to its neighbours but increasingly on a global scale. Agreements reached in the 1990s to suspend North Korean plutonium production in return for economic aid recently broke down when the North Koreans, confronted by the US, admitted that they had also embarked on a secret programme to enrich uranium.

98.   In December 2002, under pressure to abandon this programme, North Korea expelled the IAEA inspectors who had been monitoring their suspended plutonium production facilities, and soon after announced its withdrawal from the Nuclear Non-Proliferation Treaty. The North Koreans probably have enough plutonium from their previous programme to make at least one nuclear weapon. Reprocessing their spent fuel stocks could produce plutonium for still more weapons. Their uranium enrichment programme

could potentially produce highly enriched uranium for yet more. At the same time, North Korea has engaged on an extensive missile development programme, based on original designs from the Soviet Union. During the 1990s, North Korea steadily increased the range and payload of these missiles and in 1998 it test fired a three-stage rocket on a trajectory which took it over Japan. While this could not deliver a nuclear warhead beyond a medium range, North Korea is now thought to be developing missiles capable of delivering nuclear weapons as far away as the continental United States and Europe.

WHAT WAS KNOWN

99.   North Korea is a particular cause for concern because of its willingness to sell ballistic missiles to anyone prepared to pay in hard currency. While the sale of the missiles themselves is not illegal, providing them to countries which are or may be developing nuclear weapons increases the global threat from such weapons. For this reason, tracking North Korea's role as a supplier of missile systems has been a top priority for the intelligence community since 1991.

100. We examined the JIC assessments and relevant intelligence reports from that date until 2003, and heard evidence from witnesses engaged in collecting intelligence on this subject. The picture that emerged was of a state-controlled, self-sustaining missile industry, which was able to fund further development by channelling profits from exports back into the programme. While the Middle East has been the main destination for North Korean missiles, we saw evidence of North Korean interest in sales on a global scale.

101. The JIC first noted in an assessment of February 1992 that North Korea had emerged as a major exporter of missiles and that it was also prepared to sell missile production technology. The sale of technology, while lucrative on a short-term basis, closed off options for future sales but, on a wider perspective, fuelled the cycle of onward proliferation, as North Korea's customers became producers themselves and developed their own export programmes.

102. Throughout the 1990s, the JIC followed details of North Korean missile sales to third world countries. It noted that, in addition to Scud B and C, which had been sold with production technology for local manufacture, North Korea had also offered the No Dong 1, a longer range version of the Scud, to foreign purchasers. By 2001, the JIC was noting that North Korea was also prepared to offer Taepo Dong missiles with an assessed range of up to 15,000 km. In its most recent assessment of 2003, the JIC assessed that North Korea was continuing its export programme, seeking new customers and offering upgrades to existing customers.

VALIDATION

103. Intelligence has fed into the work of the Restricted Enforcement Unit, an inter-departmental organisation in the UK working to prevent the export of sensitive materials to North Korea and other countries of concern.

104. Apart from interdictions, which were the result of specific leads from intelligence, photographs of the Pakistani Ghauri missiles show that they are almost identical to the No

Dong, confirming intelligence that they were based on North Korean technology. Access to the Libyan missile programme has also confirmed earlier intelligence that the North Koreans helped the Libyans to develop an 800km-range Scud missile.

CONCLUSIONS

105.   We have studied the steady flow of intelligence on North Korean proliferation activities. North Korea is a difficult target because of tight state control. But the intelligence agencies have co-operated closely to tackle this problem, with cross-correlation of intelligence producing a total result which has been greater than the sum of the parts. The intelligence agencies have employed a range of ingenious tactics patiently and skilfully to piece together an intelligence picture of North Korean activity. This has provided important insights that have enabled the British Government to take decisive action to limit the extent of North Korean exports of missile delivery systems

106.   Intelligence continues to contribute to specific actions against missile exports in the context of the US-led Proliferation Security Initiative, which provides a framework for international co-operation aimed at disrupting the proliferation activities of states such as North Korea. Intelligence on specific activities is vital to the success of this operation. Close co-operation with liaison services is also important and we have seen clear evidence of this in the work of the intelligence agencies.

2.6 GENERAL CONCLUSIONS

107.   **All four of the case studies we discuss were to a greater or lesser extent success stories. To a degree, that was inevitable – we chose those cases where intelligence about nuclear, biological, chemical and ballistic missile programmes and proliferation activities can be discussed precisely because it has contributed to disclosure of those activities. But that should not detract from what has clearly been an impressive performance by the intelligence community and policy-makers in each case, and overall.**

108.   **A number of common threads have become clear from our examination of each case. The first and most obvious is the powerful effect of exploiting the linkages where they exist between suppliers (AQ Khan; North Korea) and buyers (Iran; Libya; others) for counter-proliferation activity. It is in the nature of proliferation that what can be discovered about a supplier leads to information about the customer, and *vice versa*. The second thread flows from this - the powerful multiplier effect of effective international (in many cases, multinational) collaboration.** This thread emerges, too, in the next Chapter, on terrorism.

109.   **Third, this is painstaking work, involving the piecing together over extended timescales of often fragmentary information. There are the surprises and 'lucky breaks'. But they often come from the foundation of knowledge developed over several years. It requires close collaboration**

between all involved, in agencies and departments, to build the jigsaw, with teams able to have access to available intelligence and to make the most of each clue. It also depends on continuity of shared purpose amongst collectors and analysts, and between the intelligence and policy communities, in gathering, assessing and using intelligence in tackling proliferation and nuclear, biological and chemical weapons programmes which are destabilising in security terms. We develop this theme further, in Chapter 4 on the UK's counter-proliferation machinery, and in Chapter 7 on our broader Conclusions.

CHAPTER 3

TERRORISM[1]

3.1 SCOPE

110.   We have examined intelligence reports and assessments on the links between terrorism and chemical, biological, radiological and nuclear weapons, and the use made of that intelligence, from when it began in the early 1990s to emerge as a topic of interest to the Joint Intelligence Committee (JIC). For the purpose of illustrating the contribution made by intelligence to policy formulation by the Government and to actions taken on the basis of that policy, we have focussed on the scope and quality of intelligence reports and assessments on the use by terrorists and extremists of unconventional weapons, and the extent to which they were validated by subsequent discoveries in Afghanistan. To avoid prejudicing current operations, we do not cover in this Report more recent intelligence assessments or findings.

3.2 THE PERIOD UP TO 1995

111.   In the late 1980s, the possibility that terrorist groups might seek to use unconventional weapons was considered remote. In surveys of nuclear, biological and chemical weapons proliferation in 1989, the JIC dealt briefly with the possibility that such technology might be used by terrorists:

> *We believe that even the most sophisticated and well-organised terrorist group is highly unlikely to be able to steal and then detonate a nuclear weapon within the foreseeable future. . . . At present the most feasible terrorist nuclear incident would probably be a credible hoax. A terrorist threat to detonate a nuclear device would be difficult to dismiss entirely in view of the increasing number of producers of fissile material in a variety of countries and the problems of accounting fully for all material produced. Terrorists might see a seemingly plausible and preferably well publicised warning of an imminent nuclear attack as potentially a very effective means of blackmailing governments.*

[JIC, 3 July 1989]

and:

> *We have no intelligence that any terrorist group makes CBW agents, possesses any such agents or is currently contemplating attacks using CBW agents or other toxic chemicals. The use of CBW agents by terrorists would generate widespread fear and could cause large numbers of casualties. The mere threat of such use could be sufficient to cause panic.*
>
> *A terrorist would need only small quantities of CW agents. The simpler ones could in principle be made by anyone with a knowledge of A-level chemistry using readily*

---

[1] This section is limited to intelligence on the use by terrorists of chemical, biological, radiological and nuclear weapons. The large majority of terrorist actions employ conventional armaments and explosives, and are not relevant to this Review.

obtainable materials. We believe that terrorist organisations could also readily obtain and handle without insurmountable difficulty, suitable bacteria, viruses and certain toxins.

Although CBW proliferation undoubtedly increases the risk that CBW agents could be stolen by or even supplied to terrorists by state sponsors . . . this prospect must be viewed against a background where many suitable agents can be manufactured in small quantities using easily available materials. So as far as terrorism is concerned, proliferation (if it comes about) may not necessarily be much affected by the actions of States with the relevant capability.

[JIC, 26 June 1989]

112. The main strands in this assessment set the standard for the next few years. There was no credible evidence of terrorist interest in nuclear, biological or chemical weapons; hoaxes and threats might be more disruptive than actual use; terrorists were very unlikely to be able to acquire nuclear devices; and the fact that some states possessed nuclear, biological or chemical weapons was unlikely to affect the risk of their use by terrorists.

113. In April 1992[2], in its first assessment specifically on the threat of attacks by terrorists using chemical, biological, radiological or nuclear weapons, the JIC considered the technical options, but emphasised the difficulties which were thought likely to render such methods unattractive options for terrorist groups:

They may be deterred by the danger to their own members, or by the risk of alienating the public and especially their own supporters. They may also fear that an attack would cause international outrage leading to determined efforts on an international scale to bring them to book. By contrast, conventional weapons are cheaper, easier to procure, and offer equal or greater effectiveness against traditional targets (such as prominent individuals, members of the security forces, government buildings).

[JIC, 23 April 1992]

This, too, was to become a feature of JIC assessments: for most terrorist uses, conventional weapons were better.

114. By October 1994, there had been a number of media reports – some correct – of fissile material being available on the black market. In the first of several such studies, the JIC did not consider that these affected its overall assessment:

Despite the possibility which now exists of obtaining fissile material, it is extremely unlikely that a terrorist group could produce even a crude nuclear device; nor is there any evidence that any group has contemplated the use of nuclear weapons. A more plausible scenario might be the dispersal of radioactive materials by conventional explosives or other means to achieve radiological contamination. The actual danger to the public from radioactivity would probably be small – smaller in some cases than to the terrorists. But such an attack (or its threat) could be highly effective in causing panic and public concern.

---

[2] It was also in 1992 that a Kurdish terrorist group tried to poison the water supply of a Turkish airbase using cyanide.

We believe that terrorists would not be able to acquire or deploy a nuclear weapon; radiological attacks are possible but unlikely. Attacks involving chemical or biological agents are also unlikely, though use of toxic chemical substances (for which there are some limited precedents) remains a possibility.

[JIC, 13–19 October 1994]

3.3 1995–1997

115. By June 1995, the JIC was assessing the threat posed by Islamist extremists; the terrorist threat was spreading outside the Middle East. The JIC commented on the use of suicide tactics, a strand which was subsequently to become significant in such assessments:

Selective interpretation of the Muslim faith enables such groups to justify terrorist violence and to recruit 'martyrs' for suicide attacks.

[JIC, 8 June 1995]

116. However, the first serious use of chemicals by terrorists was not by Islamist extremists. The sarin gas attack in the Tokyo underground by the Aum Shinrikyo sect came in March 1995[3]. In a 1996 assessment of the nuclear, biological and chemical threat to the UK[4] (which responded to the G7 declaration at the Lyons summit in June that year that special attention should be paid to the threat of use of nuclear, biological and chemical materials for terrorist purposes) the JIC stuck to its previous line, though noting the Aum Shinrikyo attack:

There is no indication of any terrorist or other group showing interest in the use of nuclear, biological or chemical (NBC) materials against the UK. For a number of reasons, conventional weapons are likely to remain more attractive for terrorist purposes. But last year's nerve agent attack in Tokyo will have heightened interest and, with ever more NBC information publicly available, hoaxes threatening NBC use are likely to become more difficult to assess.

[JIC, 4 July 1996]

3.4 1998–1999

117. Usama bin Laden first became known as a high-profile supporter of Islamist extremism while fighting against Soviet forces in Afghanistan during the 1980s. Expelled from Saudi Arabia in 1991 and from Sudan in 1996, he returned to Afghanistan. Evidence of his interest in unconventional weapons accumulated, and was summarised by the JIC in November 1998:

He has a long-standing interest in the potential terrorist use of CBR materials, and recent intelligence suggests his ideas about using toxic materials are maturing and being developed in more detail. . . . There is also secret reporting that he may have obtained some CB material – and that he is interested in nuclear materials. We

---

[3] The sect had carried out sporadic and unsuccessful open-air attacks using a range of agents since 1990. One attack (using sarin) in Matsumoto in June 1994 caused 7 deaths and 264 people were hospitalised. These earlier attacks were little noticed outside Japan.

[4] Because of its limited ambit this paper did not take note of the then recent Chechen guerrilla operation to place minute quantities of caesium-137 in a Moscow park.

assess that he lacks the expertise or facilities even to begin making a nuclear weapon, but he might seek to make a radiological device.

[JIC, 25 November 1998]

118.   Seven months later, in June 1999, the JIC had received more intelligence, and re-assessed the threat from Usama bin Laden's organisation accordingly:

> *Most of UBL's planned attacks would use conventional terrorist weapons. But he continues to seek chemical, biological, radiological and nuclear material and to develop a capability for its terrorist use. There is insufficient evidence to conclude that he has yet acquired radiological or nuclear material. In contrast, we now assess that his followers have access to some unspecified chemical or biological material. Some have received basic training in its use against individuals or in confined spaces.*

> *In April a leading Egyptian terrorist, apparently believing the information was already known to the authorities, told an Egyptian court that UBL had CB 'weapons' which he would use against US or Israeli targets.*

[JIC, 9 June 1999]

Intelligence reports of bin Laden's associates falling for nuclear materiel frauds suggested, however, that they were not well advised on nuclear matters.

119.   A month later, in July 1999, the JIC explained an important change in one of the major assumptions underpinning its previous assessments – some terrorists were no longer reluctant to cause mass casualties, for example some Islamist extremist terrorists and Aum Shinrikyo:

> *Over the 1990s there has been a significant increase in the quantity and quality of intelligence that some terrorists are interested in CBRN – and particularly in chemical and biological – materials as weapons. The risk of a CBRN terrorist incident has risen, albeit from a low base. In part this increase reflects the rise of Islamic extremism and ethnic hatred as terrorist motivations: some of the terrorists thus motivated are less constrained by considerations such as public support, casualties among innocent bystanders, or the prospect of retaliation. It may also reflect the increasing availability of information about making and using CB materials, and the publicity attracted by major incidents and hoaxes. Whether the attacker's aim is political or economic blackmail, or severe disruption, society's vulnerability to terrorist attack from CB or radiological materials is high, exacerbated by the lack of a tried and tested CB counter-terrorist response in some countries.*

[JIC, 15 July 1999]

120.   In the same assessment, the JIC made its own judgement, in the absence of specific intelligence, that Usama bin Laden had after several years been successful in acquiring non-conventional weapons. That judgement was later shown to be correct:

> *There have been important developments in [Islamist extremist] terrorism. It has become clear that Usama Bin Laden has been seeking CBRN materials . . . His wealth permits him to fund procurement, training and experimentation to an extent*

unmatched by other terrorists. ... Given the quality and quantity of intelligence about his interest in CB materials, the length of time he has sought them, and the relative ease with which they can be made, we assess that he has by now acquired or made at least modest quantities of CB materials – even if their exact nature and effectiveness are unclear. The significance of his possession of CB materials is that, in contrast to other terrorists interested in CB, he wishes to target US, British and other interests worldwide. There is also intelligence on training in the use of chemicals as weapons in a terrorist camp in Afghanistan, although it is not yet clear if this is under Bin Laden's auspices. The CB threat is likely to be higher abroad than in the UK, reflecting the location of Bin Laden and his allies, the vulnerability of potential targets, and the effectiveness of local security authorities. Targets may include British official sites or related facilities overseas. That said, Bin Laden's attacks remain more likely to employ conventional weapons than CB materials.

[JIC, 15 July 1999]

121. However the JIC still retained its overall conclusion, that:

... the indications of terrorist interest in CBRN materials have yet to be matched by a comparable amount of evidence about possession and intent to use CBRN. Most terrorists continue to favour conventional weapons, as easier to use, more reliable, safer and more controllable than CBRN materials.

[JIC, 15 July 1999]

3.5 2000–2001

122. By January 2000, in an assessment of conventional threats, the JIC summarised bin Laden's aspirations for non-conventional weapons:

UBL retains his interest in obtaining chemical, biological, radiological and nuclear (CBRN) materials and expertise. In autumn 1999 there was intelligence that he had recruited ... chemicals specialists ... . Our assessment remains that UBL has some toxic chemical or biological materials, and an understanding of their utility as terrorist weapons. But we have yet to see hard intelligence that he possesses genuine nuclear material.

[JIC, 12 January 2000]

123. By August 2000, the JIC was clear that, although there were other Islamist extremist groups[5] with an interest in non-conventional weapons, Usama bin Laden posed the most severe threat:

Some [Islamist extremist groups] *are interested in exploring the use of chemical or biological materials as weapons. In the forefront is UBL ...*

[JIC, 9 August 2000]

124. In January 2001, the JIC reported at length on the terrorist threat from unconventional weapons and emphasised the unique nature of the threat from Usama bin Laden:

---

[5] The JIC was a year later to comment that the word 'groups' can be misleading in the context of Islamist extremist terrorists. *"There are established groups in different countries, usually working to a national agenda, but the networks associated with UBL are changeable ad hoc groupings of individuals who share his agenda, and who may come together only for a particular operation. Nevertheless, 'groups' is used as a short form for want of another available term."*

The actual threat does not match the media hype. Almost all the available intelligence refers to terrorist interest in CB materials, rather than to specific attack plans. There is no credible intelligence that any terrorist except UBL has the capability or serious intent to explore the use of weapons-grade nuclear materials – nor, except for Chechen extremists, radiological material. Terrorists interested in CB are generally those least constrained by public opinion or their members' or supporters' sensitivities. Their resources and targets tend to be abroad rather than in Britain, so the risk of attacks using toxic materials has always been greater overseas.

UBL has sought CBRN materials for use as terrorist weapons . . . . From his public statements and interviews it is clear that he believes it is legitimate to use them as weapons and his wealth has allowed him to fund procurement, experimentation and training. There is plentiful intelligence that this interest is sustained, mostly relating to toxic materials.

In 1999 he sought equipment for a chemical weapons lab in Afghanistan, and claimed already to have . . . experts working there.

[JIC, 10 January 2001]

3.6 THE AFTERMATH OF 9/11

125.   In an important paper shortly after the attacks of 11 September 2001, the JIC made clear the way in which Usama bin Laden's philosophy, combined with suicide attacks, had changed the calculus of threat. This assessment summarised the new security challenge which, as we describe further in the context of Iraq at Chapter 5, was to become dominant in the thinking of British Ministers – the desire of terrorists and extremists to cause casualties on a massive scale, undeterred by the fear of alienating the public or their own supporters that had been noted as a constraining factor in JIC assessments in the early 1990s or by considerations of personal survival. To this fundamental shift in the JIC's judgement on the likely motivation and goals of terrorists and extremists was added a corresponding shift in its conclusions about the attractiveness of nuclear, biological or chemical weapons. Thus, in September 2001 the JIC noted that:

Many defensive and preventive measures taken against terrorism (such as ensuring that passenger and luggage travel together) still presuppose that the terrorist will want to survive the attack. But suicide attackers, especially those backed by sophisticated planning and pursuing non-negotiable objectives, negate many security measures and widen society's vulnerability. New strategies are required to counter the threat of terrorists willing, or even eager, to sacrifice their lives as martyrs in Islamic extremist or other causes – although there can be no complete protection against them.

In the context of UBL's jihad, casualties and destruction could be an end in themselves as much as a means to an end (Footnote: UBL's stated objective is to secure US withdrawal from the Middle East or, failing that, to provoke a reaction which would further demonise the US in the eyes of Muslims and destabilise moderate Arab states that he perceives as un-Islamic). He has no interest in negotiation and there is no indication that he can be deterred.

[JIC, 18 September 2001]

126.   The JIC also went on in this paper to note Usama bin Laden's interest in nuclear devices.

127.   The British Government's dossier of 4 October 2001[6], which attributed the attacks of 11 September 2001 to Usama bin Laden, also reflected the attractiveness to him of nuclear, biological and chemical weapons, saying that:

> *From the early 1990s Usama bin Laden has sought to obtain nuclear and chemical materials for use as weapons of terror.*

and reminding its readership that:

> *When asked in 1998 about obtaining chemical or nuclear weapons he said "acquiring such weapons for the defence of Muslims (was) a religious duty"'.*

[Government's dossier, 4 October 2001]

3.7 INTELLIGENCE ON UBL'S CAPABILITIES AND ITS VALIDATION

128.   A considerable quantity of evidence of Usama bin Laden's capabilities in the nuclear, biological and chemical fields was uncovered after the US-led military action in Afghanistan in October 2001. This section compares these discoveries with JIC judgements beforehand.

NUCLEAR

129.   In 1999, the JIC reported Usama bin Laden's claims to be setting up a laboratory in Afghanistan. Following the collapse of the Taliban regime, in January 2002 the United Nations Security Council listed a former Pakistani nuclear scientist Bashir Mahmoud as associated with the Taliban or Al Qaida.

CHEMICAL

130.   Intelligence reporting from 1999 onwards testified to the activities of Abu Khabbab, an explosives and chemicals expert who ran training courses which included information on how to make and use poisons. This was confirmed by discoveries in Afghanistan such as a video showing chemical experiments being carried out on animals, and by the finding of numerous training manuals.

BIOLOGICAL

131.   In 1999, the JIC reported that:

> *In February 1999 one of his followers claimed that UBL intended to attack US and UK targets in India, Indonesia and the US, by using means which even the US could*

---

[6] *"Responsibility for the Terrorist Atrocities in the United States, 11 September 2001".*

not counter, implying the use of chemical or biological material.

[JIC, 9 June 1999]

132. Some work with biological agents was also attributed to Abu Khabbab, though the evidence was not detailed. However, the JIC's judgement that Al Qaida was developing biological weapons was confirmed by the discovery in Afghanistan of the Kandahar laboratory, and evidence that scientists had been recruited.

3.8 INTELLIGENCE RESPONSES TO INTERNATIONAL TERRORISM

133. Few of the measures being taken by the Government to improve the response to the terrorist threat are unique to attacks using chemical, biological, radiological and nuclear materials. The threat is international, and has motivated intelligence organisations to intensify both national and international collaboration on an unprecedented scale. **All of the UK intelligence agencies are developing new techniques, and we have seen clear evidence that they are co-operating at all levels.**

134. The most obvious embodiment of enhanced inter-departmental co-operation in the UK is the Joint Terrorism Analysis Centre (JTAC). This is a multi-agency organisation, hosted by the Security Service but staffed by personnel seconded from all of the agencies, law enforcement organisations and relevant departments. Its staff retain links to their parent departments and, operating on a round-the-clock basis, pool information to produce continuous assessments of threats within the UK, to British interests abroad and of terrorist activities generally. **JTAC has now been operating for over a year and has proved a success.**

135. The Security Service and Home Office are improving public education, through web sites and by other means, for both long-term and immediate appreciation of terrorist threats.

136. **International counter-terrorism collaboration has also been significantly enhanced in the past six or seven years. Though we understand that other countries have not yet achieved the same level of inter-departmental synthesis, considerable developments have taken place. Staff of the UK intelligence and security agencies are today in much wider contact with their opposite numbers throughout the world.** We have, for example, been briefed on a recent successful counter-terrorist operation which involved eight different countries working together. **We note these initiatives, but remain concerned that the procedures of the international community are still not sufficiently aligned to match the threat.**

CHAPTER 4

COUNTER-PROLIFERATION MACHINERY

4.1 INTRODUCTION

137.   The proliferation of nuclear, chemical and biological weapons and their delivery systems has been recognised by successive British Governments as a major threat to the country's interests. Internationally, those concerns have been manifested not least through the UK's support for the Nuclear Non-Proliferation Treaty, the Chemical Weapons Convention, the Biological and Toxin Weapons Convention and the Missile Technology Control Regime. Since the Cold War, the UK has had a range of mechanisms to prevent or limit proliferation and sensitive technology transfers. In this Chapter, we describe the current UK counter-proliferation machinery in relation to countries of concern and non-state actors such as terrorist groups.

4.2 DEPARTMENTAL RESPONSIBILITIES

138.   The Foreign and Commonwealth Office (FCO) is responsible for advice on all aspects of counter-proliferation policy including treaties and conventions, sanctions and export control policy.

139.   The Department of Trade and Industry (DTI) is responsible for the implementation of the UK's international obligations relating to the Chemical Weapons Convention and the International Atomic Energy Agency, and, through the Export Control Organisation (ECO), for processing all applications for export licenses. The DTI is also responsible for export control legislation and contributes to the formulation of general policy on United Nations sanctions.

140.   The Ministry of Defence is responsible for the defence response to nuclear, chemical and biological threats and ensures that defence considerations are taken into account in the Government's counter-proliferation policy. The Defence Intelligence Staff provides detailed advice across the full range of counter-proliferation issues, including technical analysis of weapons, production programmes, delivery systems and procurement networks.

141.   HM Customs and Excise are responsible for the enforcement of export licensing controls including the investigation and prosecution of suspected offences.

142.   Within the Cabinet Office, the Joint Intelligence Committee, supported by the Assessments Staff, provides strategic national intelligence assessments which inform counter-proliferation policy decisions. The Head of the Defence and Overseas Secretariat of the Cabinet Office is responsible for co-ordinating policy on counter-proliferation across Whitehall through the Counter-Proliferation Committee (CPC), which he chairs.

4.3 CO-ORDINATION

143.   The CPC is the principal co-ordination mechanism for strategic counter-proliferation policy. It was formed in July 2002, bringing together policy and operational issues that had

previously been addressed by separate bodies. It includes senior officials from the relevant policy departments, and the intelligence community.

144. The Counter-Proliferation Implementation Committee (CPIC) is responsible for actions to put into effect the strategies and initiatives agreed by the CPC. Among its other functions, the CPIC co-ordinates more tactical or technical policy development and provides guidance on priorities for the work of individual Whitehall departments. Representation on CPIC is the same as the CPC with the addition of the Assessments Staff and HM Customs and Excise.

145. When Ministerial decisions are needed, the usual practice is for the department which leads on the particular issue to consult its own Secretary of State noting the views of the CPC and CPIC. As appropriate, the responsible Secretary of State may consult the Prime Minister and other Ministerial colleagues.

146. The Restricted Enforcement Unit (REU) is the working level group that acts on intelligence relating to attempted breaches of UK export controls or other attempts to supply sensitive items to countries of concern. It is chaired by the DTI and includes representatives of all CPIC member departments.

147. The Official Committee on Strategic Exports (OSE) has a very broad remit and membership. It does not address specific counter-proliferation issues, but deals with general aspects of the control of exports and the licensing of military goods and other goods of strategic importance.

4.4 THE ROLE OF INTELLIGENCE

148. As we note in Chapter 1, proliferating states usually represent difficult targets for intelligence collectors, and weapons programmes are usually particularly difficult targets within them. Intelligence will as a result usually provide only a part of the picture, but the alternative is usually no picture at all. Countries of concern go to great lengths to conceal weapons programmes because they represent some of the most sensitive and secret work undertaken in those countries. For example, because procurement is illegal, they use networks of companies to conduct procurement; and production and storage facilities are often sited in remote locations.

149. **Intelligence performs an important role in many aspects of the Government's counter-proliferation work. It helps to identify proliferating countries, organisations and individuals through JIC assessments, DIS proliferation studies and operational intelligence. It can help to interdict or disrupt the activities of proliferators either nationally or in co-operation with other countries. It can support diplomatic activity by revealing states' attitudes to counter-proliferation or by informing the assessments of international partners. It can also support inspection, monitoring and verification regimes and on occasions military action.**

150. **Intelligence can play an important part in enforcing export controls, particularly in relation to 'dual-use' goods and technologies.** The ECO

processes some 10,000 intelligence reports a year and about 9,000 applications for individual export licences. The Restricted Enforcement Unit regularly considers the latest intelligence relating to potential breaches of export controls or other exports of concern and co-ordinates action by its member departments. These actions can include alerting UK exporters to the activities of proliferators, seizing goods, investigating potential breaches of UK export controls and informing the authorities in other countries of proliferation activities under their jurisdiction and encouraging them to take action against them.

CHAPTER 5

IRAQ

5.1 INTRODUCTION

151.   A great deal of information on Iraq's nuclear, chemical, biological and ballistic missile programmes has already been published - more so, it seems to us, than on the other countries we have studied. We do not therefore seek to tell the full story here. Rather, we focus mainly on the intelligence assessments made by the British intelligence community; on how they were derived, and especially on the reliability of the underpinning intelligence; and on the use made of intelligence in a range of activities of Ministers and their departments.

152.   We have sought in our examination of departmental papers and in our questioning of witnesses to assess the intelligence on Iraqi capabilities to enable us to answer three broad questions:

   a.   What was the quality of the intelligence and other evidence, and the assessments made of it, about the **strategic intent** of the Iraqi regime to pursue nuclear, biological, chemical or ballistic missile programmes in contravention of its obligations under United Nations Security Council Resolution 687?

   b.   What was the quality of the intelligence or other evidence, and the assessments made of it, about Iraq seeking to sustain and develop its indigenous knowledge, skills and materiel base which would provide it with a **'break-out' capability** in each of those fields? Was there in particular good intelligence or other evidence of Iraq pursuing activities to extend and enhance those capabilities in contravention of its obligations under United Nations Security Council Resolutions?

   c.   What was the quality of the intelligence or other evidence, and the assessments made of it, about Iraqi **production** or **possession** of prohibited chemical and biological agents and weapons, nuclear materials and ballistic missiles?

153.   We have studied the assessments of the Joint Intelligence Committee (JIC) and the intelligence reports that underlay them as far back as 1990, for two reasons. First, we have sought to establish whether there are any detectable systemic issues surrounding the effective operation of the intelligence process over more than a decade which might have affected JIC assessments in the period prior to the second Gulf war. Secondly, we have sought to establish whether assessments made about the scale of Iraq's nuclear, biological, chemical and ballistic missile weapons programmes at the time of the first Gulf war and during the early- and mid-1990s had a lasting impact which was reflected in JIC assessments made in 2002 and 2003.

154. We have sought in particular to examine whether there is anything in JIC assessments made over the period from 1990 to 2003 which might illuminate the central conundrum that underlay the establishment of our Review – the apparent absence, against expectations, of significant stocks of chemical and biological agents and weapons, and of longer-range ballistic missiles, when coalition forces entered Iraq in 2003. We recognise that we have the advantage of hindsight in doing so.

5.2 1990–1998

155. We looked first at JIC assessments and underpinning intelligence reports in the period from 1990, prior to the first Gulf war, to the departure of United Nations inspectors in 1998. We set out the JIC's judgements in some detail (as we do throughout this Chapter). We have chosen not to comment in as much detail in this Section on the underpinning intelligence reports or on the sources. In part, this is because many of the JIC's judgements changed in later years as new intelligence was received. In part, it is because the most authoritative information on the status of Iraq's nuclear, biological, chemical and ballistic missile programmes in this period came from reports produced by the United Nations Special Commission (UNSCOM) and by the International Atomic Energy Agency (IAEA) derived from their inspection activities on the ground. But it may help in setting the context for what follows to record that our Review has shown that the intelligence agencies contributed to a steady flow of intelligence covering Iraqi procurement activities, attempts to break United Nations sanctions, concealment of prohibited programmes and plans for handling UNSCOM and IAEA inspections. Intelligence reporting increased in volume as the dispute between the Iraqi regime and the United Nations developed in 1998.

IRAQ'S NUCLEAR WEAPONS PROGRAMME

156. A JIC assessment produced in September 1990 noted that:

Our assessment is that, unless it receives significant external assistance, it will take Iraq:

- *at least three years to establish a production capability for fissile material;*

- *one more year before sufficient weapons-grade material would be available for the production of one nuclear device; and*

- *a further year or more (ie 1995 at the earliest) before there would be enough material for a small stockpile of 3–4 weapons.*

[JIC, 27 September 1990]

157. That assessment was based on the Iraqis using only a centrifuge route to the enrichment of fissile material, an assumption later shown to be incorrect. But it did cover, on the basis of intelligence, the ability of the Iraqi regime to implement a 'crash programme' to acquire a nuclear device in a considerably shorter time. The JIC noted that doing so would require Iraq to order diversion to military purposes of nuclear material stored at civil sites, in breach of the IAEA safeguards regime; to recover unburnt uranium from reactor fuel; and

to have advanced with work on firing systems and high explosive parts to the stage where they could be incorporated into a nuclear device. The JIC noted that:

> *If and only if all of these conditions were met, and assuming that reprocessing of diverted fuel started at the time of the invasion of Kuwait, then it is conceivable that Iraq could have the capability to make an untested nuclear weapon (though not a series of weapons) with a yield of approximately 20 kilotonnes by the end of this year.*

[JIC, 27 September 1990]

158.　The JIC noted that there were some indications that Saddam Hussein might have authorised a development project on those lines. It also concluded, however, that those indications did not lead it to alter its judgement that:

> *. . . the technical difficulties would be so great as to be virtually insurmountable in the short time available.*

[JIC, 27 September 1990]

159.　In a further assessment in December 1990, produced following an IAEA inspection in November, the JIC noted that:

> *We have no intelligence that would cause us to change our assessment of Iraq's current nuclear capability. Without significant foreign assistance, Iraq is still at least three years away from the capability to produce fissile material itself; and at least a further year away from being able to turn it into a weapon.*

[JIC, 4 December 1990]

160.　The JIC also reconsidered its previous judgements on the possibility of Iraq having a 'crash programme' to build a nuclear device, concluding that:

> *We continue to believe that the most obvious short cut for Iraq to produce at least one nuclear device would be by diverting the material from its civil reactor programme, which was inspected by the IAEA. We have no reason to believe that the IAEA inspection was flawed. This means that the material had not been diverted by 22 November. If, however, material were diverted immediately after the inspection . . .* [Iraq] *might, in ideal circumstances, be able to produce a single, untested device by mid-1991. But we continue to believe that the technical problems would be so great as to be virtually insurmountable in such a short timescale.*

[JIC, 4 December 1990]

161.　Finally, the JIC noted that:

> *The only other way in which Iraq could have a nuclear weapon within the next few months would be for it to acquire, or to have acquired, the necessary material, or a complete weapon, from an outside supplier.*

[JIC, 4 December 1990]

162.　The JIC dismissed this option, on the grounds that, of the countries with access to fissile material, only a few might conceivably have the motivation to supply the necessary materiel or weapons and that the JIC did not in any case consider such supply likely.

163. The period after the war was marked by periodic reports by the JIC on the progress made by the IAEA in supervising the dismantlement of Iraq's nuclear weapons programme, and re-assessments of Iraq's indigenous capabilities and the timescales within which it might be able to build a viable nuclear device. It is clear that two IAEA discoveries in 1991 had a significant impact on JIC assessments of Iraqi capabilities in the nuclear field.

164. The first was the discovery that, rather than focusing only on the centrifuge route, Iraq had been pursuing a number of routes for the production of fissile material. The JIC reported that, on the basis of post-war intelligence, it now knew that:

> ... in the 1980s Iraq investigated four methods of uranium enrichment, including the use of centrifuges. But the route that had made most progress was electromagnetic isotope separation (EMIS).

[JIC, 11 July 1991]

165. The JIC noted also that, according to the intelligence:

> ... enough fissile material had been produced before the coalition air attacks to produce one nuclear device.

[JIC, 11 July 1991]

166. The JIC concluded that, whilst it found the new intelligence generally credible, it did not believe that Iraq could have obtained enough fissile material for a bomb by the route described in the new intelligence - a judgement later supported by the IAEA. It nevertheless cautioned that:

> Nonetheless, given our lack of intelligence about the Iraqi nuclear programme, we cannot exclude the possibility that Iraq might have produced more fissile material than we have previously believed.

[JIC, 11 July 1991]

167. The second discovery was that made by an IAEA inspection team in September 1991 of significant volumes of documents about Iraq's nuclear weapons programme. The JIC noted that the inspection had confirmed the existence of a comprehensive Iraqi nuclear weapons programme. It concluded that:

> On the basis of the evidence so far of the programme's progress before Desert Storm, Iraq could have made its first nuclear weapon by 1993, had its work not been interrupted by the war.

[JIC, 3 October 1991]

that is, at least two years earlier than its pre-war assessment.

168. It is clear from the papers we have seen and from oral evidence given by witnesses that the IAEA's discovery in 1991 of the full scale of Iraqi capabilities had a significant impact on JIC assessments thereafter.

169.	A JIC assessment of August 1995 included an assessment of evidence provided by Saddam Hussein's son-in-law, Hussein Kamil, after his defection, and of new information which was drawn out from the Iraqi regime as a result of that defection. The JIC noted that:

> *Iraq also admits it previously concealed the full extent of its nuclear programme. It has revealed that in August 1990 it began a crash programme, later abandoned, to build a nuclear weapon within a year.*

> [JIC, 24 August 1995]

170.	The JIC also noted that Iraq:

> *. . . intended to use nuclear material held under IAEA safeguards in Iraq. The Iraqis claim the plan was abandoned because they concluded that the IAEA would detect their activities. In fact, they had insufficient fissile material to make a nuclear device. Hussein Kamil's reported claim that, at the time of the Gulf conflict, Iraq was only three months from completing a nuclear weapon probably refers to the 'crash programme'. It is very unlikely to be true.*

> [JIC, 24 August 1995]

171.	JIC assessments in the period after 1995 to the departure of the United Nations inspectors focussed on continuing IAEA activities, and on Iraq's residual indigenous capabilities. They included a consistent JIC assessment that, if all United Nations controls on Iraq's nuclear activities were removed, Iraq could possibly develop a nuclear device in around five years. We have taken as a useful summary of Iraqi capabilities at that time a JIC assessment in February 1998 that:

> *UNSCOM and the IAEA have succeeded in destroying or controlling the vast majority of Saddam's 1991 weapons of mass destruction (WMD) capability.*

> [JIC, 4 February 1998]

IRAQ'S CHEMICAL WEAPONS PROGRAMME

172.	In reviewing JIC assessments of Iraq's chemical weapons programme, we were struck at the outset by the impact of a single intelligence report received in November 1990 on the then Iraqi chemical warfare capability. (We cover at Chapter 6 the impact of reporting from this source on JIC assessments of Iraqi possession and production of plague and 'dusty mustard'.) The report added new detail to the JIC's existing body of knowledge, covering the types of chemical agents held in the Iraqi stockpile; the capabilities of those agents; their weaponisation into free-fall bombs; the availability of suitable ballistic missiles for the delivery of particular agents; and the volumes of each type of agent, and hence of the total chemical agent stockpile. JIC assessments picked up key details from this report, including putting Iraq's total chemical agent stocks in the range 15,000–22,000 tonnes - a figure adopted briefly by the JIC.

173.	We can understand how such a detailed report, received only a little before the onset of hostilities, would have caught the attention of the intelligence community. We can also understand how, in such circumstances, the JIC might have felt that it needed to present a worst case assessment, and to let those responsible for operational planning have all available intelligence, even if uncorroborated. But we have noted that the report turned out to be wrong on several counts: on the total stockpile of chemical agent, on the availability of particular types of agent and on the ballistic missile systems available for their delivery.

174. Estimates of the size of the Iraqi chemical agent stockpile were revised radically downwards in the immediate pre-war period, from the November 1990 estimate described above to an assessed range of 6,000–10,000 tonnes. This was drawn up to provide military commanders with an indication of the possible scale of Iraq's use of chemical weapons, and of how long such use could be sustained. We questioned the derivation of the figures. We were told that the calculation started from an estimate of Iraq's chemical agent production capacity, derived from past intelligence about production at individual plants, pieced together to provide a figure for the combined capacity of Iraq's production plants of 3,000–5,000 tonnes per annum[1]. Estimates of the possible size of the stockpile were derived by assuming two years' production at full capacity over the period from the end of the Iran/Iraq war until the start of the first Gulf war. Such estimates assumed that no chemical agent stocks had been left over from the Iran/Iraq war. The sizeable range given is a reflection of the uncertainty inherent in this estimate, and especially in the scale of operation of the production plants. Less agent would have been available had the plants been operating at less than full capacity; more would have been available had some stocks remained after the Iran/Iraq war.

175. We understand why the JIC chose that method of calculation, given the limited evidence available in the immediate post-war period of residual Iraqi chemical weapons capabilities. We also noted that the assumptions behind the estimate were clearly spelt out in the JIC assessment. But we have also concluded that one consequence was to leave the intelligence community with an estimate for the size of the Iraqi chemical agent stockpile which was over-cautious, and at its upper end worst case. We have also noted that, after May 1991, JIC assessments did not spell out that the figures inside them were calculated on the same worst case basis. There will inevitably have been a risk that that estimate, shorn of its assumptions, may have become the 'prevailing wisdom', with subsequent Iraqi declarations being tested against it for truthfulness, especially in circumstances where intelligence was sparse. If so, that process would have tended to lead to deductions by analysts and policy-makers that there were shortfalls in Iraqi declarations. Furthermore, suspicions here will have been exacerbated by Iraqi prevarication, concealment and deception in the early- and mid-1990s, reinforcing any suspicions that Iraq had substantial stocks to hide.

176. We have also noted, however, that by 1994/95 the JIC was becoming more sanguine about the size of the Iraqi chemical agent stockpile and indeed of the value to Iraq of retaining a stockpile at all. A JIC assessment in September 1994 noted that:

> *. . . we do not believe the full extent of the CW programme has yet been revealed*

but also that:

---

[1] Iraq later declared to UNSCOM that, during the entire period of its chemical warfare programme, it produced 3,859 tonnes of chemical agent. Of this quantity, it weaponised 3,315 tonnes, of which about 80% was used during the Iran/ Iraq war. UNSCOM was unable to verify this information fully.

Although UNSCOM has destroyed the large declared stocks of CW agents, precursors and weapons, Iraq may have retained a secret stockpile but we have no direct evidence. Hidden stockpiles are probably unnecessary as the Iraqi civil chemical industry can produce all the precursors needed to make mustard agent and most of those for nerve agents.

[JIC, 8 September 1994]

177.   In the same vein, in August 1995, drawing on evidence provided by Hussein Kamil after his defection, the JIC concluded that:

We assess [Iraq] may also have hidden some specialised equipment and stocks of precursor chemicals but it is unlikely they have a covert stockpile of weapons or agent in any significant quantity; Hussein Kamil claims there are no remaining stockpiles of agent.

[JIC, 24 August 1995]

178.   The JIC assessed at the same time that Iraq:

. . .could begin to make chemical weapons within a matter of weeks, and produce significant quantities within months, if UN constraints were removed.

[JIC, 24 August 1995]

179.   That assessment represented the low point in estimates of the size of Iraqi chemical agent stocks. Thereafter, the JIC had growing suspicions and concerns. In an assessment in June 1996, it noted that:

We doubt that all agents, munitions, precursor chemicals and equipment have been accounted for.

[JIC, 12 June 1996]

180.   In October 1997, the JIC expressed its doubts more strongly:

Iraq nevertheless remains capable of regenerating a CW capability in a matter of months. We assess that some CW agents, munitions, precursor chemicals and production equipment remain hidden . . .

[JIC, 8 October 1997]

181.   Notwithstanding its overall assessment in February 1998 that:

UNSCOM and the IAEA have succeeded in destroying or controlling the vast majority of Saddam's 1991 weapons of mass destruction (WMD) capability.

[JIC, 4 February 1998]

the JIC also later that year repeated its view that:

. . . some CW agents, munitions, precursor chemicals and production equipment remain hidden.

[JIC, 24 September 1998]

182. We conclude that the impression left by JIC assessments in the mind of readers at the time of departure of United Nations inspectors will have been of suspicion and concern about Iraq's break-out capability, coupled with possible possession of chemical agent stockpiles, in breach of its United Nations obligations.

IRAQ'S BIOLOGICAL WEAPONS PROGRAMME

183. A JIC assessment produced in June 1992 included the JIC's judgement that:

> ... Iraq retains a potential BW agent production capability and has hidden BW weapons.

[JIC, 4 June 1992]

184. The JIC reached broadly the same conclusion in two assessments in 1993. As with chemical weapons, however, by 1994/95 the JIC was becoming more sanguine about the size of the biological agent stockpile. In an assessment in September 1994, the JIC noted that:

> There is little need for hidden stockpiles of BW weapons or agents. Small quantities of agent could be quickly and covertly produced ...

[JIC, 8 September 1994]

185. As with JIC assessments on Iraq's chemical weapons programmes, that judgement represented the low point in assessments of the status of the Iraqi biological weapons programme. Thereafter, following the defection of Hussein Kamil and the Iraqi admission of an extensive biological weapons programme, the JIC had growing concerns that Iraq was concealing biological agent stocks. Thus, in an assessment in June 1996, the JIC noted that:

> We do not believe Iraqi statements that the BW programme has been destroyed. Possibly substantial elements, including some production equipment and weaponised agent, continue to be concealed.

[JIC, 12 June 1996]

186. We enquired into the reason for this shift in the JIC's view, in the apparent absence of underpinning reliable intelligence. We were told that the changed assessment was based on the impact of Hussein Kamil's defection, UNSCOM's inability to reconcile Iraqi claims for production and destruction, unaccounted-for growth media and a total lack of co-operation from the Iraqis.

187. The JIC included a similar judgement in an assessment in December 1997, which noted that Iraq:

> ... may have retained hidden BW production equipment, agent and delivery systems.

and that it:

> ... could, in any event, regenerate a significant offensive BW capability within months ...

[JIC, 4 December 1997]

188.	Thus, as with assessments of Iraq's chemical weapons programme, notwithstanding the JIC's assessment in February 1998 that:

> UNSCOM and the IAEA have succeeded in destroying or controlling the vast majority of Saddam's 1991 weapons of mass destruction (WMD) capability.

[JIC, 4 February 1998]

the JIC concluded later that year that:

> Some biological warfare (BW) production equipment, stocks of agents and even weapons are probably retained by Iraq.

[JIC, 24 September 1998]

189.	We conclude that the impression left by JIC assessments in the mind of readers at the time of departure of United Nations inspectors will have been of concern about Iraq's break-out capability, coupled with possible biological agent stockpiles, in breach of its United Nations obligations.

IRAQ'S BALLISTIC MISSILE PROGRAMME

190.	As with its assessments on Iraq's chemical weapons programme, JIC assessments on Iraq's ballistic missile capabilities in the period before the first Gulf war were done on what was effectively a worst case basis. The JIC did not make this explicitly clear, although it did caution that:

> There are considerable uncertainties about Iraq's current ballistic missile capability and deployments.

[JIC, 20 September 1990]

191.	Given these uncertainties, the JIC could only provide an estimate which, in September 1990, was that Iraq had a stockpile of "about 700" ballistic missiles. The JIC broke down this figure between the three primary SCUD-based missile systems, concluding that:

> . . . there could be about 300 SCUD-B missiles . . .

that:

> The Iraqis may have converted some 250 SCUD-B missiles to the longer-range Al Hussein variant.

and that:

> The second SCUD derivative is the Al-Abbas missile, of which the Iraqis could now have up to 150.

[JIC, 20 September 1990]

192.	In the event, the Al Abbas was probably never deployed operationally, although it underwent a number of flight tests. No Al Abbas missiles were fired in the first Gulf war, and UNSCOM made no mention of them in their Final Report of January 1999. At the time of production of the assessment, there was much uncertainty not only over the number of ballistic missiles available to Iraq but also over the status of the domestically-modified

Scud variants (Al Hussein and Al Abbas). We have been told that Iraq later declared to the United Nations that it had produced 17 Al Abbas and 387 Al Hussein missiles between 1987 and 1990. Thus, if the Iraqi figures are taken at face value, while the JIC paper was approximately correct in its estimate of the overall number of about 400 Scud missile variants produced by Iraq, it was inaccurate in the ratio of production between Al Abbas and Al Hussein. A possible explanatory factor is that the JIC's performance estimate for one of the two versions of the Al Abbas missile was not greatly different from that of the Al Hussein. The episode illuminates, however, the complexities surrounding estimates of Iraqi ballistic missile stocks, against which later JIC estimates should be considered.

193. By contrast to pre-war assessments, JIC assessments prepared in April and May 1991 on the residual Iraqi ballistic missile stockpile did declare explicitly that they had been prepared on a worst case basis and in the absence of any direct intelligence. On the basis of somewhat fewer than 100 Iraqi missile firings during the war, the JIC concluded that Iraq:

> *. . . may have up to 600 left (but probably less), both standard Scud and extended-range variants.*
>
> [JIC, 17 April 1991]

194. On that basis, the JIC said that:

> *We cannot be precise, but we are confident that the Iraqis have substantially under-reported the numbers of missiles.*
>
> [JIC, 9 May 1991]

195. As in the chemical and biological weapons fields, we detect a risk here that, by making comparisons with worst case assessments (especially those not declared as such), analysts and policy-makers may have come to conclude that there were shortfalls in Iraqi declarations, with suspicions being exacerbated by Iraqi prevarication, concealment and deception.

196. A further JIC assessment in January 1992 described Iraqi declarations and included a substantial downwards revision in its estimates of Iraq's ballistic missile stockpile. The JIC reported that:

> *Although we do not know the true figure, we assess that around 100 Scud B remain concealed.*
>
> [JIC, 16 January 1992]

197. The JIC did not show fully the basis on which it derived that calculation. It has not therefore been possible for us to investigate whether the assumptions that underpinned it might have had an impact on assessments in later years about whether Iraq was concealing ballistic missiles and, if so, how many.

198. The JIC also noted in the same assessment that there might be:

> *. . . as many as 250 complete Soviet built SCUD B guidance and engine packages which cannot be accounted for, and would be critical for future production. Provided the raw material was available, Iraq could build its own replacement mid-body sections and assemble new missiles from this stockpile.*
>
> [JIC, 16 January 1992]

The possibility of Iraq reassembling missiles from hidden components was to be a major feature of JIC estimates of the Iraqi ballistic missile stockpile in the years ahead.

199. JIC assessments in 1992 and 1993 reported on progress on UNSCOM inspections and remaining uncertainties; and included judgements on the ability of the Iraqi regime to resume production of missiles with ranges longer than those permitted under United Nations Security Council Resolution 687. As in the nuclear, biological and chemical weapons fields, the JIC assessment of August 1995 included an analysis of Iraq's residual ballistic missile capabilities, taking into account information provided by Hussein Kamil after his defection. We noted in particular that the JIC recorded that:

> *UNSCOM has verified destruction of the declared Scuds (and the Iraqi derivatives) and their launchers and believes it has a satisfactory account of what happened to the rest. UNSCOM has also supervised destruction of components and much of the missile-related infrastructure . . .*
>
> [JIC, 24 August 1995]

200. In the same reassuring vein, the JIC said that:

> *We would expect Kamil to know a lot about the missile programme . . . He has also said that all the Scuds and their components have been destroyed . . .*
>
> [JIC, 24 August 1995]

201. The JIC also noted, however, that:

> *Iraq will retain a technology and production base because SCR 687 allows it to continue to develop and manufacture missiles with ranges less than 150 km. But intelligence reports that some current missile R&D work is being hidden from UNSCOM inspectors. Iraq has now revealed that it developed domestic Scud-type missile motors. This re-introduces uncertainty into an area where UNSCOM had previously expressed itself to be satisfied.*
>
> [JIC, 24 August 1995]

202. This inherent uncertainty was reflected in the next JIC assessment, in June 1996, in which the JIC said that:

> *Information obtained in the wake of the August defection has, however, led UNSCOM to judge that missile components, launchers and possibly complete SCUD missiles remain hidden. We doubt whether there are any concealed missiles in Iraq but it is likely that components remain.*
>
> [JIC, 12 June 1996]

203. The JIC also included an assessment of Iraq's ability to regenerate a longer-range missile capability:

> *If all UN controls were to be removed and Iraq could purchase the technology and expertise required to produce a long-range missile, an accurate 1,000km range missile could probably be produced within three to five years. A 300–500km range SCUD type missile could be indigenously manufactured within two years.*
>
> [JIC, 12 June 1996]

204.   In the period from 1996 to the withdrawal of United Nations inspectors in December 1998, the JIC continued to assess that, because of the inherent uncertainties, Iraq might retain variously *"a small number"*, *"a handful"* or *"some"* ballistic missiles. While UNSCOM concluded in 1997 that all but two Scud missiles acquired by Iraq from the Soviet Union had been accounted for, this did not cover some other indigenously produced missiles which Iraq claimed to have destroyed. We have observed in this context remarks attributed to Ambassador Ekeus (Executive Chairman of UNSCOM, 1991–1997) that a number of Iraqi missiles, put variously in the range 6–25, remained unaccounted for. We have also noted information from one intelligence source in 1998 suggesting that Iraq retained sufficient complete missiles and components to allow it to assemble up to 16 missiles in total.

205.   The JIC's final assessment before the withdrawal of United Nations inspectors in December 1998 was that:

> *We cannot rule out the possibility that Saddam retains a handful of missiles ... these could be available for use within a matter of weeks or perhaps even days. Provided it still has key components - and that is unclear - Iraq could within a few months build, with little risk of detection, missiles capable of hitting Israel and key targets in Saudi Arabia. If it needs to make or acquire the components, production of such missiles could begin within a year ...*

[JIC, 24 September 1998]

206.   We conclude that the impression left by JIC assessments in the mind of readers at the time of departure of the United Nations inspectors will have been of concern about the ability of Iraq to regenerate a small number of ballistic missiles, either through bringing back into use missiles that had been hidden or by re-assembling missiles from hidden components.

SUMMARY

207.   From our analysis of JIC assessments in this period, we are left with four strong impressions. First, of effective - but not demonstrably complete - work carried out by the IAEA and UNSCOM to supervise the dismantlement of Iraq's nuclear, biological and chemical weapons programmes, together with those missile programmes prohibited under United Nations Security Council Resolution 687. Secondly, of a progressive reduction in JIC estimates of Iraq's indigenous capabilities in the period to 1994/95. Thirdly, however, of growing suspicions and concerns underlying JIC assessments between 1995 and 1998 of Iraq's chemical, biological and ballistic missile capabilities, which were exacerbated and reinforced by Iraqi prevarication, concealment and deception. We detect signs that this context led to the JIC making its estimates of Iraqi capabilities on an over-cautious or worst case basis (not always declared as such).

208.   Our fourth impression is of differences in the quality of the assessments carried out by the JIC. We have been impressed by intelligence assessments on Iraq's nuclear capabilities. They were generally thorough; drew fully on both open and secret material; brought together human and technical intelligence; offered a view where appropriate on the

quality of the underlying intelligence sources; were balanced and measured; identified explicitly those areas where previous assessments had been wrong, and the reasons why, to correct the record; and at each significant stage included consideration of alternative hypotheses and scenarios, and provided an explanation of the consequences were any to arise, to aid readers' understanding.

209.   We recognise that assessments in the chemical and biological weapons fields are intrinsically more difficult, and that analysis draws on different intelligence techniques. We are conscious in particular that, because chemical and biological weapons programmes can draw heavily on 'dual use' materials, it is easier for a proliferating state to keep its programmes covert. The intelligence community will also have had in mind that Iraq had used its chemical weapons in the past, and was engaged in a sustained programme to try to deceive United Nations inspectors and to conceal from them evidence of its prohibited programmes. Even so, we have found JIC assessments in these areas less assured. Our impression is that they were less complete, especially in their considerations of alternative hypotheses; used a different 'burden of proof' in testing Iraqi declarations; and hence inclined towards over-cautious or worst case estimates, carrying with them a greater sense of suspicion and an accompanying propensity to disbelieve. We return to this point in our Conclusions.

5.3 1998 – MARCH 2002

THE POLICY CONTEXT

210.   In this Section, we consider the intelligence and the use made of it in the period from the withdrawal of United Nations inspectors in 1998 to early 2002.

211.   1998 was marked by rising tensions between the United Nations and Iraq over the ability of UNSCOM and IAEA inspectors to carry out their work, in particular their ability to carry out inspections at presidential compounds and palaces. We judge that this tension had an impact on the way in which the intelligence community assessed the intelligence available to it, and in particular contributed to the climate of suspicion on which we have remarked in the previous Section.

212.   It will also have had an influence on policy-makers, in shaping the overall context within which they read JIC assessments. The Government's policy position at that time was encapsulated in the statement by the Prime Minister to the House of Commons on 24 February 1998 on the most recent crisis over UNSCOM and IAEA inspections. That provides an insight not only into the way in which the Government viewed events in Iraq itself but also the broader context within which policy towards Iraq was made, both then and over the next few years. In his statement in 1998, the Prime Minister said that:

> . . . *This has not been an artificial argument about some theoretical threat, but a reflection of real alarm on the part of UN inspectors about the use of* [Presidential compounds] *to conceal both evidence and actual weapons* . . .

> *Saddam began by saying that there could be no access to the sites. Then, under intense pressure, not least from the start of build-up of forces in the Gulf, he*

eventually agreed that they could be visited once. That was clearly unacceptable, but he refused to move further. Meanwhile, we and the Americans, together with our other allies, continued to make it clear that, if he did not back down, we saw no alternative in the end to the use of force. We made preparations to ensure that we were ready to use force, if absolutely necessary. . . .

We should never forget that if we do not stop Saddam Hussein acting in breach of his agreement on weapons of mass destruction, the losers will be not just those threatened by him, but the authority and standing of the UN itself. . . .

The Saddam Hussein we face today is the same Saddam Hussein we faced yesterday. He has not changed. He remains an evil, brutal dictator. The only thing that has changed is that he has changed his mind in the face of effective diplomacy and firm willingness to use force. . . .

We will not tolerate any repetition of the Iraqi behaviour that has led to this agreement. We are not going to play more elaborate diplomatic games that allow Saddam Hussein to thwart the inspections regime that has now been agreed. . . .

Throughout the dispute, our aim has been a peaceful, diplomatic settlement. There was no desire on either side of the Atlantic to use force, but it was also clear to us throughout that Saddam Hussein only understands and respects force. . . .

Saddam Hussein has spent seven years playing for time, but has been thwarted by the resolve of the international community. It is now clearer than ever that his games have to stop once and for all. If they do not, the consequences should be clear to all.

[Hansard, 24 February 1998, Col 173]

213. A joint memorandum submitted by the then Foreign and Defence Secretaries to the Cabinet Ministerial Committee on Defence and Overseas Policy in May 1999 covered future strategy towards Iraq. That paper set out the Government's policy objectives towards Iraq as being:

> *. . . in the short term, to reduce the threat Saddam poses to the region, including by eliminating his Weapons of Mass Destruction (WMD) programmes; and, in the longer term, to reintegrate a territorially intact Iraq as a law-abiding member of the international community.*

214. The paper noted that the Government had sought to achieve these aims:

> *. . . by a policy of containment, through active support of UNSCOM/IAEA efforts to complete WMD disarmament in Iraq, diplomatic pressure and sanctions, backed by the threat and, as necessary, use of military force.*

215. The paper made judgements on the success of that policy and its longer-term prospects:

> *Containment has kept the lid on Saddam. . . . But containment has disadvantages: it does not produce rapid or decisive results; it is resource-intensive, requiring constant diplomatic effort and a significant military presence; and it is not always easy to justify to public opinion, as criticisms of UK/US air strikes and of the humanitarian impact of sanctions has shown.*

216. Following the withdrawal of United Nations inspectors, the paper stressed the importance of an effective, in-country arms control regime:

An important tool of containment has hitherto been a reasonably effective in-country arms control regime. . . . External controls and sanctions can constrain, though not eradicate, the importation of military and dual-use materials . . . external monitoring has serious limitations . . . and would be less of a constraint on Saddam than an intrusive in-country regime. Moreover, it would be unable to pursue disarmament, and thus offer no realistic prospect of being able to give Iraq a clean bill of health as required by the UNSCRs before sanctions can be lifted.

217. Finally, the paper, after considering humanitarian and other policy issues, concluded that the policy of containment should be sustained, on the grounds that:

However difficult it may be to sustain a policy of containment, it is not clear what the alternatives would be. To simply walk away from the problem would be an admission of failure, and leave Saddam free to pose once more a major threat to regional security and British interests. On the other hand, a policy of trying to topple Saddam would command no useful international support. . . .

Containment, therefore, remains the only usable option for achieving our policy objectives. If Iraq complied with UNSCRs, we should then lift sanctions. . . . If, on the other hand, Iraq does not co-operate with the UN (let alone comply with the UNSCRs), we face the prospect of indefinite containment from outside Iraq, based on sanctions, external monitoring and control, and the threat of military force if Saddam seeks to threaten his neighbours or reconstitute his WMD capabilities.

IRAQ'S NUCLEAR WEAPONS PROGRAMME

218. A substantial JIC assessment on Iraq's nuclear weapons capabilities in December 2000 sustained the JIC's prior assessment that:

Iraq still lacks fissile material and the infrastructure to make it. With trade sanctions but no UN monitoring, we judge that it would be difficult in these circumstances for Iraq to build a nuclear weapon. It would take at least five years, probably longer, and only in the context of evading sanctions and foreign assistance, for Iraq to make such a weapon; . . .

[JIC, 1 December 2000]

219. The JIC noted, however, that:

Iraqi entities, some formerly associated with its nuclear programme, seek dual use equipment that could be used in association with a centrifuge programme . . .

and that:

Unconfirmed intelligence indicates Iraqi interest in acquiring uranium . . .

[JIC, 1 December 2000]

220. The intelligence underpinning the latter relates to an Iraqi trade mission to Africa and is covered at Chapter 6; we judge it to have been represented correctly by the JIC in its assessment. We are also satisfied that the JIC reflected fairly the intelligence underpinning its statements about Iraqi attempts at procurement of 'dual use' equipment. The assessment also contained a full options analysis of the impact of the continued application (or otherwise) of United Nations sanctions, and of any resumption of United Nations inspections, on the date by which Iraq could acquire a nuclear device.

221. A further assessment by the JIC of the status of Iraq's nuclear, biological, chemical and ballistic missile programmes in May 2001 signalled a clear change in the JIC's perception. In the first Key Judgement to its assessment, the JIC noted that:

> *Our knowledge of developments in Iraq's WMD and ballistic missile programmes since Desert Fox air operations in December 1998 is patchy. But intelligence gives grounds for concern and suggests that Iraq is becoming bolder in conducting activities prohibited by UNSCR 687.*

[JIC, 10 May 2001]

222. The JIC cautioned that, on Iraq's nuclear programme:

> *We have no clear intelligence . . .*

[JIC, 10 May 2001]

223. It did, however, include the Key Judgement that:

> *There is evidence of increased activity at Iraq's only remaining nuclear facility and a growing number of reports on possible nuclear related procurement. We judge but cannot confirm that Iraq is conducting nuclear related research and development into the enrichment of uranium and could have longer term plans to produce enriched uranium for a weapon. If successful, this could reduce the time needed to develop a nuclear warhead once sanctions were lifted.*

[JIC, 10 May 2001]

224. In support of this Key Judgement, the JIC noted once again Iraqi efforts to acquire items for possible inclusion in a uranium enrichment programme using centrifuges, including 'dual use' items and aluminium tubes. Intelligence and its interpretation on the latter, which became an issue of some controversy, is covered more fully at Chapter 6. The assessment also noted that Iraq had

> *. . . recalled its nuclear scientists in 1998.*

[JIC, 10 May 2001]

225. This judgement was based on two human intelligence reports, both from new sources and neither speaking from direct, current experience. Unusually in the nuclear field, we conclude that those reports were given more weight in the JIC assessment than they could reasonably bear.

IRAQ'S CHEMICAL WEAPONS PROGRAMME

226. The JIC produced a further substantial assessment of Iraq's chemical (and biological) weapons programme in April 2000. It started with a warning that:

Our picture is limited.

a warning expanded in the body of the paper:

Since the departure of United Nations Special Commission for Iraq (UNSCOM), in December 1998, our limited picture of Iraqi chemical and biological warfare activities has been further reduced.

[JIC, 19 April 2000]

227.   Nevertheless, it included as the first Key Judgement of the assessment:

It is likely that Iraq is continuing to develop its offensive chemical warfare (CW) and biological warfare (BW) capabilities.

[JIC, 19 April 2000]

228.   Underpinning this judgement, it noted that:

After the Gulf War, we know that a large proportion of Iraq's CW capability was destroyed under UNSCOM supervision. But we assess that some was not destroyed.

and that:

Iraq could have hidden dual use precursor chemicals, and production equipment, since the Gulf War. Using these we continue to assess that, even with UNMOVIC and other UN controls, Iraq could produce mustard agent within weeks of a decision to do so. Iraq could produce limited quantities of nerve agent within months of such a decision.

[JIC, 19 April 2000]

229.   The JIC also noted:

. . . continuing Iraqi procurement activities which could be associated with a chemical weapons programme . . .

that:

Facilities formerly associated with Iraq's chemical warfare programme at its Habbaniyah I and II sites are being reconstructed.

and that:

. . . Iraq is restoring its civil chemical production capability, including pesticides, at one of its former chemical warfare related facilities. We assess that this would help any revival of its CW programme.

[JIC, 19 April 2000]

230.   In contrast to its warning about the limited amount of intelligence on Iraq's nuclear weapons programme, the JIC's assessment in May 2001 noted that it had:

. . . good intelligence of Iraq's former chemical and biological warfare (CBW) facilities, their limited reconstruction and civil production. Taken together, this suggests a continuing research and development programme.

[JIC, 10 May 2001]

231.   The JIC went on to say:

> We believe that Iraq retains some production equipment, stocks of CW precursors, agent and weapons, . . .

[JIC, 10 May 2001]

232.   It also noted that:

> . . . intelligence of other related CW activity, including possible weaponisation, is less clear.

[JIC, 10 May 2001]

233.   As well as the prior intelligence, described above, these judgements appear to have been based on three main pieces of evidence:

   a.   A single report from a new source who reported details of a project three years earlier to integrate the nerve agent VX into rocket artillery warheads and the subsequent filling of 60 warheads.

   b.   A further single report from a new source, passing on the comments of a subsource that he had been part of a project to produce the nerve agent VX in the period to 1998, again three years earlier.

   c.   Intelligence pointing to the restoration of a facility formerly used for the production of chemical agent precursors and on shipments to the plant, although there was no positive evidence that precursors had been produced.

234.   A further report from a liaison service on the establishment of a group of chemical experts to work on the production of chemical agent using mobile facilities appears to have been discounted by the JIC.

235.   We conclude that the JIC reflected these reports fairly in its assessments of the status of Iraq's chemical weapons programme, especially those on the production and weaponisation of the nerve agent VX. The intelligence applied mainly to historical (as opposed to current) activity and, even so, was by no means conclusive.

IRAQ'S BIOLOGICAL WEAPONS PROGRAMME

236.   In an assessment of January 1999, in the immediate aftermath of Operation Desert Fox, the JIC reached somewhat firmer judgements than in 1997 on Iraq's biological weapons capabilities. On Iraqi possession of biological agents, the JIC concluded that:

> Following the 1991 Gulf War, Iraq concealed BW production equipment, stocks of agents and perhaps even BW weapons; . . .

and on Iraqi production capabilities, that:

> . . . Iraq has sufficient expertise, equipment, and materials to produce BW agents within weeks.

[JIC, 7 January 1999]

237. We were told that the reason for the shortening of timescales in the JIC's judgements about likely biological agent production - from months in earlier JIC assessments to weeks - was intelligence of Iraqi requests for large quantities of growth media. We were told that these were judged to be greatly in excess of Iraq's likely legitimate requirements, on which advice had been sought from medical experts familiar with commercial and hospital requirements for growth media. It is not known if the growth media were actually obtained by Iraq. If they had been, this would have decreased the time needed to produce biological warfare agents.

238. JIC assessments on Iraq's biological warfare capabilities changed once again in its assessment of April 2000. As well as the warning and Key Judgement that:

> *Our picture is limited. But it is likely that Iraq is continuing to develop its offensive chemical warfare (CW) and biological warfare (BW) capabilities.*

the JIC also concluded as a Key Judgement that:

> *There is clear evidence of continuing Iraqi biological warfare activity, including BW related research and the production of BW agent. Iraq seems to be exploring the use of mobile facilities to give its BW activities greater security. But we have no evidence for Iraq filling weapons with biological agent since the Gulf War.*

and, as before, noted in the main body of the text that:

> *We continue to assess that, even without procurement from abroad, Iraq has retained sufficient expertise, equipment and materials to produce BW agents within weeks using its legitimate biotechnology facilities.*

[JIC, 19 April 2000]

239. This firmer assessment was based on two new strands of evidence. The first was intelligence reports on aspects of Iraqi research and development activities in 1997/98. The second, and more significant, was new intelligence from a liaison service[2] received a few days before the production of the JIC assessment on the use by Iraq of mobile facilities to produce biological agent. This intelligence and the judgements drawn from it are described more fully at Chapter 6. We note that the JIC confined itself in the main body of its assessment to saying that:

> *Iraq seems to be exploring the use of mobile facilities to give its biological warfare activities greater security.*

[JIC, 19 April 2000]

and to an assessment of the technical feasibility of production of the volumes of biological agent described in the intelligence reporting. We believe that this language was appropriate for a new source whose reporting had not by then been validated, although the Key Judgement was somewhat more firmly expressed than the subsequent analysis in the assessment might bear.

---

[2] During the course of our Review, we were told by SIS that, as a result of their post-war validation of intelligence sources, they had concluded that important aspects of the intelligence reports received by them on this issue were incorrect. A fuller description is at Section 5.9.

240. The JIC assessment of May 2001 cautioned that:

> *Our picture of Iraq's BW programme is unclear.*

[JIC, 10 May 2001]

241. It went on to record, however, that it had:

> *. . . good intelligence of one facility that could be used to support BW agent production.*

and that:

> *Other intelligence which points to the possible research and production of BW agent is unconfirmed. We believe Iraq retains equipment and materials to produce BW. . . .*

[JIC, 10 May 2001]

242. In support of these judgements, the assessment pointed to additional intelligence on:

> *Iraqi attempts to recruit new scientists by people formerly associated with Iraq's BW programme to work on BW related research, including genetic engineering.*

and:

> *Evidence of increased activity at a former BW associated plant in Amiriyah.*

[JIC, 10 May 2001]

243. The new intelligence came from human intelligence and imagery. Although the human intelligence was recording events that had taken place some time previously, we conclude that it was fairly reflected by the JIC.

244. Continuing intelligence reports from the liaison service on Iraqi mobile biological agent production facilities had a significant impact on the next JIC assessment, produced in February 2002, which noted that:

> *Iraq . . . if it has not already done so, could produce significant quantities of BW agent within days. . . .*

[JIC, 27 February 2002]

245. We were told that this further shortening of production timescales - from weeks to days - was based on a more thorough understanding of the capabilities of the mobile production facilities, and on refurbishment of an Iraqi facility involved in biological agent production and research before the first Gulf war.

IRAQ'S BALLISTIC MISSILE PROGRAMME

246. A substantial JIC assessment in December 2000 covered Iraqi ballistic missile stocks and indigenous research, development and production capabilities. The JIC sustained its estimate of the late-1990s of the size of residual Iraqi ballistic missile stocks:

> *. . . a handful of ageing SCUD-derived missiles, with a range of up to 650 km, are probably disassembled and concealed. These could be re-assembled quickly and*

used (albeit with little accuracy) against targets in Kuwait, Saudi Arabia and even Israel; . . .

[JIC, 1 December 2000]

247.   On Iraq's indigenous capabilities, the JIC noted that:

Iraq has increased the pace and scope of its missile research and development programmes. Series production of the 150 km range Al Samoud could begin within months. A longer range version (up to 200 km) is being worked on. We have no evidence of a revival in the 650 km range Al Hussein missile programme. But according to intelligence, preliminary work is under way on another missile with a possible range of over 700 km; . . .

[JIC, 1 December 2000]

248.   Intelligence supporting the JIC's judgements on Iraqi research and development programmes came from a range of sources, and was in our view substantial.

249.   The JIC produced further assessments of Iraq's ballistic missile programme in February 2001 and May 2001. That in February 2001 put for the first time an actual number to the size of the residual Iraqi stockpile of Al Hussein missiles:

We know that Iraq has retained key components of disassembled 650 km range Al Hussein missiles. Recent intelligence suggests that they may have assembled up to 20 of these missiles.

[JIC, 9 February 2001]

250.   The JIC appears to have based this judgement on its long-standing view, going as far back as the mid-1990s, that Iraq had concealed missile components; and three pieces of human intelligence from three separate sources on Iraqi possession of Al Hussein missiles. One of those sources provided the actual number of "*up to 20*" missiles being concealed, which was subsequently reflected in all future JIC assessments (and Government statements). That source was in our view in a position to comment authoritatively; and we have established that he reported reliably both before and after that report. But we note that he was passing on the comments of a sub-source, who reported only once. SIS had not, by the time we finished our Review, been able to contact the sub-source to validate the reliability of his reporting.

251.   The same assessment also commented further on Iraqi research and development activities, as did the JIC's further assessment in May 2001 on the status of Iraq's nuclear, biological, chemical and ballistic missile programmes. Of those, the JIC clearly felt most confident about the intelligence on Iraq's ballistic missile programmes, leading it to say in a Key Judgement to the assessment that:

We know most about Iraq's ballistic missile programme. Over the past two years, there has been a step change in progress. In addition to its permitted programmes for missile up to 150 km range, we know that Iraq is developing longer range systems possibly up to 2000km. We have good intelligence on research and development facilities but we do not know where the longer range missiles will be built.

[JIC, 10 May 2001]

252.   On Iraq's shorter-range missile programmes, the JIC noted that:

> We have reliable intelligence of Iraq's current short range ballistic missile programmes ... there is a growing body of evidence that Iraq intends to develop missiles well beyond its permitted range of 150km. This would represent a step change in Saddam Hussein's military capabilities.

that:

> ... [Iraq] appears to have accelerated progress over the past year. This includes:
>
> ...
>
> •   work on extending the range of the Al Samoud missile to 200–300km - production could start within the year;
>
> •   work on a further missile engine test stand with the capacity for much larger engines than the Al Samoud, including SCUD ...

and that:

> We assess that within a year Iraq will begin production of Al Samoud and possibly its extended range version. Both could deliver a conventional, chemical or biological warhead.

[JIC, 10 May 2001]

253.   On Iraq's long-range missile programmes, the JIC cautioned that:

> We have intelligence which is less clear on longer term missile objectives.

but reported on:

> ... tests on pairs of solid propellant motor cases. These are at a very early stage of development, but if combined in a missile, they could have a range of up to 2000km with a 500kg payload. Developed individually into missiles, using the same payload, they could achieve a range of between 700–1200km.

although:

> We do not know enough about the possible 2000 km range missile to judge a timescale for its completion.

[JIC, 10 May 2001]

254.   We have examined the intelligence to support these statements and consider the JIC's judgements to be well-founded and properly expressed.

SUMMARY

255. By early 2002, therefore, readers of JIC assessments will have had an impression of:

   a. The continuing clear strategic intent on the part of the Iraqi regime to pursue its nuclear, biological, chemical and ballistic missile programmes.

   b. Continuing efforts by the Iraqi regime to sustain and where possible develop its indigenous capabilities, including through procurement of necessary materiel.

   c. The development, drawing on those capabilities, of Iraq's 'break-out' potential in the chemical, biological and ballistic missile fields, coupled with the proven ability to weaponise onto some delivery systems chemical and biological agent.

256. It is right to remember, too, the international context within which those making and reading the JIC assessments were working. For the small group of policy-makers with access to the most sensitive JIC assessments, there were increasing concerns about proliferation elsewhere, including in the countries and through the networks described at Chapters 2 and 3. Thus, by early 2002, the JIC was concluding that AQ Khan had been marketing components and expertise related to the production of highly enriched uranium, suitable for use in nuclear weapons, for more than a decade; and, worse, that Khan had moved his base outside Pakistan and demand for his products had increased to the extent that he had now established his own production facilities and a network of associates and suppliers. It was also reporting on the evidence found, as a result of military operations in Afghanistan, of Usama bin Laden's efforts to seek unconventional weapons. Finally, senior policy-makers were also pre-occupied with the crisis between India and Pakistan and the nuclear risks which that posed.

257. All of this will have contributed to a strong sense of what one witness called a "*creeping tide*" of proliferation and growth in the nuclear, biological, chemical and ballistic missile capabilities of countries of concern. The Prime Minister described it to us as follows:

> *. . . what I was getting was a picture of, not that there were extra States necessarily coming into the proliferation and WMD business but that those States that were pushing on this were very determined, they were mainly States that you would not want to have this type of stuff because of their unstable and repressive nature and there were certainly suggestions that the potential link with terrorism, and there was also . . . quite a lot of stuff about Bin Laden and his desire to acquire WMD of one sort or another and I was quite often saying . . . "what are we actually doing about this" . . . there was a lot to make me concerned about this and actually at the first meeting I had with George Bush in February 2001 I raised it with him but . . . after September 11th it took on a completely different aspect. . . . what changed for me with September 11th was that I thought then you have to change your mindset . . . you have to go out and get after the different aspects of this threat . . . you have to deal with this because otherwise the threat will grow . . . you have to take a stand, you have to say "Right we are not going to allow the development of WMD in breach of the will of the international community to continue".*

258.   We consider the shift in UK policy towards Iraq in early 2002, and the Government's subsequent decision to take stronger action to enforce Iraqi disarmament, against that background.

5.4 MARCH – SEPTEMBER 2002

THE POLICY CONTEXT

259.   We have described in the previous Section how the Government's thinking developed in the period from 1998 to early-2002. President Bush's 'Axis of Evil' speech of 29 January 2002, supplemented by reporting of comments made by a range of US interlocutors of emerging thinking within the US Administration, and coupled with the sense of a *creeping tide*' of proliferation described at the end of the previous Section, provided the background to inter-departmental advice to Ministers in early March 2002.

260.   Officials restated the Government's objectives towards Iraq:

Within our objectives of preserving peace and stability in the Gulf and ensuring energy security, our current objectives towards Iraq are:

- *the reintegration of a law-abiding Iraq, which does not possess WMD or threaten its neighbours, into the international community. Implicitly, this cannot occur with Saddam in power; and*

- *hence, as the least worst option, we have supported containment of Iraq, by constraining Saddam's ability to re-arm or build up WMD and to threaten his neighbours.*

Subsidiary objectives are:

- *Preserving the territorial integrity of Iraq;*

- *improving the humanitarian situation of the Iraqi people;*

- *protecting the Kurds in northern Iraq;*

- *sustaining UK/US co-operation, including, if necessary, by moderating US policy; and*

- *maintaining the credibility and authority of the Security Council.*

261.   They set against those objectives an analysis of whether the policy of containment had worked, drawing heavily on JIC assessments, concluding that:

Since 1991, the policy of containment has been partially successful:

- *Sanctions have effectively frozen Iraq's nuclear programme;*

- *Iraq has been prevented from rebuilding its chemical arsenal to pre-Gulf War levels;*

- *Ballistic missile programmes have been severely restricted;*

- *Biological weapons (BW) and Chemical Weapons (CW) programmes have been hindered;*

- *No Fly Zones established over northern and southern Iraq have given some protection to the Kurds and the Shia. Although subject to continuing political pressure, the Kurds remain autonomous; and*

- *Saddam has not succeeded in seriously threatening his neighbours.*

but also that:

Iraq continues to develop weapons of mass destruction, although our intelligence is poor. Iraq has up to 20 650km range missiles left over from the Gulf War. These are capable of hitting Israel and the Gulf states. Design work for other ballistic missiles over the UN limit of 150km continues. Iraq continues with its BW and CW programmes and, if it has not already done so, could produce significant quantities of BW agents within days and CW agent within weeks of a decision to do so. We believe it could deliver CBW by a variety of means, including in ballistic missile warheads. There are also some indications of a continuing nuclear programme. Saddam has used WMD in the past and could do so again if his regime were threatened.

262. We consider this part of the advice to be a fair and balanced summary of the most recent JIC assessments.

263. On the basis of that analysis, officials then considered two broad options for securing the objectives set out above - a toughening of the existing containment policy; and regime change by military means. Much of their analysis on those options is not relevant to the scope of our Review. But two aspects are directly related to Iraqi nuclear, biological, chemical and ballistic missile programmes and options for dealing with them.

264. First, in the context of the policy option of toughening containment, the analysis noted amongst other things:

   a. The need for full implementation of all relevant United Nations Security Council resolutions, and the introduction in May 2002 of the Goods Review List, intended to focus sanctions exclusively on preventing shipments of unconventional weapons and other arms while allowing other business without scrutiny, in particular facilitating legitimate Iraqi commerce under the Oil for Food programme.

   b. That unity amongst members, especially Permanent Members, of the United Nations Security Council would facilitate a specific demand for Iraq to re-admit United Nations inspectors:

   Our aim would be to tell Saddam to admit inspectors or face the risk of military action.

   c. The need for tougher action against states breaking sanctions.

265. Officials went on to note that:

> The return of UN weapons inspectors would allow greater scrutiny of Iraqi WMD programmes ... If they found significant evidence of WMD, were expelled or, in face of an ultimatum, not re-admitted in the first place, then this could provide legal justification for large-scale military action ...

but cautioned that:

> Saddam is only likely to permit the return of inspectors if he believes the threat of large-scale US military action is imminent and that such concessions would prevent the US from acting decisively. Playing for time, he would then embark on a renewed policy of non co-operation ...

and that:

> ... although containment has held for the past decade, Iraq has progressively increased its international engagement. Even if the [Goods Review List] makes sanctions more sustainable, the sanctions regime could collapse in the long-term.

266. Secondly, in the context of the policy option of regime change by military means, officials noted that a full opinion would need to be sought from the Government's Law Officers if the policy option were to be taken further. The paper advised that regime change of itself had no basis in international law. It noted the judgement of the JIC that there was no recent evidence of Iraqi complicity with international terrorism, and thus no justification for action against Iraq based on action in self-defence to combat imminent threats of terrorism. It therefore concluded that offensive military action against Iraq could only be justified if Iraq were held to be in breach of United Nations Security Council Resolution 687, which imposed obligations on Iraq in regard to the elimination of its prohibited weapons programmes. It also noted that Resolution 687 did not terminate the authority to use force mandated in Security Council Resolution 678, so that a violation of Resolution 687 could revive the authorisation to use force in Resolution 678.

267. Officials noted, however, that for the five Permanent Members of the Security Council and the majority of the 15 members of the Council to take the view that Iraq was in breach of its obligations under Resolution 687:

> * They would need to be convinced that Iraq was in breach of its obligations regarding WMD, and ballistic missiles. Such proof would need to be incontrovertible and of large-scale activity. Current intelligence is insufficiently robust to meet this criterion ...

or

> * If P5 unity could be obtained, Iraq refused to readmit UN inspectors after a clear ultimatum by the UN Security Council.

or

> * The UN inspectors were re-admitted to Iraq and found sufficient evidence of WMD activity or were again expelled trying to do so.

268. Officials concluded on the basis of this analysis that:

> *In sum, despite the considerable difficulties, the use of overriding force in a ground campaign is the only option that we can be confident will remove Saddam and bring Iraq back into the international community.*

269. We have drawn out from amongst the paper's conclusions four factors in implementing this policy relevant to intelligence and its use, to which the policy-making community returned repeatedly in the following twelve months and to which we therefore return in the rest of this Chapter:

    a.   The value of increasing the pressure on the Iraqi regime, through tougher containment, stricter implementation of sanctions and a military build-up.

    b.   The importance of the United Nations dimension, in particular getting inspectors back into Iraq, noting that a refusal to admit inspectors, or their admission and subsequent frustration which resulted in an appropriate finding by the Security Council, would provide a basis for military action.

    c.   In that context, the justification for any military action in terms of international law. We cover this at Section 5.7.

    d.   The importance of presentational activity on Iraq's breaches (and other issues) to persuade other members of the United Nations Security Council as well as domestic audiences of the case for action to enforce disarmament.

IRAQ'S PROHIBITED PROGRAMMES

270. The JIC produced in parallel a 'status report' on Iraq's nuclear, biological, chemical and ballistic missile programmes. It warned in the text (although not in the Key Judgements) that:

> *Intelligence on Iraq's weapons of mass destruction (WMD) and ballistic missile programmes is sporadic and patchy. Iraq is also well practised in the art of deception, such as concealment and exaggeration. A complete picture of the various programmes is therefore difficult. But it is clear that Iraq continues to pursue a policy of acquiring WMD and their delivery means. Intelligence indicates that planning to reconstitute some of its programmes began in 1995. WMD programmes were then given a further boost in 1998 with the withdrawal of UNSCOM inspectors.*

[JIC, 15 March 2002]

271. On Iraq's **nuclear weapons programme**, the JIC noted that:

> *Iraq is pursuing a nuclear weapons programme. But it will not be able to indigenously produce a nuclear weapon while sanctions remain in place, unless suitable fissile material is purchased from abroad.*

[JIC, 15 March 2002]

272. Underpinning this assessment, the JIC noted that:

> *Although there is very little intelligence we continue to judge that Iraq is pursuing a nuclear weapons programme. We assess the programme to be based on gas centrifuge uranium enrichment ... Recent intelligence indicates that nuclear scientists were recalled to work on a nuclear programme in the autumn of 1998, but we do not know if large scale development work has yet recommenced. Procurement of dual-use items over the past few years could be used in a uranium enrichment programme.*

[JIC, 15 March 2002]

273. Overall, the JIC judged that:

> *... while sanctions remain effective, Iraq cannot indigenously develop and produce nuclear weapons; if sanctions were removed or became ineffective, it would take at least five years to produce a nuclear weapon. This timescale would shorten if fissile material was acquired from abroad.*

[JIC, 15 March 2002]

274. On Iraq's **chemical weapons programme**, the JIC reported in Key Judgements to its assessment that:

> *Iraq may retain some stocks of chemical agents.*

and that:

> *Following a decision to do so, Iraq could produce:*
>
> • *significant quantities of mustard within weeks;*
>
> • *significant quantities of sarin and VX within months, and in the case of VX may have already done so.*

[JIC, 15 March 2002]

275. Underpinning these judgements, the JIC said that:

> *We continue to judge that Iraq has an offensive chemical warfare (CW) programme, although there is very little intelligence relating to it. From the evidence available to us, we believe Iraq retains some production equipment, and some small stocks of CW agent precursors, and may have hidden small quantities of agents and weapons. Anomalies in Iraqi declarations to UNSCOM suggest stocks could be much larger.*

[JIC, 15 March 2002]

276. We conclude that this assessment reflects fairly the intelligence position on Iraq's chemical weapons programme prior to the receipt of new intelligence (described below) in summer 2002, which was considered substantial at the time (although some has subsequently been withdrawn and doubt cast on some of the rest). We note that the JIC said that it had very little intelligence in this area. We also note the way in which, through the use of the word *'may'*, the JIC reflected previous intelligence reports on Iraqi

production and weaponisation of chemical agent, although we believe the position is best described by a DIS commentary at the time:

Since 1998, there have been numerous claims that Iraq has continued to weaponise agent, but much of the reporting has come from dubious sources and that worth closer examination has lacked collateral and remains unsubstantiated.

277.   On Iraq's **biological weapons programme**, the JIC sustained its prior judgement that:

Iraq currently has available, either from pre Gulf War stocks or more recent production, a number of biological agents. Iraq could produce more of these biological agents within days.

[JIC, 15 March 2002]

278.   Underpinning this judgement, the JIC reported that:

BW work continued throughout the period of UNSCOM inspections and intelligence indicates that this programme continues. Key figures from the pre-Gulf War programme are reported to be involved. Research and development is assessed to continue under cover of a number of legitimate institutes and possibly in a number of covert facilities . . . There is no intelligence on any BW agent production facilities but one source indicates that Iraq may have developed mobile production facilities.

[JIC, 15 March 2002]

279.   On Iraq's ballistic missile capabilities, the JIC sustained its previous judgement that:

Iraq retains up to 20 Al Hussein ballistic missiles . . .

noting that:

The location and condition of these is unknown, but there is sufficient engineering expertise to make them operational.

[JIC, 15 March 2002]

280.   The JIC also commented on the programme to extend the range of the Al Samoud missile beyond limits set by the United Nations:

Iraq has reportedly succeeded in developing a number of 200km range variants of Al Samoud, although it is unclear if these are for operational use or research and development for longer-range systems.

[JIC, 15 March 2002]

281.   On the longer-range systems themselves, and Iraq's indigenous capabilities, the JIC said that:

Iraq has rebuilt much of the military production infrastructure associated with the missile programme damaged in the Gulf War and the few high profile sites targeted in Operation Desert Fox in 1998. New infrastructure is being built, with a particular focus on improving the support to the solid propellant missile programme.

and that:

Iraq is seeking to develop new, larger liquid and solid propellant missiles, contrary to UN limits. Recent intelligence indicates personnel associated with the Al Samoud programme have now been tasked to concentrate on designing liquid propellant systems with ranges of 2000–3000km. New intelligence indicates the main focus may be on the development of a SCUD derivative, which we judge has an intended range of around 1200km ... Providing sanctions remain effective, Iraq is unlikely to be able to produce a longer-range missile before 2007.

[JIC, 15 March 2002]

We have examined the intelligence underpinning these judgements and on missile development found it substantial.

POLICY DEVELOPMENT, APRIL-AUGUST 2002

282. The inter-departmental advice and JIC assessment we have described above formed part of the background for the Prime Minister's meeting with President Bush at Crawford on 6–7 April 2002. Policy advice was not influenced so much by changing intelligence on Iraq as by two other factors which reinforced each other.

283. One was a general concern about proliferation and the intelligence becoming available about the AQ Khan network, and what this added to the concerns already felt about North Korea, Libya and Iran as well as Iraq - the sense of a '*creeping tide*' we discuss above. The second was the absence of physical inspection of Iraqi programmes and activities following the withdrawal of United Nations inspectors in 1998 and fears about what the Iraqi regime might be able to achieve in terms of building up its prohibited weapons programmes if left unchecked.

284. Both those were increased by the heightened sensitivity following the terrorist attack on the World Trade Center and the changed 'calculus of threat' we describe at Chapter 3 - the desire of terrorists and extremists to cause casualties on a massive scale, undeterred by the fear of alienating the public or their supporters, or by considerations of personal survival. The Prime Minister confirmed to us that his position was accurately represented by a statement in one of the policy papers that:

What has changed is not the pace of Saddam Hussein's WMD programmes but our tolerance of them post 11 September.

285. We have also noted that departments and agencies saw the <u>direct</u> challenges to British interests caused by the proliferation activities of states other than Iraq as being more serious. But it is clear from the papers we have seen and from the evidence we have heard from witnesses that the Government, as well as being influenced by the concerns of the US Government, saw a need for immediate action on Iraq because of the wider historical and international context, especially Iraq's perceived continuing challenge to the authority of the United Nations. It also saw in the United Nations and a decade of Security Council Resolutions calling for Iraqi disarmament a basis for taking action to enforce Iraqi disarmament. The Prime Minister said to us on this that:

... the place to start was Iraq because you have the history of the United Nations Resolutions and you have the ... fact that we'd taken action in respect of WMD in

the aftermath of the Gulf War, then again in 1998, the fact that he had actually used chemical weapons ... my view was and still is that you have to take a stand, you have to say "Right we are not going to allow the development of WMD in breach of the will of the international community to continue" ...

and:

Now you have different strategies for different countries. In respect of Iraq it's going back to where we were before the inspectors were kicked out ...

286. The papers show that, of the four continuing themes set out at paragraph 269 above, sustaining the pressure on the Iraqi regime and the need for effective presentational activity were discussed between the Prime Minister and President Bush at Crawford; and the Prime Minister reverted to the need to get United Nations inspectors back into Iraq in his speech on 7 April following those discussions:

> *... the moment for decision on how to act is not yet with us. But to allow WMD to be developed by a state like Iraq without let or hindrance would be grossly to ignore the lessons of September 11 and we will not do it. The message to Saddam is clear: he has to let the inspectors back in, anyone, any time, any place that the international community demands.*

[Prime Minister, George Bush Senior Presidential Library, 7 April 2002]

287. The next key stage was a meeting on 23 July chaired by the Prime Minister with those Ministers and officials primarily involved in UK policy formulation and military contingency planning. This meeting considered, on the basis of a briefing from the Chairman of the JIC, the current intelligence assessment of Iraq's nuclear, biological, chemical and ballistic missile programmes, noting that Iraqi capabilities were smaller in scale than those of other states of concern. The meeting discussed the re-engagement of United Nations inspectors, against the background of intelligence advice that the Iraqi regime would allow inspectors into Iraq only when the threat of military action was thought to be real. It also commissioned work on legal issues.

288. The role of the United Nations - in building an international consensus on the need for action to tackle Iraq's prohibited weapons programmes; in the re-engagement of inspectors to investigate the extent and scale of those programmes; and ultimately in providing legitimacy for any military action to enforce disarmament - was discussed further at a meeting between the Foreign Secretary and Secretary of State Powell at a meeting at the Hamptons, New York, on 20 August 2002, and between the Prime Minister and the President at Camp David on 7 September 2002. It is clear from the departmental papers we have seen that the UK championed the role of the United Nations at that meeting.

JIC ASSESSMENTS, AUGUST-SEPTEMBER 2002

289. It is clear to us from departmental papers and from the evidence we have heard that the Government became increasingly concerned in August and early September 2002 about the nature of the media debate in the UK (stimulated by the media debate in the US). The

Prime Minister described to us his impression of a growing media picture of military action being imminent, and of a growing clamour for information from the media and from Parliamentarians about why the Government thought that military action was necessary. That led him to conclude that there was a need to put fuller information about Iraq's nuclear, biological, chemical and ballistic missile programmes into the public domain:

> ... I remember that during the course ... of July and August ... I was increasingly getting messages saying ... "are you about to go to war?" and I was thinking "this is ridiculous" and so I remember towards the end of the holiday actually phoning Bush and saying that we have got to put this in the right place straight away ... we've not decided on military action ... he was in absolute agreement ... So we devised the strategy, and this was really the purpose of Camp David ... where we would go down the UN route and ... the purpose of the dossier was simply to say "this is why we think this is important because here is the intelligence that means that this is not a fanciful view on our part, there is a real issue here" ... there was a tremendous clamour coming for it and I think a clamour to the extent that had we resisted it would have become completely impossible.

290. The dossier was commissioned on 3 September. Its preparation was informed by the existing body of JIC assessments; by drafts covering various aspects of Iraq's programmes which had been prepared for possible publication during the Spring and Summer; by JIC assessments on Iraq's nuclear, biological, chemical and ballistic missile programmes produced before the summer break; and also by two further JIC papers published on 21 August on "*Saddam's Diplomatic and Military Options*" and on 9 September on "*Iraqi use of Chemical and Biological Weapons – Possible Scenarios*".

291. The JIC assessment of 21 August was prepared at the request of the Ministry of Defence, to:

> ... consider what diplomatic options Saddam has to deter, avert or limit the scope and effectiveness of a US-led attack [and] ... his military options for facing a US-led attack.

[JIC, 21 August 2002]

292. The Key Judgements of that assessment would rightly have been prepared on a precautionary basis. Perhaps for that reason, we have observed that, when set against intelligence on Iraqi programmes contained in advice to Ministers in March, the JIC assessment reflected more firmly the premise that Iraq had chemical and biological weapons and would use them in war. Underpinning this must have been a presumption that, if Iraq did not have stocks of those weapons, it would quickly produce agent, weaponise it and deploy weapons to units. We have noted, for example, the JIC's judgements in this context that:

> We judge that Saddam would probably order missile attacks on Israel and the coalition early on in a conflict in an attempt to attract Israeli retaliation and thus widen the war, split the coalition and arouse popular opinion in the Arab states. Such missiles could be armed with chemical or biological warfare (CBW) agents.

that:

Although we have little intelligence on Iraq's CBW doctrine, and know little about Iraq's CBW work since late 1998, we judge it likely that Saddam would order the use of CBW against coalition forces at some point, probably after coalition attacks had begun. Iraqi CBW use would become increasingly likely the closer coalition forces came to Baghdad. Military targets might include troop concentrations or important fixed targets in rear areas such as ports and airfields.

and that:

Should he feel his fate is sealed, Saddam's judgement might change to 'bring the temple down' on his enemies no matter what the cost to the country as a whole. We judge that at this stage, Saddam would order the unrestrained use of CBW against coalition forces, supporting regional states and Israel, although he would face practical problems of command and control, the loyalty of his commanders, logistics problems and the availability of chemical or biological agents in sufficient quantities to be effective and the means to deliver them.

[JIC, 21 August 2002]

293. We were told that the JIC's conclusions were based in part on one human intelligence report from one source, but mainly on the JIC's own judgements. They thus represent an insight into the views of JIC members of Iraq's chemical and biological weapons capabilities at that time.

294. The JIC assessment of 9 September also focused on Iraq's use of chemical and biological weapons (indeed, although issued later, it was prepared in parallel with the assessment of 21 August). Its tone was set by its first Key Judgement, which reflected a significant change from previous JIC judgements on Iraqi possession of chemical and biological weapons:

Iraq has a chemical and biological weapons capability and Saddam is prepared to use it.

[JIC, 9 September 2002]

295. The paper recorded that:

Recent intelligence casts light on Iraq's holdings of weapons of mass destruction and on its doctrine for using them.

[JIC, 9 September 2002]

but warned that, nevertheless:

Intelligence remains limited and Saddam's own unpredictability complicates judgements about Iraqi use of these weapons. Much of this paper is necessarily based on judgement and assessment.

[JIC, 9 September 2002]

296. It then went on to judge that:

Iraq currently has available, either from pre Gulf War stocks or more recent production, a number of biological warfare (BW) and chemical warfare (CW) agents and weapons; . . .

to note that:

Other recent intelligence indicates that production of chemical and biological weapons is taking place; . . .

and that:

Iraq may have other toxins, chemical and biological agents that we do not know about.

[JIC, 9 September 2002]

297. On Iraq's chemical weapons capabilities, the JIC sustained its earlier judgement that:

. . . following a decision to do so, Iraq could produce significant quantities of mustard agent within weeks; significant quantities of the nerve agents sarin and VX within months (and in the case of VX may already have done so).

[JIC, 9 September 2002]

298. On Iraq's biological weapons capabilities, the JIC sustained its earlier judgement that:

Iraq could produce more biological agents within days.

[JIC, 9 September 2002]

299. On delivery means, the JIC sustained its earlier judgement that:

. . . Iraq retains up to 20 Al Husseins . . .

[JIC, 9 September 2002]

300. The more definite judgements inside the assessment were based on the receipt of significant new intelligence in August and September 2002, in response to the routine requirement on SIS to obtain information to support the drafting of JIC assessments (and which in this case supported the drafting of the Government's dossier). Four reports were received in total, from three sources, which were influential in the JIC's assessment.

301. The first provided material from a range of original informants reporting via an intermediary to the source[3]. We have noted, however, that the individual items from the informants did not confirm directly that Iraq had chemical weapons. They came from senior Iraqi officials who were believed at the time to have direct knowledge of Iraq's intentions, use, deployment or concealment of chemical weapons, but were based for most of the informants on an assumption (not direct knowledge) that Iraq had such weapons.

302. The second and third were from a source who had previously reported reliably and who continued to do so in the following months. This source, too, could not confirm from direct experience that Iraq had chemical weapons, resting on reporting "*common knowledge*" within his circle that chemical agent production was taking place. The second report from this source seems to us to duplicate much of the first.

303. The fourth was a single report, from a reliable and established source reporting a new sub-source who did not subsequently provide any further reporting, which was described as

---

[3] We were told by SIS during the course of our Review that there is now doubt about the reliability of this reporting chain and hence of the reports derived from it. Section 5.9 provides further detail.

"confirming" the intelligence on Iraqi mobile biological agent production facilities received from the liaison service. Contrary to the JIC view at the time, we believe that this report would have been more accurately described as *"complementary"* to, rather than *"confirming"*, it[4].

304. The JIC made clear that much of the assessment was based on its own judgement, drawing on the work done for its assessment of 21 August. But we were struck by the relative thinness of the intelligence base supporting the greater firmness of the JIC's judgements on Iraqi production and possession of chemical and biological weapons, especially the inferential nature of much of it. We also noted that the JIC did not reflect in its assessment, even if only to dismiss it, material in one of those reports suggesting that most members of the Iraqi leadership were not convinced that it would be possible to use chemical and biological weapons.

305. One further intelligence report which has been described to us as being significant was received between the production of the JIC's assessment of 9 September and the publication of the Government's dossier. This source[5] reported that production of biological and chemical agent had been accelerated by the Iraqi regime, including through the building of further facilities throughout Iraq.

306. By mid-September 2002, therefore, readers of JIC assessments will have had an impression of continuity with, but also some change from, the JIC assessment of 15 March:

   a. The continuing clear strategic intent on the part of the Iraqi regime to pursue its nuclear, biological, chemical and ballistic missile programmes.

   b. Continuing efforts by the Iraqi regime to sustain and where possible develop its indigenous capabilities.

   c. The apparent considerable development, drawing on these capabilities, of Iraq's 'break-out' potential. Although Iraq's nuclear programme continued to be constrained, there was strong evidence of continuing work on ballistic missiles, including the development and production of systems with ranges in excess of limits set by the United Nations. There was also evidence from one source, supported by one complementary report, of Iraq having the ability to produce biological agent in mobile facilities, and additional evidence of activity at one site formerly associated with Iraq's biological warfare programme. Finally, there were recent intelligence reports, albeit mainly inferential, that Iraq was producing chemical agent. For analysts, intelligence on Iraqi production of biological and chemical agent would have been put alongside Iraq's proven ability to weaponise agent onto at least some delivery systems, and separate intelligence reports on Saddam Hussein's intention to use chemical and biological weapons if attacked.

---

4 Chapter 1 sets out our view of the difference.
5 Reporting from this source was withdrawn by SIS in July 2003 as being unreliable. See Section 5.9.

307.   We consider the Government's dossier against this background.

5.5 THE GOVERNMENT'S DOSSIER OF SEPTEMBER 2002

INTRODUCTION

308.   The Government's dossier on *Iraq's Weapons of Mass Destruction*, published on 24 September 2002, had antecedents, including the information made public[6] in October 2001 on Al Qaida's responsibility for the attacks of 11 September. But it broke new ground in three ways:

   a.   The JIC had never previously produced a public document.

   b.   No Government case for any international action had previously been made to the British public through explicitly drawing on a JIC publication.

   c.   The authority of the British intelligence community, and of the JIC in particular, had never been used in such a public way. As the Prime Minister said in his Foreword to the dossier:

   It is unprecedented for the Government to publish this kind of document.

309.   We return below to the Government's reasons for publishing the dossier, and for drawing on intelligence material and the authority of the JIC in doing so, in response to growing Parliamentary and media debate about the imminence of war and questioning of the reasons for it.

310.   It is, however, fair to say at the outset that the dossier attracted more attention after the war than it had done before it. When first published, it was regarded as cautious, and even dull. Some of the attention that it eventually received was the product of controversy over the Government's further dossier of February 2003. Some of it arose over subsequent allegations that the intelligence in the September dossier had knowingly been embellished, and hence over the good faith of the Government. Lord Hutton dismissed those allegations. We should record that we, too, have seen no evidence that would support any such allegations.

311.   The September dossier also subsequently attracted attention because of the fact that, contrary to the expectation reflected in it, military forces entering Iraq did not find significant stocks of chemical or biological weapons or evidence of recent production of such weapons. We therefore consider here the genesis of the document, the challenge of presenting intelligence judgements effectively to the general public and the extent to which intelligence on particular areas of Iraqi activity was accurately reflected in the dossier.

312.   A number of specific elements in the dossier have subsequently attracted controversy. We examine the most prominent of these - the '45-minute' claim, uranium procurement activity in Africa, procurement of aluminium tubes and mobile biological agent production facilities – in Chapter 6.

---

[6] *"Responsibility for the Terrorist Atrocities in the United States, 11 September 2001".*

THE GENESIS OF THE DOSSIER

313. The dossier had its origins early in 2002 in an analysis of the threat posed by Iraq and three other countries known to be pursuing nuclear, chemical, biological and ballistic missile programmes. Work on this 'Four Country' analysis was dropped in the course of 2002 in favour of a document dedicated to Iraq alone for which a range of material had been produced. It was intended to inform public understanding of the case for stronger action (although not necessarily military action) to enforce Iraqi compliance with its obligations contained in United Nations Security Council resolutions over more than a decade. The timing of publication of the dossier was driven by concern within the Government over increasing media speculation in the UK (stimulated by media debate in the US) during the summer of 2002 that war was imminent, and growing questioning of the reasons for the UK going to war, which contributed to the decision to recall Parliament on 24 September to debate policy towards Iraq. The Prime Minister told us that:

> . . . in the course of July and August . . . I was increasingly getting messages saying . . . "are you about to go to war?" . . . I was thinking this is ridiculous . . . we've not decided on military action, we've not decided on what we're going to do . . . and the purpose of the dossier was simply to say "this is why we think this is important . . . here is the intelligence that means that this is not a fanciful view on our part, there is a real issue here" . . . there was a tremendous clamour coming for it and I think a clamour to the extent that had we resisted it would have become completely impossible.

314. The dossier was commissioned by the Prime Minister on 3 September. The timescale for its production was accelerated so that it would be ready when Parliament was recalled on 24 September.

315. We have considered carefully whether the dossier was explicitly intended to make a case for war. We have seen no evidence that this was the Government's purpose. The dossier was a broadly-based document which could support a range of policy options. The Foreign Secretary told us that:

> . . . there was a clear understanding by Government about the purpose of the document, which is that it was to meet the demand for intelligence-based information about Iraq and to make a case for the world to recognise the importance of the issue and hopefully to galvanise the international community into taking it seriously.

316. The Defence Secretary said in evidence to us:

> . . . if we were going to be able to make out a case for war against Iraq, we were going to have to publish the material. Of course we published the material if you recall in relation to Afghanistan for the same reason. . . . otherwise we would have just faced day in and day out a constant complaint that we had no basis, that we had no proper reason.

317. When we asked Dr Hans Blix if he saw the dossier as making a case for war, he said:

> No it was not. I saw it as a case for inspection . . .

318. Members of the JIC from whom we took evidence consistently told us that they did not see the dossier as making a case for <u>anything</u>. The Chairman of the JIC (Mr John Scarlett) said to Lord Hutton's Inquiry:

> *As far as I was concerned, this was an objective which was a very worthwhile objective if quite a difficult one; and it was to put into the public domain and to share, as far as it could be done safely, the intelligence assessment on this issue which was being provided to the Prime Minister and the Government. It was no more or less than that. And in no sense, in my mind, or in the mind of the JIC, was it a document designed to make a case for anything.*

319. We conclude that the dossier was not intended to make the case for a particular course of action in relation to Iraq. It was intended by the Government to promote domestic and international understanding of, and gain support for, the general direction in which Government policy had been moving since the early months of 2002, away from containment to a more proactive approach to enforcing Iraqi disarmament.

PRESENTING INTELLIGENCE TO THE PUBLIC

320. Once a decision had been taken to publish such a document, and to draw on intelligence in doing so, the question of authorship arose. The Security and Intelligence Co-ordinator (Sir David Omand) and the Chairman of the JIC took the view that the JIC should be responsible for the production of the dossier, to ensure that its content properly reflected the judgements of the intelligence community and did not prejudice national security. This was agreed at the outset. From then on, the dossier was in the ownership of the JIC generally and of its Chairman in particular, drawing on the members of the Assessments Staff and the wider intelligence community who had drafted the classified JIC assessments on this subject.

321. Many witnesses, both Ministers and officials, put it to us that there was no real alternative to the JIC taking on this role. In the view of these witnesses, a Government document that claimed to be underpinned by intelligence would have been met with immediate scepticism unless it was evident that the JIC had endorsed its content.

322. Against this, it may be said that the information published by the Government on Al Qaida's responsibility for the attacks of 11 September 2001 was put out without any public reference to the JIC. There was no conspicuous pressure on that occasion for the JIC to make its own view public. However, nor was there on that issue as much controversy and scepticism about the grounds for the Government's policy.

323. The advantage to the Government of associating the JIC's name with the dossier was the badge of objectivity that it brought with it and the credibility which this would give to the document. We have noted that Mr Alastair Campbell said in his minute to the Chairman of the JIC on 9 September, following a meeting to discuss the drafting of the dossier:

> *The first point is that this must be, and be seen to be, the work of you and your team, and that its credibility depends fundamentally on that.*

324. As the Prime Minister noted in his statement in the House of Commons on 24 September:

The dossier is based on the work of the British Joint Intelligence Committee ...
Normally, its work is obviously secret. Unusually, because it is important that we
explain our concerns about Saddam to the British people, we have decided to
disclose its assessments.

[Hansard, 24 September 2002, Col 3]

325. We record above the Foreign Secretary's evidence to us that the Government's understanding of the purpose of the dossier was that it was to:

> *... meet the demand for intelligence-based information about Iraq ...*

and to:

> *... make a case for the world to recognise the importance of the issue and hopefully to galvanise the international community into taking it seriously.*

326. As we also record above, the Chairman of the JIC, too, saw its purpose as informing public debate by putting:

> *... into the public domain ... the intelligence assessment on this issue ...*

but not as making a case:

> *... in no sense, in my mind or that of the JIC, was it a document designed to make a case for anything.*

327. The Government wanted a document on which it could draw in its *advocacy* of its policy. The JIC sought to offer a dispassionate *assessment* of intelligence and other material on Iraqi nuclear, biological, chemical and ballistic missile programmes. The JIC, with commendable motives, took responsibility for the dossier in order that its content should properly reflect the judgements of the intelligence community. They did their utmost to ensure that this standard was met. But this will have put strain on them in seeking to maintain their normal standards of neutral and objective assessment. Intelligence assessment is necessarily based heavily on judgement, relying on such material as intelligence has provided. It is not simply a matter of reporting this material but of presenting the judgements which flow from it to an experienced readership. Explaining those judgements to a wider public audience is a very different and difficult presentational task.

THE INTELLIGENCE BEHIND THE DOSSIER

328. As the Intelligence and Security Committee noted in its report[7] in September 2003:

> *The dossier was founded on the assessments then available.*

329. In this Section we examine the way in which judgements in JIC assessments prepared during 2002 were translated into the dossier. We are acutely aware of the danger of being unfair through selective quotation. The dossier did not follow the format of JIC assessments exactly, nor should it have done so. It was written for a different purpose and

---

[7] "*Iraqi Weapons of Mass Destruction - Intelligence and Assessments.*" Cm 5972. September 2003.

a different audience. Furthermore, to be comprehensive it brought together the key parts of a number of past JIC assessments, together with some intelligence that had not featured in JIC assessments, about Iraq's nuclear, biological, chemical and ballistic missile programmes. It is as a result difficult to make a direct comparison between judgements in any one JIC paper and the language in the dossier. We are therefore publishing, at Annex B, substantial extracts from three key JIC assessments issued in 2002 alongside relevant extracts from the Government's dossier, the Prime Minister's Foreword and his accompanying statement to the House of Commons so that readers can check our judgements and reach their own conclusions.

330.   We have noted that the JIC assessment of 9 September exercised considerable influence over the dossier, which was being prepared almost in parallel. That assessment was written to inform military and other contingency planning, and examined a range of possible scenarios in which chemical and biological weapons might be used by Iraq. But these precautionary JIC judgements about the scenarios (as was right for a document to inform military planning) were subsequently taken up into the dossier, and were taken up in an abbreviated form in which points were run together and caveats on the intelligence were dropped. The most significant difference was the omission of the warnings included in JIC assessments about the limited intelligence base on which some aspects of those assessments were being made. We set out below the warnings on this point from JIC assessments between March and September 2002 (in the left-hand column) against extracts from the dossier (in the right-hand column) addressing the size and quality of the intelligence base:

Quotations from JIC Assessments	Quotations from the dossier
"Iraqi Use of Chemical and Biological Weapons – Possible Scenarios" (9 September 2002)	
Recent intelligence casts light on Iraq's holdings of weapons of mass destruction and on its doctrine for using them. Intelligence remains limited and Saddam's own unpredictability complicates judgements about Iraqi use of these weapons. Much of this paper is necessarily based on judgement and assessment.	*As well as the public evidence, however, significant additional information is available to the Government from secret intelligence sources, described in more detail in this paper. This intelligence cannot tell us about everything. However, it provides a fuller picture of Iraqi plans and capabilities.*
"Iraq; Saddam's Diplomatic and Military Options" (21 August 2002)	
. . . we have little intelligence on Iraq's CBW doctrine, and know little about Iraq's CBW work since late 1998 . . .	*Intelligence rarely offers a complete account of activities which are designed to remain concealed. The nature of Saddam's regime makes Iraq a difficult target for the intelligence services. Intelligence, however, has provided important insights into Iraqi programmes and Iraqi military thinking. Taken together with what is already known from other sources, this intelligence builds our understanding of Iraq's capabilities and adds significantly to the analysis already in the public domain. But intelligence sources need to be protected, and this limits the detail that can be made available.*
"The Status of Iraqi WMD Programmes" (15 March 2002)	
Intelligence on Iraq's weapons of mass destruction (WMD) and ballistic missile programmes is sporadic and patchy. Iraq is also well practised in the art of deception, such as concealment and exaggeration. A complete picture of the various programmes is therefore difficult. But it is clear that Iraq continues to pursue a policy of acquiring WMD and their delivery means.	*Part 1 of this paper includes some of the most significant views reached by the JIC between 1999 and 2002.*

331.   The ISC has observed[8] that the 9 September assessment:

> *. . . did not highlight in the key judgements the uncertainties and gaps in the UK's knowledge about the Iraqi biological and chemical weapons.*

The same was true of the 21 August and 15 March assessments. In each paper, a description of the limitations of the intelligence underlying some aspects of those assessments was given in the <u>body</u> of each paper. Experienced readers would have seen these warnings in the original JIC assessments and taken them into account in reading them. But the public, through reading the dossier, would not have known of them. The dossier did include a first chapter on the role of intelligence, as an introduction for the lay reader. But, rather than illuminating the limitations of intelligence either in the case of Iraq or more generally[9], the language in that Chapter may have had the opposite effect on readers. Readers may, for example, have read language in the dossier about the impossibility for security reasons of putting all the detail of the intelligence into the public domain as implying that there was fuller and firmer intelligence behind the judgements than was the case: our view, having reviewed all of the material, is that judgements in the dossier went to (although not beyond) the outer limits of the intelligence available. The Prime Minister's description, in his statement to the House of Commons on the day of publication of the dossier, of the picture painted by the intelligence services in the dossier as "*extensive, detailed and authoritative*" may have reinforced this impression.

332.   We believe that it was a serious weakness that the JIC's warnings on the limitations of the intelligence underlying some of its judgements were not made sufficiently clear in the dossier.

THE ACCURACY OF THE DOSSIER

333.   In general, subject to the points below and others identified in Chapter 6, the statements in the dossier reflected fairly the judgements of past JIC assessments. In the tables in the paragraphs below, quotations from JIC assessments are set out in the left-hand column and from the dossier are set out in the right-hand column.

---

[8] "*Iraqi Weapons of Mass Destruction - Intelligence and Assessments*". Cm 5972. September 2003.
[9] See, for example, the section on this subject at Chapter 1 of this Report.

334.   Regime intent:

Quotations from JIC Assessments	Quotations from the dossier
Saddam attaches great importance to having CBW, is committed to using CBW if he can and is aware of the implications of doing so. Saddam wants it to dominate his neighbours and deter his enemies who he considers are unimpressed by his weakened conventional military capability. [9 September]	*Saddam continues to attach great importance to the possession of weapons of mass destruction and ballistic missiles which he regards as being the basis for Iraq's regional power. He is determined to retain these capabilities.* [Chapter 3, paragraph 1]
Iraq has a chemical and biological weapons capability and Saddam is prepared to use it. [9 September]	*It* [the intelligence] *shows that he does not regard them only as weapons of last resort.* [Executive Summary, paragraph 4]
Faced with the likelihood of military defeat and being removed from power, Saddam is unlikely to be deterred from using chemical and biological weapons by any diplomatic or military means. [9 September]	
The use of chemical and biological weapons prior to any military attack would boost support for US-led action and is unlikely. [9 September]	
Intelligence indicates that Saddam has identified Bahrain, Jordan, Qatar, Israel, Kuwait as targets. Turkey could also be at risk. [9 September]	*Iraq possesses extended-range versions of the SCUD ballistic missile in breach of UNSCR 687 which are capable of reaching Cyprus, Eastern Turkey, Tehran and Israel.* [Chapter 3, paragraph 1]
Saddam is prepared to order missile strikes against Israel, with chemical or biological warheads, in order to widen the war once hostilities begin. [9 September]	

335.   The first extract from the dossier fairly reflects the 9 September JIC assessment. While the context of the last three extracts from the assessment, that Iraq would use chemical and biological weapons only in the event of an attack, is not repeated in the dossier, this was because the dossier was dealing with the overall picture, while the JIC's assessment of 9 September was only looking at attack scenarios.

336.   Chemical and biological agents:

Quotations from JIC Assessments	Quotations from the dossier
Following a decision to do so, Iraq could produce significant quantities of mustard agent within weeks; significant quantities of the nerve agents sarin and VX within months (and in the case of VX Iraq may already have done so). Production of sarin and VX would be heavily dependent on hidden stocks of precursors [9 September]	[Iraq has] *the capability to produce the chemical agents mustard gas, tabun, sarin, cyclosarin, and VX capable of producing mass casualties.* [Chapter 3, paragraph 16]
Iraq could produce more biological agents within days. At the time of the Gulf War Iraq had developed the lethal BW agents anthrax, botulinum toxin and aflatoxin. [9 September]	*Iraq has a biological agent production capability and can produce at least anthrax, botulinum toxin, aflatoxin and ricin.* [Chapter 3, paragraph 16]
Iraq may have other toxins, chemical and biological agents that we do not know about; [9 September]	
. . . the former Habbaniyah chemical weapons site may provide the base for producing ricin, although there is no evidence that Iraq is currently doing so. [15 March]	
Iraq has developed for the military, fermentation systems which are capable of being mounted on road-trailers or rail cars. These could produce BW agents. [9 September]	[Iraq has] *developed mobile laboratories for military use, corroborating earlier reports about the mobile production of biological warfare agents.* [Executive Summary, paragraph 6]
Iraq has a variety of delivery means available for both chemical and biological weapons, some of which are very basic. These include free fall bombs, artillery shells, helicopter and aircraft borne sprayers and ballistic missile warheads. Although the exact numbers are unknown. Iraq is also continuing with the L-29 remotely piloted vehicle programme, which could have chemical and biological weapons delivery applications. [15 March]	

337. The dossier did not refer explicitly to the JIC's uncertainty about the size of stocks of sarin and VX precursors, and hence Iraq's ability to produce these agents. Nor did it, like the JIC assessments, refer explicitly to the lack of intelligence on the location of facilities for producing biological and chemical agent, although it did draw attention to the difficulty of assessing the use made of 'dual use' facilities.

338. Delivery systems:

Quotations from JIC Assessments	Quotations from the dossier
Iraq told UNSCOM in the 1990s that it filled 25 warheads with anthrax, bolulinum toxin and aflatoxin for its Al Hussein ballistic missile (range 650km). Iraq also admitted it had developed 50 chemical warheads for Al Hussein. We judge Iraq retains up to 20 Al Husseins and a limited number of launchers. [9 September]	*Iraq told UNSCOM that it filled 25 warheads with anthrax, botulinum toxin and aflatoxin. Iraq also developed chemical agent warheads for al-Hussein. Iraq admitted to producing 50 chemical warheads for al-Hussein which were intended for the delivery of a mixture of sarin and cyclosarin.* [Chapter 3, paragraph 14]
Iraq is also developing short-range systems Al Samoud/Ababil 100 ballistic missiles (range 150kms plus) - One intelligence report suggests that Iraq has "lost" the capability to develop warheads capable of effectively disseminating chemical and biological agent and that it would take six months to overcome the "technical difficulties". However, both these missile systems are currently being deployed with military units and an emergency operational capability with conventional warheads is probably available. [9 September]	*Al-Samoud/Ababil 100 ballistic missiles (range 150kms plus): it is unclear if chemical and biological warheads have been developed for these systems, but given the Iraqi experience on other missile systems, we judge that Iraq has the technical expertise for doing so.* [Chapter 3, paragraph 14]
Iraq has probably dispersed its special weapons, including its CBW weapons. Intelligence also indicates that chemical and biological munitions could be with military units and ready for firing within 20–45 minutes. [9 September]	*[The dossier] discloses that his military planning allows for some of the WMD to be ready within 45 minutes of an order to use them.* [Prime Minister's Foreword] *Iraq has: ... military plans for the use of chemical and biological weapons, including against its own Shia population. Some of these weapons are deployable within 45 minutes of an order to use them* [Executive Summary, paragraph 6]

Quotations from JIC Assessments	Quotations from the dossier
	Iraq's military forces are able to use chemical and biological weapons, with command, control and logistical arrangements in place. The Iraqi military are able to deploy these weapons within 45 minutes of a decision to do so. [Chapter 3, paragraph 1] *. . . intelligence indicates that as part of Iraq's military planning Saddam is willing to use chemical and biological weapons, including against his own Shia population. Intelligence indicates that the Iraqi military are able to deploy chemical or biological weapons within 45 minutes of an order to do so.* [Chapter 3, paragraph 5]

339. JIC judgements on Iraq's ballistic missile capabilities were reflected fairly in the dossier. The '45 minute' issue was, because of the context of the JIC assessment[10], run together in the dossier with statements on Iraqi intentions for use of its capabilities. It was also included in the Prime Minister's Foreword.

340. Nuclear:

Quotations from JIC Assessments	Quotations from the dossier
We judge that Iraq does not possess a nuclear weapons capability. . . . Although there is very little intelligence, we continue to judge that Iraq is pursuing a nuclear weapons programme. [15 March]	*Iraq continues to work on developing nuclear weapons, in breach of its obligations under the Non-Proliferation Treaty and in breach of UNSCR 687.* [Chapter 3, paragraph 1]
We have an unclear picture of the current status of Iraq's nuclear programme. There is intelligence that Iraq continued its nuclear research after the Gulf War and recalled its nuclear scientists in 1998. [10 May 2001]	*In mid-2001 the JIC assessed that Iraq had continued its nuclear research after 1998. The JIC drew attention to intelligence that Iraq had recalled its nuclear scientists to the programme in 1998.* [Chapter 3, paragraph 17]

341. The dossier did not repeat the JIC's warning about the limited intelligence available on Iraq's nuclear weapon programme, but it did make clear separately that Iraq would not be able to develop a nuclear weapon without procuring key equipment and materiel.

---

[10] See the fuller analysis at Chapter 6.

LESSONS FOR THE FUTURE

342. Many witnesses have told us that they expect that the nature of the security challenges faced by the UK in the 21st century, and public expectations of government openness, will increase the frequency of demands on government to put intelligence into the public domain when arguing the case for a particular course of action. On this view, the production of the dossier has set a precedent for openness that the public will wish to see repeated in future. We recognise this argument. We conclude that, if intelligence is to be used more widely by governments in public debate in future, those doing so must be careful to explain its uses and limitations. It will be essential, too, that clearer and more effective dividing lines between assessment and advocacy are established when doing so.

5.6 SEPTEMBER 2002 – MARCH 2003

THE SCOPE OF JIC ASSESSMENTS

343. There was a marked shift in the nature of JIC assessments after the production of the Government's dossier. Before 24 September, they had focused on the status of Iraq's nuclear, biological, chemical and ballistic missile programmes, and on Iraqi options for the use of its capabilities. After that date, the JIC and intelligence community turned their attention to intelligence reporting on and assessments of:

    a. Links between the Iraqi regime, its chemical and biological weapons capabilities and terrorism (covered more fully at Chapter 6).

    b. The likely nature of Iraq's dealings with the United Nations, and in particular its handling of staff of the United Nations Monitoring, Verification and Inspection Commission (UNMOVIC) and of the IAEA undertaking inspection activities in Iraq.

    c. Iraqi military preparations and options.

344. Intelligence was also collected and used to inform contingency planning for a possible military campaign, especially in the selection of targets that should be attacked.

345. Apart from an assessment of Iraq's declaration of 7 December to the United Nations[11] (covered further below), Iraq's nuclear, biological, chemical and ballistic missile capabilities were covered only tangentially in those assessments. We summarise these assessments below.

IRAQI CAPABILITIES

346. No new JIC assessment of the status of Iraq's **nuclear weapons programme** was prepared during the period, notwithstanding the findings of the IAEA inspectors. On Iraq's **chemical weapons programme**, the JIC noted in October that:

---

[11] Security Council Resolution 1441 adopted on 8 November 2002 called for Iraq to provide "*a currently accurate, full, and complete declaration of all aspects of its programme to develop chemical, biological, and nuclear weapons, ballistic missiles, and other delivery systems . . .*".

> *We continue to judge . . . that Iraq has an offensive CW programme and intelligence indicates that it has continued to produce chemical agent.*

and that:

> *Iraq can weaponise CBW agents into missile warheads, bombs, artillery rockets and shells.*

> [JIC, 28 October 2002]

347.   The judgement that Iraq was continuing to produce chemical agent was supported by one new human intelligence report[12] received on 30 September.

348.   On Iraq's **biological weapons programme**, the JIC concluded in its October assessment that:

> *We assess that Iraq has continued with an offensive BW programme. Research, development and production is assessed to continue under cover of a number of outwardly legitimate institutes and covert facilities. Confirmed intelligence reveals that transportable BW production facilities have been constructed. Iraq has possibly already made significant quantities of BW agents and intelligence indicates it has continued to produce biological agents. We judge that Iraq is self-sufficient in its BW programme and currently has available, either from pre-Gulf War stocks or more recent production, anthrax spores, botulinum toxin, aflatoxin, and possibly plague and ricin.*

> [JIC, 28 October 2002]

349.   We cover JIC assessments on Iraqi possession of plague more fully at Chapter 6. The most significant change in this assessment was in the JIC's indication to readers of its new judgement that intelligence on mobile biological agent production facilities had been "*confirmed*". The greater firmness of the JIC's judgement in this area was based on the receipt of one intelligence report, from a reliable and established source quoting a new sub-source. That report reinforced the large volume of reports on those facilities received from a single source through a liaison service since April 2000, although our view is that the new report was complementary to rather than confirming those from the liaison service.

350.   On Iraq's **ballistic missile programme**, a JIC assessment of December 2002 sustained the judgement it had made over the past two years that Iraq had: . . .

> *. . . retained up to 20 Al Hussein missiles . . . though their condition is not known . . .*

> [JIC, 6 December 2002]

---

[12] This report was withdrawn when all reporting from this source was withdrawn by SIS in July 2003 as being unreliable. Section 5.9 provides fuller detail.

351.　It also noted that:

> *Intelligence indicates that the Iraqis may have developed an extended al-Samoud,*
> *which sources claim has a range of over 300 Kms. We judge such ranges are*
> *technically possible, but would result in a significant decrease in payload.*

[JIC, 6 December 2002]

DECEPTION AND CONCEALMENT

352.　In contrast to reporting on Iraqi nuclear, biological, chemical and ballistic missile capabilities, intelligence reporting between mid-October 2002 and March 2003 on Iraqi deception and concealment activities was voluminous. Reports covered Iraqi preparations for the arrival of UNMOVIC and IAEA inspectors following the adoption of United Nations Security Council Resolution 1441, and plans to obstruct their activity once they had arrived. Human intelligence reports again played an important role in informing JIC assessments during this period.

353.　Two full JIC assessments addressed Iraqi deception and concealment in depth. The issue was covered, sometimes extensively, in four Weekly Intelligence Summaries on Iraq, 32 Intelligence Updates and 19 Daily Intelligence Highlights provided to relevant Ministers and officials.

354.　Those reports, together with the findings of the United Nations inspectors, were available to the Prime Minister when deciding whether Iraq was in further material breach of its obligations under United Nations Security Council Resolution 1441, an issue to which we return in the next Section. We have therefore examined their quality, both in terms of the reliability of the original sources and by validation against the discoveries made by UNMOVIC and the IAEA on the basis of the intelligence reports they received from the UK.

Reliability of human intelligence reports

355.　Of the human intelligence reports which had a material influence on JIC assessments on Iraqi deception and concealment, over four-fifths came from two principal sources, and two-thirds from one in particular. Both were believed at the time to be reporting reliably[13]. There will therefore have been a tendency for the intelligence community to assume that they were similarly reporting reliably on Iraqi concealment and deception.

Use of the Intelligence

356.　The British Government, drawing on intelligence reports, passed leads to UNMOVIC via the '*Rockingham*' cell (see box) and SIS to assist them in their search for weapons, materiel, documents and personnel related to Iraq's nuclear, biological, chemical and ballistic missile programmes.

---

[13] We have, however, been told that post-war validation by SIS of its sources has led to doubts about the reliability of the reports provided by the source who provided the smaller proportion of the reporting.

Operation Rockingham

At the end of the first Gulf war, the United Nations Security Council passed a series of resolutions aimed at eliminating Iraq's nuclear, biological and chemical weapons capabilities, and programmes covering ballistic missiles with ranges in excess of 150 kilometres. These established the United Nations Special Commission (UNSCOM), which worked closely with the International Atomic Energy Agency (IAEA) in pursuit of this goal. UK support to UNSCOM and the IAEA was provided as a cross-departmental initiative through a new organisation within the Defence Intelligence Staff known as Operation Rockingham.

From 1991 until the end of 1998, Rockingham was responsible for briefing some of the personnel who formed part of UNSCOM and IAEA inspection teams. It processed information received as a result of the inspections, and acted as a central source of advice on continuing inspection activity. Rockingham also advised FCO and MOD policy branches on the provision of UK experts from government and industry to work with UNSCOM and the IAEA as members of inspection teams. Rockingham included an officer detached to Bahrain to staff an organisation known as GATEWAY to co-ordinate briefings to, and debriefings of, inspection team members as they deployed to, and returned from, Iraq.

With the withdrawal of UNSCOM from Iraq in December 1998, Rockingham was reduced to a single member of staff. It continued to maintain a watching brief on matters related to possible future United Nations inspections in Iraq. GATEWAY was closed.

Rockingham was expanded again to provide UK support to UNMOVIC. Unlike UNSCOM, UNMOVIC inspectors were United Nations employees, and did not deploy in a national capacity. As a result, no official feedback from UNMOVIC was offered, nor expected. Rockingham did not brief or debrief individual inspectors. It did, however, continue to provide UNMOVIC and the IAEA with all-source UK intelligence assessments of the extent of Iraq's nuclear, biological, chemical and ballistic missile programmes, and information about sites of potential significance. Rockingham also assisted in the briefing of senior UNMOVIC staff and responded to a number of requests from UNMOVIC for specific information to assist its work. It acted as the focus for the work tasked by the JIC on the analysis of the Iraqi declaration of 7 December 2002.

After the second Gulf war, Rockingham became the UK focal point for intelligence support to the work of the Iraq Survey Group. In that role, Rockingham receives and distributes reporting from the ISG, and provides additional guidance and support to the ISG and UK customers, as required.

357. About 30 separate pieces of intelligence from human sources and satellite imagery, covering 19 sites in all, were involved in the leads provided to the inspectors. UNMOVIC visited seven of those sites, made a partial examination of one more and subjected one further site to examination by ground-penetrating radar. In terms of the results:

    a.   At two sites, United Nations inspectors found relevant material – 223 Volga engines for Al Samoud missiles at one, and at the other documents on the Iraqi nuclear programme dating from 1991.

    b.   At one site, inspectors found conventional munitions (they were also aware of conventional munitions concealed at another site that they did not visit, and found conventional munitions near a site they planned to visit).

    c.   At three sites, inspectors found no evidence of either prohibited or conventional Iraqi programmes. (The inspection by ground-penetrating radar of one site also produced no results.) One of these three sites was the Al Kut hospital, where the first inspection was disrupted by a demonstration; nothing was found when the inspectors returned (although we note that this was carried out 15 days later).

    d.   At the final site, the inspectors took samples.

358.   We have noted a reasonable correlation between the intelligence provided by one source and discoveries made by UNMOVIC. Leads provided on the basis of intelligence received from other sources do not appear to have borne fruit. In the time available UNMOVIC followed up a little over half of the leads provided by the British Government.

359.   In total, UNMOVIC carried out, in a little under four months, 731 inspections, covering 411 sites, 88 of which had not been inspected before. It found and, where relevant, supervised the destruction of:

    a.   The illegally-imported Volga engines, and historic documents on the Iraqi nuclear programme, described above, flowing from leads given by the British Government.

    b.   Over 70 illegal Al-Samoud 2 missiles and over 50 warheads. When UNMOVIC's operations were suspended in mid-March 2003, 25 more missiles and nearly 40 warheads remained to be destroyed. (As noted above, British intelligence had led to the discovery of the engines for the missiles.)

    c.   Two propellant casting chambers capable of producing rocket motors for missiles with ranges greater than 150km.

    d.   A small number of unfilled chemical munitions (all old).

    e.   244.6 kg of declared but expired growth media and 40 vials of expired 'toxin standards'.

360.   Dr Blix in early 2003 told the United Nations in addition that:

    a.   He had information indicating that Iraq had worked on purifying and stabilising VX, and had achieved more than it had declared.

    b.   UNMOVIC thought that 10,000 litres of anthrax might still exist, and was concerned generally about biological agent growth media.

    c.   Iraq had worked on a possible anthrax simulant (*Bacillus thuringiensis*).

    d.   Of the 157 biological agent-filled munitions which Iraq had declared but UNSCOM had considered unaccounted for, UNMOVIC, with Iraq's co-operation, had accounted for 128. Two were found to have definitely contained anthrax.

    e.   UNMOVIC inspections had confirmed that unmanned aerial vehicles capable of autonomous flight had been developed and produced, but did not know whether they were intended for chemical and biological warfare use.

361. By the time United Nations inspectors left on 17 March 2003, the IAEA had not found any evidence or plausible indication of the revival of Iraq's nuclear programme.

362. As we have described above, there was throughout this period a substantial volume of intelligence reports on Iraqi deception and concealment activities, coupled with - as UNMOVIC reported - a lack of active co-operation with inspectors. There were also the UNMOVIC discoveries listed above. Even so, we are surprised that neither policy-makers nor the intelligence community, as the generally negative results of UNMOVIC inspections became increasingly apparent, conducted a formal re-evaluation of the quality of the intelligence and hence of the assessments made on it. We have noted in departmental papers expressions of concern about the impact on public and international opinion of the lack of strong evidence of Iraqi violation of its disarmament obligations. But those involved appear to have operated on the presumption that the intelligence was right, and that it was because of the combination of Iraqi concealment and deception activities and perceived UNMOVIC weaknesses that such evidence was not found.

363. We also noted the limited time given to evaluation of the Iraqi declaration of 7 December. Considerable effort was made by DIS staff immediately on its receipt to sift and analyse its contents. Their initial findings were reported by the Assessments Staff on 13 December. Further DIS work on the declaration was captured in a JIC paper on 18 December, properly described as "*An Initial Assessment of Iraq's WMD Declaration*". Thereafter, despite its importance to the determination of whether Iraq was in further material breach of its disarmament obligations under United Nations Security Council Resolution 1441[14], the JIC made no further assessment.

364. The JIC's attitude will have been shaped by intelligence received in late-November that Iraq's declaration would omit references to its prohibited programmes and more generally would seek to overload the United Nations with information. Predictions on the extreme length[15] and nature of the declaration were subsequently borne out. Even so, we find it odd that after the '*Initial Assessment*' of 18 December, the JIC produced no further assessment.

SUMMARY

365. We consider in the next Section those legal issues surrounding the decision to take military action to enforce Iraqi disarmament that fall within our terms of reference. From our Review, we believe that those involved will, in taking that decision, have had the following evidence derived from intelligence reports and assessments made by the UK intelligence community[16]:

    a. Judgements which became increasingly firm during summer 2002 about the extent of Iraq's prohibited programmes, drawing in particular on new intelligence on Iraqi biological and chemical weapons programmes received from 2000 onwards.

---

[14] Operative Paragraph 4.
[15] The eventual document was almost 12,000 pages long.
[16] They will, of course, also have taken into account the findings of UNMOVIC and the IAEA, and the conclusions of the United Nations Security Council.

b. The initial assessment of the Iraqi declaration of 7 December.

c. Intelligence reports from September 2002 onwards on the extent of Iraqi concealment of evidence of prohibited programmes, together with the results of inspections undertaken on the basis of those reports.

5.7 THE ROLE OF INTELLIGENCE IN ASSESSING THE LEGALITY OF THE WAR[17]

366. We have examined the Attorney General's advice on the legality of war in Iraq, and taken oral evidence from him on two occasions.

367. The Attorney General was briefed on relevant intelligence issues in September 2002 and February 2003.

368. At our request, the Legal Secretariat to the Law Officers submitted to us a background note on the usual procedure by which the Government obtains legal advice from the Law Officers, who are the Government's principal legal advisers. In view of the public interest in this matter, we judge that it may be worth setting this out.

369. There is no set procedure for seeking the advice of the Law Officers. The usual practice is for a Government lawyer in the Whitehall department with the lead interest in the issue to write to the Legal Secretary to the Law Officers, or to one of the officials in the Legal Secretariat, with a request for Law Officers' advice. It is not, however, the invariable practice for advice to be sought in this way. On occasion, Ministers write directly to the Law Officers to seek their advice. Paragraph 22 of the Ministerial Code describes the type of case where it will normally be appropriate to consult the Law Officers.

370. Requests for advice normally set out the background and provide the department's own legal analysis of the issue. Depending on the circumstances, a number of things might happen once the request is received. The lead department might be asked for further information or further analysis of the legal question if the Legal Secretariat felt that this was needed; it might be necessary to convene a meeting between the Law Officers and relevant departmental lawyers to discuss the matter; the Law Officers might ask for the views of outside counsel on the issue before giving their advice; or the letter might simply be submitted by the Legal Secretariat to the Law Officers for their views.

371. Once the Law Officers have formed a view on the matter, officials in the Legal Secretariat would normally write back to the lead department recording the Law Officers' advice. In some cases, the Law Officers may communicate their advice directly to the Minister of the lead department.

372. There is a long-standing convention, adhered to by successive Governments (and reflected in paragraph 24 of the Ministerial Code), that neither the fact that the Law Officers

---

[17] The Government made clear to us that Government legal advice, whether from the Attorney General or from other legal advisers, was shown to us in confidence and without intending to waive the legal professional privilege to which the advice is subject. We have therefore referred to legal advice in general terms only and have not disclosed the contents of that advice in this Report, except to the very limited extent that this is done in this Section. Those limitations are deliberately constructed in a way which does not give rise to the risk of waiver of legal professional privilege in the underlying advice which was given, which the Attorney General has made clear to us remains confidential.

have been consulted in relation to a particular matter nor the substance of any advice they may have given is disclosed outside Government. The purpose of the convention is to enable the Government, like everyone else, to obtain full and frank legal advice in confidence. There is a strong public interest in the Government seeking legal advice so that it acts in accordance with the law. If there were a risk that Law Officers' advice would be made public, this might inhibit the provision of full and frank legal advice. The rationale for the convention is the same as that which underpins the doctrine of legal professional privilege, which also applies to Law Officers' advice.

373.   We have been advised of only three examples in the past 100 years of the actual advice of the Law Officers being disclosed publicly. Two of those examples relate to the provision of documents in judicial proceedings, namely the Factortame litigation and the Scott Inquiry. In both of those cases, the advice given by the Law Officers was central to the issues in the proceedings. The third example arose from the Westland affair when a letter from the then Solicitor General to the then Secretary of State for Defence was published by the Government. This followed, however, the unauthorised disclosure of part of the Solicitor General's letter in breach of the convention, which gave rise to serious consideration of prosecutions under the Officials Secrets Act and led to, or contributed to, the resignation of two Cabinet Ministers.

374.   In the case of Iraq, the Attorney General offered initial advice to the Government prior to the adoption of United Nations Security Council Resolution 1441, when consideration was being given to the enforcement of Iraq's compliance with its disarmament obligations under United Nations Security Council Resolution 687 and subsequent relevant resolutions. That advice mainly concerned legal interpretation of relevant United Nations Security Council resolutions. But the Attorney General did conclude that, on the basis of the information he had seen, there would be no justification for the use of force against Iraq on grounds of self-defence against an imminent threat.

375.   Following the passing of United Nations Security Council Resolution 1441, there was disagreement inside the FCO on whether a further decision of the Security Council would be needed before the UK could lawfully use force against Iraq to secure compliance by Iraq with its disarmament obligations. The Foreign Secretary told us that he took the view that, particularly in the light of the negotiating history of Security Council Resolution 1441, such a further decision was not essential but that all concerned in the FCO accepted that the final word would belong to the Attorney General.

376.   In the ultimate event, a Deputy Legal Adviser in the FCO, Ms Elizabeth Wilmshurst, disagreed with the Government's position and felt it necessary to resign. We took evidence from Ms Wilmshurst and she told us that her view rested on a difference over legal arguments and was not related to intelligence.

377.   The Attorney General has told us that, during the course of negotiation of Resolution 1441 and in the weeks following the adoption of that resolution, he had a number of discussions with the Prime Minister, the Foreign Secretary and senior officials from their departments about what happened during the negotiations, and on the interpretation of Resolution 1441, including whether it was of itself sufficient to authorise the use of force in the event that Iraq failed to take the 'final opportunity' afforded to it by the Security Council to comply

with its disarmament obligations. The Attorney General has also told us that, in order to assist him in reaching a concluded view of the proper interpretation of the resolution, he also spoke to Sir Jeremy Greenstock, the UK Permanent Representative to the United Nations, and in February 2003 met members of the US Administration who as co-sponsors of the Resolution had detailed knowledge of the negotiation of the resolution.

378.   The Attorney General informed the Prime Minister's Chief of Staff (Mr Powell), his Foreign Policy Adviser (Sir David Manning) and Baroness Morgan of his view of the legal position at a meeting on 28 February 2003. The Prime Minister's office subsequently asked the Attorney General to put those views in writing, which he did in a formal minute to the Prime Minister on 7 March 2003.

379.   We have received an account from the Attorney General of that advice, and have read it. It was based on the legal interpretation of relevant United Nations Security Council resolutions and negotiating history in the United Nations, and not on WMD-related intelligence. It did, however, require the Prime Minister, in the absence of a further United Nations Security Council resolution, to be satisfied that there were strong factual grounds for concluding that Iraq had failed to take the final opportunity to comply with its disarmament obligations under relevant resolutions of the Security Council and that it was possible to demonstrate hard evidence of non-compliance and non-co-operation with the requirements of Security Council Resolution 1441, so as to justify the conclusion that Iraq was in further material breach of its obligations.

380.   On the basis of the Attorney General's advice, the Government drew up its military campaign objectives (set out at Annex C) which made it clear that the Government's overall objective for the military campaign was to bring about Iraq's disarmament in accordance with its obligations under the relevant United Nations Security Council resolutions and that the obstacle to achieving this was the then current Iraqi regime, supported by the security forces under its control. The Government therefore concluded that military action was necessary to remove the Iraqi regime from power, in order to secure compliance by Iraq with its disarmament obligations. The Attorney General confirmed to us his view that, while the assessment that it was necessary to remove the current regime to enforce compliance with its disarmament obligations was not for him, he saw no reason to regard this as being other than a proper and reasonable political and military assessment for the Government to make.

381.   The Attorney General decided that it was in the interests of public servants, both military and civil, who would have to carry through any decision to take military action that a statement should be made in clear and simple terms as to his view of the legal position. The Attorney General informed Lord Falconer and Baroness Morgan at a meeting on 13 March of his clear view that it was lawful under Resolution 1441 to use force without a further United Nations Security Council resolution.

382.   The Legal Secretary to the Law Officers informed the Legal Adviser to the Ministry of Defence on 14 March of the Attorney General's view, the Legal Adviser to the Ministry of Defence having written to the Legal Secretary on 12 March asking for confirmation of the legal position in order that the Chief of the Defence Staff could issue the order to commit armed forces to military action.

383. Following the end of negotiations in the United Nations on a further Security Council resolution, the Legal Secretary to the Attorney General wrote to the Private Secretary to the Prime Minister on 14 March 2003 seeking confirmation that:

> *. . . it is unequivocally the Prime Minister's view that Iraq has committed further material breaches as specified in paragraph 4 of resolution 1441.*

384. The Prime Minister's Private Secretary replied to the Legal Secretary on 15 March, confirming that:

> *. . . it is indeed the Prime Minister's unequivocal view that Iraq is in further material breach of its obligations, as in OP4[18] of UNSCR 1441, because of 'false statements or omissions in the declarations submitted by Iraq pursuant to this resolution and failure by Iraq to comply with, and co-operate fully in the implementation of, this resolution'.*

385. We have been told that, in coming to his view that Iraq was in further material breach, the Prime Minister took account both of the overall intelligence picture and of information from a wide range of other sources, including especially UNMOVIC information.

386. The Attorney General set out his view of the legal position to the Cabinet on 17 March, by producing and speaking to the Written Answer he gave to Parliament on that date:

> **Baroness Ramsay of Cartvale:** *What is the Attorney General's view of the legal basis for the use of force against Iraq.*
>
> **The Attorney General:** *Authority to use force against Iraq exists from the combined effect of Resolutions 678, 687 and 1441. All of these resolutions were adopted under Chapter VII of the UN Charter which allows the use of force for the express purpose of restoring international peace and security:*
>
> 1. *In Resolution 678, the Security Council authorised force against Iraq, to eject it from Kuwait and to restore peace and security in the area.*
>
> 2. *In Resolution 687, which set out the ceasefire obligations after Operation Desert Storm, the Security Council imposed continuing obligations on Iraq to eliminate its weapons of mass destruction in order to restore international peace and security in the area. Resolution 687 suspended but did not terminate the authority to use force under Resolution 678.*
>
> 3. *A material breach of Resolution 687 revives the authority to use force under Resolution 678.*
>
> 4. *In Resolution 1441, the Security Council determined that Iraq has been and remains in material breach of Resolution 687, because it has not fully complied with its obligations to disarm under that resolution.*
>
> 5. *The Security Council in Resolution 1441 gave Iraq "a final opportunity to comply with its disarmament obligations" and warned Iraq of the "serious consequences" if it did not.*

---

[18] Operative Paragraph 4 of the resolution.

6.   The Security Council also decided in Resolution 1441 that, if Iraq failed at any time to comply with and co-operate fully in the implementation of Resolution 1441, that would constitute a further material breach.

7.   It is plain that Iraq has failed so to comply and therefore Iraq was at the time of Resolution 1441 and continues to be in material breach.

8.   Thus, the authority to use force under Resolution 678 has revived and so continues today.

9.   Resolution 1441 would in terms have provided that a further decision of the Security Council to sanction force was required if that had been intended. Thus, all that Resolution 1441 requires is reporting to and discussion by the Security Council of Iraq's failures, but not an express further decision to authorise force.

387.   On the same date, the Foreign Secretary gave a more detailed statement of the legal position in his letter to both Houses of Parliament which included a note summarising Iraq's record on non-compliance with United Nations Security Council Resolution 1441 (reproduced at Annex D).

5.8 WHAT HAS BEEN FOUND IN IRAQ SINCE THE WAR

INTRODUCTION

388.   In the period immediately following hostilities, there was much disorder and looting in Iraq. Coalition activities were initially directed to mopping up outlying resistance, establishing internal security and repairing public utilities. Although the 75th Exploitation Task Force was set up to find and destroy chemical or biological weapons deployed on the battlefield or stockpiled in position near Iraqi military units, circumstances on the ground made their operations very difficult.

389.   During this period, much potential evidence about prohibited Iraqi weapons programmes may have been destroyed. The systematic destruction of computers and other forms of records at some sites suggested that it was not the work of looters but was part of a scheme of orchestrated destruction. There was also evidence of sanitisation of sites which may have been used for research.

390.   Iraqi concealment activities may also have hidden evidence from Coalition forces. Items were buried. A complete fighter aircraft was, for example, dug out of the sand by US Air Force troops after the end of military action. It would not have been difficult to conceal in this way a complete Al Hussein missile. It would have been even easier to conceal such missiles if they were broken down into components, as some intelligence suggested.

391.   We were told that the volume of biological and chemical agents unaccounted for at the time of UNSCOM's departure, even if they were all held together, would fit into a petrol tanker. If they were dispersed and hidden in small quantities, they would be even harder to discover; and they could be concealed in containers bearing an innocent description which would not raise suspicion if they were standing in the open.

392.   We conclude that it would be a rash person who asserted at this stage that evidence of Iraqi possession of stocks of biological or chemical agents, or even of banned missiles, does not exist or will never be found.

WHAT THE IRAQ SURVEY GROUP HAS FOUND

393.   In June 2003, the US-led Iraq Survey Group (ISG) was established to investigate *'weapons of mass destruction developed by Iraq under the previous regime'* and took over from the 75th Exploitation Task Force.

394.   Following initial investigations, the ISG noted that it was unlikely that the Iraqis had deployed chemical and biological weapons on the battlefield for use. In March 2004, the ISG published an interim "Status Report" in which it projected key priorities for future investigation, including:

      a.   Further research into a complex and well-developed procurement system hidden by an effective denial and deception strategy.

      b.   New leads on plans to develop an indigenous capability to produce a range of chemicals, some of them subject to sanctions.

      c.   New information related to potential dual-use facilities.

      d.   Information indicating Iraqi interest in maintaining the knowledge needed to support a potential nuclear programme.

395.   As we note in the introduction to this report, the ISG have not yet produced any publicly available comprehensive report. But we have been advised that, in their work over the past year, they have developed the following key concerns:

      a.   On Iraq's nuclear programme, the ISG are continuing to investigate Iraqi attempts to sustain the necessary intellectual capital, both human and documentary, to reconstitute such a programme.

      b.   On Iraq's chemical weapons programme, the ISG found a small number of pre-1991 weapons.

      c.   On Iraq's biological weapons programme, the ISG are continuing to investigate the evidence of post-1991 biological research, including potential laboratories run by the Iraqi Intelligence Service.

      d.   On Iraq's ballistic missile programme, there is evidence of clear decisions by the Iraqi leadership to proceed with the development and production of ballistic missiles beyond permitted ranges, but no corroboration that new warheads capable of chemical and biological payloads were developed for ballistic missiles.

396.   The ISG are continuing to investigate the decisions and plans of the former Iraqi regime, and we have been told that the debriefing of detainees has included:

      a.   Admissions that chemical weapons were used in the Iran-Iraq war, but assertions that any remaining stocks were destroyed in 1991.

b.   Statements that after 1991 the Iraqi regime was determined to maintain the intellectual capital necessary for reconstruction of nuclear, biological and chemical weapons programmes once sanctions were significantly eroded or lifted.

CONCLUSIONS

397.   For the reasons given above, even now it is premature to reach conclusions about Iraq's prohibited weapons. But from the evidence which has been found and de-briefing of Iraqi personnel it appears that prior to the war the Iraqi regime:

a.   Had the strategic intention of resuming the pursuit of prohibited weapons programmes, including if possible its nuclear weapons programme, when United Nations inspection regimes were relaxed and sanctions were eroded or lifted.

b.   In support of that goal, was carrying out illicit research and development, and procurement, activities.

c.   Was developing ballistic missiles with a range longer than permitted under relevant United Nations Security Council resolutions.

d.   Did not, however, have significant - if any - stocks of chemical or biological weapons in a state fit for deployment, or developed plans for using them.

5.9 VALIDATION OF HUMAN INTELLIGENCE SOURCES

INTRODUCTION

398.   During the course of our Review, SIS provided a series of commentaries on the results of their post-war validation of the main sources of human intelligence in the run-up to the war on Iraqi chemical and biological weapons, their use and their concealment. The good faith and reliability of some of those sources have been verified. But doubts - and in some cases serious doubts - have emerged about the reliability of intelligence from three sources whose intelligence helped to underpin JIC assessments and the Government's dossier of September 2002. We set out below the position at the time of conclusion of our Review.

CONTEXT

399.   Before doing so, however, we believe that it would be helpful to set in context the relative influence of each of the main SIS sources whose reporting underpinned JIC assessments. We cannot here set out in full the analysis we made; doing so would present an unacceptable risk to the continued security of sources and to the confidence of other current and potential SIS sources that their secrets will remain safe with SIS. But we can provide a description both of the subjects on which SIS's main sources reported and of the volume of their reporting. We are also able to include our conclusions on their validation.

400.   SIS's main sources reported on the production and possession of stocks of chemical and biological agents; on the weaponisation and deployment of those agents; on the use by

the Iraqi regime of chemical and biological weapons; and on the concealment of evidence of prohibited programmes from United Nations inspectors. One main source reported only on the mobile biological agent production facilities. Reporting from SIS's main sources represented in total some three-quarters of all SIS intelligence reports on those subjects circulated during 2002.

401. Two of the main sources were dominant, in terms of both the number of reports and influence on JIC assessments. During 2002, they provided some two-thirds of all intelligence reports that were circulated; and from summer 2002 onwards their reporting had a significant influence on intelligence assessments on Iraqi use of chemical and biological weapons. As noted in Chapter 1, however, volume is not necessarily a measure of influence; even single intelligence reports can have a significant impact. That was certainly the case with one report from one of these sources which had a major effect on the certainty of statements in the Government's dossier of September 2002 that Iraq possessed and was producing chemical and biological weapons. (This report was subsequently withdrawn.)

SIS MAIN SOURCES

402. Of the two dominant sources, the first reported accurately and authoritatively on some key issues. On production and stocks of chemical and biological weapons and agents, he could only report what he learned from others in his circle of high-level contacts in Baghdad.

403. The second dominant source remains the subject of continuing SIS validation. In 2002, SIS considered him to be an established and reliable source. His intelligence on other subjects had previously been corroborated. We therefore understand why SIS decided that it should issue a number of reports from him quoting a new sub-source on Iraqi chemical and biological programmes and intentions. Even then, they properly included a caution about the sub-source's links to opposition groups and the possibility that his reports would be affected by that. We have been told that post-war validation by SIS has raised serious doubts about the reliability of reporting from this new sub-source. We conclude that this stream of reporting that underpinned JIC assessments on Iraqi production and possession of chemical and biological weapons must be open to serious doubt.

404. In addition to these two dominant sources, SIS's post-war validation has led them to conclude that two further main sources should continue to be regarded as reliable. We have, however, noted that reports from those sources tended to present a less worrying view of Iraqi chemical and biological weapons capability than that from the sources whose reporting is now subject to doubt.

405. Finally, in mid-September 2002 SIS issued a report, described as being from '*a new source on trial*', on Iraqi production of chemical and biological agent. Although this report was received too late for inclusion in the JIC assessment of 9 September, it did provide significant assurance to those drafting the Government's dossier that active, current production of chemical and biological agent was taking place. A second report from the

new source, about the production of a particular chemical agent, was received later in September 2002. In July 2003, however, SIS withdrew the two reports because the sourcing chain had by then been discredited. SIS also interviewed the alleged sub-source for the intelligence after the war, who denied ever having provided the information in the reports. We note, therefore, that the two reports from this source, including one which was important in the closing stages of production of the Government's September dossier, must now be treated as unsafe.

LIAISON SERVICE SOURCES

406. As noted above, one source provided the vast majority of the intelligence that suggested that Iraq had developed mobile facilities for the production of biological agent. In oral evidence to our Review in May, the Chief of SIS said that this source's reports had been received through a liaison service and that he had not therefore been under the control of SIS. SIS had been able to verify that he had worked in an area which would have meant that he would have had access to the sort of information he claimed to have. But they had not been able to question him directly until after the war.

407. Following this initial post-war debrief of the source, SIS told us that:

It has become apparent that significant detail did not appear in the original liaison reports . . . But based on the information derived from the limited access to [the source] *to date we continue to judge that it is premature to conclude . . . that all the intelligence from the source must be discounted.*

408. SIS also noted, however, that their own debriefing of the source had led them to conclude that the product from the mobile facilities would have been in slurry form, which would have had a shorter life than would dried agent. As a result, SIS concluded that:

This indicates that the concept for use of the [mobile facilities] *was not to produce material to stockpile . . . Whilst further work needs to be done, at the moment it appears that the most likely function of the trailers was to provide a breakout production capability and not the continued production of material for stockpiling.*

409. SIS have informed us that they will continue to debrief the source. But, for the purposes of our Review, we conclude that there must be some doubts about the reliability of all the reports received from this source via the liaison service. We also conclude that intelligence reports received in 2000 which suggested that Iraq had recently-produced biological agent were seriously flawed. We therefore also conclude that the grounds for the JIC assessments drawing on those reports that Iraq had recently-produced stocks of biological agent no longer exist.

SUMMARY OF MAIN SOURCES

410. The overall picture therefore is that, of the main human intelligence sources described above:

    a.   One SIS main source reported authoritatively on some issues, but on others was passing on what he had heard within his circle.

b.   Reporting from a sub-source to a second main SIS source that was important to JIC assessments on Iraqi possession of chemical and biological weapons must be open to serious doubt.

c.   Reports from a third SIS main source have been withdrawn as unreliable.

d.   Reports from two further main SIS sources continue to be regarded as reliable, although it is notable that their reports were less worrying than the rest about Iraqi chemical and biological weapons capabilities.

e.   Reports received from the liaison service on Iraqi production of biological agent were seriously flawed, so that the grounds for JIC assessments drawing on those reports that Iraq had recently-produced stocks of biological agent no longer exist.

OTHER SOURCES

411.   A handful of other sources, and liaison reporting, comprised the remaining quarter of the human intelligence base reporting on Iraqi nuclear, biological, chemical and ballistic missile programmes in 2002. Very few of their reports were judged by the JIC to be material to the judgements reached in its assessments, although some were seen as providing some additional confidence to reporting from the sources described above, including a single report received from a reliable and established source quoting a new sub-source on the mobile biological agent production facilities.

412.   In addition to seeking to validate after the war the sources described above, SIS told us that they had planned to interview scientists associated with Iraqi chemical and biological weapons programmes but that this operation had had to be suspended because of practical and legal difficulties in Iraq. We understand those constraints.

SIS VALIDATION PROCEDURES

413.   We commend SIS for the thoroughness with which they have sought to validate their sources after the war and for the frankness they have shown in sharing with us on a continuing basis the results of their investigations. Nevertheless, the fact that reporting from one of their important pre-war sources has been withdrawn, and that from two other main sources is open to doubt, led us to question the standard procedures adopted by SIS to ensure that their sources are valid and that their reporting is subjected to quality control, and to ask whether these procedures were followed in the case of Iraq.

414.   Two witnesses made contributions on this process. The first said that, in areas relevant to our Review, SIS's organisational structure changed in the mid-1990s in a way that unintentionally undermined the effectiveness of the quality assurance process. Before the re-organisation, the 'Requirements' function, which was responsible for quality assurance in respect of agents' reporting, was independent of the 'Production' function responsible for producing reports. There was also a separation between UK-based case officers and their 'Production' team. According to this witness, in order to make overall staff savings and, within the staff that remained, to free resources for operational work, SIS brought

together the different functions of running sources and controlling their reporting into one unified team, whose leader was responsible for the total output. The consequence of this was thought by the witness to be that the quality assurance function of the SIS 'Requirements' officer, responsible for checking the validity and quality of source reporting, became subjected to the operational imperative of the team leader to produce results. At the same time, we were told, 'Requirements' posts were increasingly staffed by more junior officers as experienced staff were put into improving the operational teeth of the Service. Their ability to challenge the validity of cases and their reporting was correspondingly reduced.

415. The second witness commented in a similar manner to the first on the impact of the organisational changes described above for the effectiveness of the quality assurance process carried out by 'Requirements' officers. The witness also said that staff effort overall, and the number of experienced case officers in particular, applied to both the geographical (Near and Middle East) and functional (counter-proliferation) areas covered by our Review, were too thin to support SIS's responsibilities. Source validation, especially that on Iraq, had suffered as a consequence of both problems, with what were in the witness's view sources with dubious motivation being over-graded for reliability.

416. The Chief of SIS commented to us that the aim of these changes had been to make:

> ... people that run the operations responsible not just for operational activity but for delivery and to give them a much, much more clear cut responsibility for the requirement side ... The primary reason for bringing together operational units into teams was to make delivery of intelligence (and part of the delivery is the ability to assess and evaluate it in terms of its accuracy), as important as operational performance.

417. In terms of their application to sources of intelligence on Iraq, he added:

> I would say now we're a victim of a lack of experience and a lack of sufficiently expert resources to apply to [one] case ... had it been under more day to day scrutiny than it was at the time. And then, of course, there is pressure on the Service to produce ... and what you have to bear in mind in the period from about the middle of 2002 is that we were trying to ramp up our coverage of Iraq.

418. He added, however, that:

> The Service has a very tough source evaluation process which was completely revised in the period late 1999 to 2001. It was a long exercise and we introduced new processes and systems. Now they, for resource reasons, obviously couldn't be immediately applied, because they are heavy duty, to every case but ... it's something that we take incredibly seriously, where we have a highly developed process.

419. The Chief of SIS agreed that these tightened up procedures had obviously not been applied fully in one case. But he also pointed out that in other cases, including the two main sources described above whose reporting is still viewed as reliable, they had worked well.

420. On the level of seniority of officers staffing the 'Requirements' desks, the Chief of SIS commented that:

. . . it's very, very difficult particularly when the pressure on the Service is to produce good intelligence, to put your officers who are the only ones that can do production as well into the Requirements tasks. I accept problems and the fact that in an ideal world you would only staff your Requirements desks with very experienced operational officers. In practice that is not possible.

421.   He added, however, that SIS had nevertheless:

. . . managed to keep significant experience in each Requirement bit and we don't allow a situation where raw recruits without experience are putting out intelligence without reference to more experienced officers who can check the process.

422.   In conclusion, the Chief of SIS said that:

We look very hard at the health of the Requirements function and one of the exercises we did post-Iraq was to look at this very carefully and try to work out whether anything remedial needed to be done . . . where we need to run more training courses for Requirements officers, whether we need to reinforce the Requirements sections with more area expertise, whether we need more operational expertise. I don't think the Requirements function in SIS is in any way diminished.

423.   Our experience of SIS reporting on other countries of concern and the AQ Khan network, described at Chapter 2, gives us assurance that these procedures work, when applied properly. But there were clearly failures in the case of intelligence on Iraq. We return to this issue in our Conclusions.

5.10 CONCLUSIONS ON IRAQ

THE POLICY CONTEXT

424.   We have deliberately started our description of the policy context in 1998. It was clear to us, especially from the evidence we heard from the Prime Minister, that the challenge posed by the Iraqi regime in 1998 to the United Nations inspections regime and the Government's response to it had a significant influence on policy towards Iraq in later years. Thus, the Prime Minister's statement in the House of Commons in February 1998 contained themes that would be equally applicable four years later – the need to preserve the authority and standing of the United Nations; the need in particular to prevent the Iraqi government thwarting the United Nations inspection regime; and in that context the need to back United Nations' demands that Iraq meet its obligations with the threat of force.

425.   A review of Government policy towards Iraq in 1999 noted that the policy of containment had *"kept the lid on"* Saddam Hussein. In the absence of internationally acceptable alternative options, it recommended continuation of the policy of containment, despite its disadvantages. In parallel, however, key policy-makers were receiving increasing intelligence on the developing nuclear, chemical and biological programmes of other states of concern and the proliferation activities of the AQ Khan network, described more fully at Chapter 2. They also had intelligence, described at Chapter 3, of efforts by Usama bin Laden to seek unconventional weapons. The Prime Minister described to us his perception of the longer-term risks to international security and stability posed by such

programmes and activities. Other witnesses spoke of a sense of a *creeping tide* of proliferation and growth in the nuclear, biological, chemical and ballistic missile capabilities of states of concern.

426. The Prime Minister told us that, even before the attacks of 11 September 2001, his concern in this area was increasingly causing him to examine more proactive policy options. He also described to us the way in which the events of 11 September 2001 led him to conclude that policy had to change. He and other witnesses told us of the impact on policy-making of the changed calculus of threat that emerged from those attacks - of the risk of unconventional weapons in due course becoming available to terrorists and extremists seeking to cause mass casualties unconstrained by the fear of alienating their supporters or the public, or by considerations of personal safety. The Prime Minister's view was that a stand had to be taken, and a more active policy put in place to prevent the continuing development and proliferation of nuclear, biological and chemical weapons and technology in breach of the will of the international community. We describe at Chapter 4 the new counter-proliferation machinery put in place in summer 2002 to implement that policy.

427. **The developing policy context of the previous four years, and especially the impact of the events of 11 September 2001, formed the backdrop for changes in policy towards Iraq in early 2002. The Government's conclusion in the spring of 2002 that stronger action (although not necessarily military action) needed to be taken to enforce Iraqi disarmament was not based on any new development in the current intelligence picture on Iraq**. In his evidence to us, the Prime Minister endorsed the view expressed at the time that what had changed was not the pace of Iraq's prohibited weapons programmes, which had not been dramatically stepped up, but tolerance of them following the attacks of 11 September 2001. **When the Government concluded that action going beyond the previous policy of containment needed to be taken, there were many grounds for concern arising from Iraq's past record and behaviour. There was a clear view that, to be successful, any new action to enforce Iraqi compliance with its disarmament obligations would need to be backed with the credible threat of force. But there was no recent intelligence that would itself have given rise to a conclusion that Iraq was of more immediate concern than the activities of some other countries**.

428. Other factors clearly influenced the decision to focus on Iraq. The Prime Minister told us that, whilst on some perspectives the activities of other states might be seen as posing more direct challenges to British interests, **the Government, as well as being influenced by the concerns of the US Government, saw a need for immediate action on Iraq because of the wider historical and international context, especially Iraq's perceived continuing challenge to the authority of the United Nations. The Government also saw in the United Nations and a decade of Security Council Resolutions a basis for action through the United Nations to enforce Iraqi compliance with its disarmament obligations**.

429. **The Government considered in March 2002 two options for achieving the goal of Iraqi disarmament – a toughening of the existing containment policy; and regime change by military means. Ministers were advised that, if regime change was the chosen policy, only the use of overriding force in a ground campaign would achieve the removal of Saddam Hussein and Iraq's re-integration with the international community. Officials noted that regime change of itself had no basis in international law; and that any offensive military action against Iraq could only be justified if Iraq were held to be in breach of its disarmament obligations under United Nations Security Council Resolution 687 or some new resolution. Officials also noted that for the five Permanent Members of the Security Council and the majority of the 15 members of the Council to take the view that Iraq was in breach of its obligations under Resolution 687, they would need to be convinced that Iraq was in breach of its obligations; that such proof would need to be incontrovertible and of large-scale activity; but that the intelligence then available was insufficiently robust to meet that criterion.**

430. This advice, and a parallel JIC assessment, formed part of the background for the Prime Minister's meeting with President Bush at Crawford on 6–7 April 2002. The themes of the British Government's policy framework established as a result of that meeting and work in subsequent months echoed those of 1998 - the importance of the United Nations; the need to get United Nations inspectors back into Iraq; and the value of increasing pressure on the Iraqi regime, including through military action.

431. **Intelligence on Iraqi nuclear, biological, chemical and ballistic missile programmes was used in support of the execution of this policy,** for three main purposes:

   a. **To inform planning for a military campaign** if that should be necessary, in particular, in relation to unconventional weapons, for providing the necessary safeguards for coalition troops, diplomatic personnel and others; and for targeting.

   b. **To inform domestic and international opinion** of the UK's assessment of Iraq's holdings, programmes and intentions, **in support of the Government's advocacy of its changing policy towards Iraq.**

   c. **To obtain and provide information to United Nations inspectors** about the likely locations of weapons and programmes which contravened the terms of United Nations Security Council resolutions.

432. We draw our Conclusions on the sources, assessment and use of intelligence in the following paragraphs against that policy background. In doing so, we are conscious that **Iraq was not the only issue on which the intelligence agencies, the JIC and the departments concerned were working during this period**. It is a common temptation for reviews of this nature to comment as if those concerned were doing nothing else and should have had their attention concentrated full-time on the subject under review. In this case, for much of the period up to mid-2002, many other issues were more

demanding of the intelligence community's and policy-makers' time and attention. Iraq loomed large from mid-2002 onwards. But even then **other matters, including terrorism and the activities of other countries of concern, were requiring intensive day-to-day observation and action**, including continuing operations in Afghanistan and the crisis between India and Pakistan.

THE SOURCES OF INTELLIGENCE

433.   Iraq was a very difficult intelligence target. **Between 1991 and 1998, the bulk of information used in assessing the status of Iraq's biological, chemical and ballistic missile programmes was derived from UNSCOM reports**. In 1995, knowledge was significantly boosted by the defection of Hussein Kamil. But, **after the departure of United Nations inspectors in December 1998, information sources were sparse, particularly on Iraq's chemical and biological weapons programmes.**

434.   In Spring 2000, intelligence was obtained from a significant new source via a liaison service on mobile biological agent production facilities. During 2002, additional human intelligence reporting was obtained by the UK. Nevertheless **the number of primary human intelligence sources remained few** (although they drew on a wider number of sub-sources and sub-sub-sources). As Section 5.9 explains, SIS had five main sources. Two of those were dominant, in terms of both the number of reports and influence on JIC assessments.

435.   Furthermore, SIS did not generally have agents with first-hand, inside knowledge of Iraq's nuclear, chemical, biological or ballistic missile programmes. As a result, intelligence reports were mainly inferential. **Other intelligence sources provided valuable information on other activity, including overseas procurement activity. They did not generally provide confirmation of the intelligence received from human sources, but did contribute to the picture of the continuing intention of the Iraqi regime to pursue its prohibited weapons programmes.**

436.   **Validation of human intelligence sources after the war has thrown doubt on a high proportion of those sources and of their reports, and hence on the quality of the intelligence assessments received by Ministers and officials in the period from summer 2002 to the outbreak of hostilities. Of the main human intelligence sources** described above:

   a.   **One SIS main source reported authoritatively on some issues, but on others was passing on what he had heard within his circle.**

   b.   **Reporting from a sub-source to a second SIS main source that was important to JIC assessments on Iraqi possession of chemical and biological weapons must be open to doubt.**

   c.   **Reports from a third SIS main source have been withdrawn as unreliable.**

d. **Reports from two further SIS main sources continue to be regarded as reliable, although it is notable that their reports were less worrying than the rest about Iraqi chemical and biological weapons capabilities.**

e. **Reports received from a liaison service on Iraqi production of biological agent were seriously flawed, so that the grounds for JIC assessments drawing on those reports that Iraq had recently-produced stocks of biological agent no longer exist.**

437. We have considered why such a high proportion of human intelligence reports should have been withdrawn or subsequently be subject to doubt.

438. One reason which is frequently suggested is that, in the case of Iraq, there was over-reliance on emigré and dissident sources, who had their own motives for exaggerating the dangers presented by the Iraq regime. But, after examination, **we do not believe that over-reliance on dissident and emigré sources was a major cause of subsequent weaknesses in the human intelligence relied on by the UK**. The important source on Iraqi biological agent production capabilities was a refugee. But his reporting was treated with some caution by the JIC until it appeared to be confirmed by other human intelligence. The subsequent need to withdraw a key part of the reporting received through the liaison service arose as a result of misunderstandings, not because of the source's status.

439. A new sub-source to another main source, who provided a significant proportion of influential human intelligence reporting, turned out to have links to opposition groups of which SIS only later became aware. But SIS, once they knew of those links, warned readers in their reports of the risk of embellishment. And the serious doubts that have subsequently arisen on the quality of his reporting do not arise from issues connected with his dissident status.

440. **One reason for the number of agents whose reports turned out to be unreliable or questionable may be the length of the reporting chains.** Even when there were sources who were shown to be reliable in some areas of reporting, they had in other areas of intelligence concern where they did not have direct knowledge to draw on sub-sources or sub-sub-sources. This was the case with the first of the two dominant sources.

441. **Another reason may be that agents who were known to be reliable were asked to report on issues going well beyond their usual territory**, leading to intelligence reports which were more speculative than they would have provided on their own specialisms. We believe this to have been the case with some aspects of the reporting of the second of the two dominant sources.

442. **A third reason may be that, because of the scarcity of sources and the urgent requirement for intelligence, more credence was given to untried agents than would normally be the case**. This was the case with the report received between the JIC assessment of 9 September 2002 and the publication of the Government's dossier in September 2002.

443. We believe that **a major underlying reason for the problems that have arisen was the difficulty of achieving reliable human intelligence on Iraq**. Part of the difficulty faced by SIS in recruiting and running reliable agents came from the nature and brutality of the Iraqi regime. The nature of Iraq <u>after</u> the war might also have had its own effect, with the risk that some of the informants may have reported reliably but had reasons after the war to deny having provided information.

444. **However, even taking into account the difficulty of recruiting and running reliable agents on Iraqi issues, we conclude that part of the reason for the serious doubt being cast over a high proportion of human intelligence reports on Iraq arises from weaknesses in the effective application by SIS of its validation procedures and in their proper resourcing**. We received evidence from two witnesses about the impact of organisational changes in parts of SIS relevant to our Review. Following reductions in SIS's budget in the mid-1990s, these were made with the goal of making overall staff savings and freeing experienced case officers for operational work. This weakened SIS's internal processes for the quality assurance of agents. One of those witnesses also noted that the level of staff effort applied to geographical and functional tasks relevant to our Review was too thin to support SIS's responsibilities. We believe that the validation of some sources on Iraq suffered as a consequence of both problems.

445. The Chief of SIS acknowledged to us that a problem had arisen. He attributed it primarily to the shortage of experienced case officers following the rundown of the size of SIS in the 1990s. **Our Review has shown the vital importance of effective scrutiny and validation of human intelligence sources and of their reporting to the preparation of accurate JIC assessments and high-quality advice to Ministers. We urge the Chief of SIS to ensure that this task is properly resourced and organised to achieve that result, and we think that it would be appropriate if the Intelligence and Security Committee were to monitor this.**

ASSESSMENT

446. We have examined the way in which raw intelligence was analysed and assessed over the period and then incorporated into JIC assessments for Ministers and other senior readers. In particular, we have looked at whether:

    a. The material in intelligence reports was correctly treated as it passed along the chain from agent reports through analysis into JIC assessments, and that it did not suffer as a result of compression or incorrect translation from one stage to the next.

    b. Analysis or assessment appears to have been coloured by departmental policy or other agendas.

    c. Assessment had access to and made full use of available technical expertise.

447. Drawing on our conclusions on these issues, we have then examined and drawn conclusions on the quality of the JIC assessments we read on Iraq's nuclear, biological,

chemical and ballistic missile programmes. We have looked in particular at the degree of analytical rigour applied across the range of assessments we have read, especially to see whether there developed within the intelligence community over a decade of analysis and assessment 'Group Think' or a 'prevailing wisdom'. That has led us to look at whether sufficient challenge was applied to analysis and assessment, and whether readers of JIC assessments and the JIC itself were sufficiently alerted to the existence of dissenting or alternative views.

448.   In doing so, we decided to study JIC assessments and the intelligence reports that underlay them as far back as 1990, to seek to establish in particular:

a.   Whether there were any issues surrounding the operation of the intelligence assessment process over more than a decade which might have affected JIC assessments in the period prior to the second Gulf war.

b.   Whether assessments made about the scale of Iraq's nuclear, biological, chemical and ballistic missile programmes at the time of the first Gulf war and during the early- and mid-1990s had an impact which was still reflected in JIC assessments made in 2002 and 2003.

The treatment of intelligence material

449.   **In general, we found that the original intelligence material was correctly reported in JIC assessments. An exception was the '45 minute' report. But this sort of example was rare** in the several hundred JIC assessments we read on Iraq. In general, we also found that the reliability of the original intelligence reports was fairly represented by the use of accompanying qualifications. **We should record in particular that we have found no evidence of deliberate distortion or of culpable negligence**.

The effect of departmental policy agendas

450.   We examined JIC assessments to see whether there was evidence that the judgements inside them were systematically distorted by non-intelligence factors, in particular the influence of the policy positions of departments. **We found no evidence of JIC assessments and the judgements inside them being pulled in any particular direction to meet the policy concerns of senior officials on the JIC**.

Access to technical and other expertise

451.   **We conclude in general that the intelligence community made good use of the technical expertise available to the Government**, for example in the DIS or from the Atomic Weapons Establishment at Aldermaston and the Defence Science and Technology Laboratory: Porton Down, both through consultation and secondments. An example of the strength of this network of expertise came in the assurances we were given that technical experts both in the DIS and elsewhere were consulted on the question of

whether the aluminium tubes were likely to have been intended for a centrifuge facility for nuclear enrichment.

452. **We accept the need for careful handling of human intelligence reports to sustain the security of sources. We have, however, seen evidence of difficulties that arose from the unduly strict 'compartmentalisation' of intelligence** which meant that experts in DIS did not have access to an intelligence report which became available in September 2002 and played a major role for the JIC in confirming previous intelligence reports that Iraq was producing chemical and biological weapons. The report was later withdrawn in July 2003. We accept that this report was from a new source who was thought to be of great potential value and was therefore of extreme sensitivity. Nevertheless, **it was wrong that a report which was of significance in the drafting of a document of the importance of the dossier was not shown to key experts in the DIS who could have commented on the validity and credibility of the report. We conclude that arrangements should always be sought to ensure that the need for protection of sources should not prevent the exposure of reports on technical matters to the most expert available analysis**.

The quality of JIC assessments

453. **We were impressed by the quality of intelligence assessments on Iraq's nuclear capabilities**. They were in our view thorough, balanced and measured; brought together effectively human and technical intelligence information; included information on the perceived quality of the underlying intelligence sources to help readers in interpreting the material; identified explicitly those areas where previous assessments were wrong, and the reasons why; and at each significant stage included consideration of alternative hypotheses and scenarios, and provided an explanation of the consequences were any one to arise, to aid readers' understanding.

454. **Partly because of inherent difficulties in assessing chemical and biological programmes, JIC assessments on Iraq's chemical and biological weapons programmes were less assured**. In our view, assessments in those areas tended to be over-cautious and in some areas worst case. Where there was a balance of inference to be drawn, it tended to go in the direction of inferring the existence of banned weapons programmes. Assessments were as a consequence less complete, especially in their considerations of alternative hypotheses, and used a different burden of proof.

455. There are some general factors which will always complicate assessments of chemical and biological weapons programmes. In our review of intelligence on the nuclear, biological and chemical programmes of other states, we saw an equivalent complexity in making judgements on their status. **The most significant is the 'dual use' issue - because chemical and biological weapons programmes can draw heavily on 'dual use' materials, it is easier for a proliferating state to keep its programmes covert**.

456. **There were also Iraq-specific factors. The intelligence community will have had in mind that Iraq had not only owned but used its chemical weapons in the past. It will inevitably have been influenced by the way in which the Iraqi regime was engaged in a sustained programme to try to deceive United Nations inspectors** and to conceal from them evidence of its prohibited programmes. Furthermore, because SIS did not have agents with first-hand knowledge of Iraq's nuclear, chemical, biological or ballistic missile programmes, **most of the intelligence reports on which assessments were being made were inferential. The Assessments Staff and JIC were not fully aware of the access and background of key informants, and could not therefore read their material against the background of an understanding of their motivations** for passing on information.

457. We have also noted in the papers we have read that the **broad conclusions of the UK intelligence community (although not some particular details) were widely-shared by other countries**, especially the assessment that it was likely that Iraq had, or could produce, chemical and biological weapons which it might use in circumstances of extremity. We note that Dr Blix, Executive Chairman of UNMOVIC, has said[19] that:

> My gut feelings, which I kept to myself, suggested to me that Iraq still engaged in prohibited activities and retained prohibited items, and that it had the documents to prove it.

Where doubts existed, they were about the extent to which the intelligence amounted to proof, as opposed to balance of probability.

458. However, **we detected a tendency for assessments to be coloured by over-reaction to previous errors**. Past under-estimates had a more lasting impact on the assessment process than past over-estimates, when both should have been as deserving of attention. We have also noted that where for good reasons[20] the JIC chose to adopt a worst case estimate (which in most cases it described as such) there was a tendency for that basis of calculation not to be made clear in later assessments. **As a result, there was a risk of over-cautious or worst case estimates, shorn of their caveats, becoming the 'prevailing wisdom'.** Subsequent Iraqi declarations being tested against such estimates for truthfulness would have been seen as falling short - a view that will have been reinforced by proven shortfalls in Iraqi declarations during the early- and mid-1990s and by Iraqi prevarication, concealment and deception.

459. **The JIC may, in some assessments, also have misread the nature of Iraqi governmental and social structures.** The absence of intelligence in this area may also have hampered planning for the post-war phase on which departments did a great deal of work. We note that the collection of intelligence on Iraq's prohibited weapons programmes was designated as being a JIC First Order of Priority whereas intelligence

---

[19] Dr Hans Blix, "*Disarming Iraq*" (Bloomsbury, London, 2004), page 112.
[20] In particular, in relation to chemical and biological weapons it would have been irresponsible in the highest degree to send armed forces into battle on the assumption that Iraq did not have chemical or biological weapons and would not use them.

on Iraqi political issues was designated as being Third Order. The membership of the JIC is broad enough to allow such wider evidence to be brought to bear. **We emphasise the importance of the Assessments Staff and the JIC having access to a wide range of information, especially in circumstances (e.g. where the UK is likely to become involved in national reconstruction and institution-building) where information on political and social issues will be vital**.

THE USE OF INTELLIGENCE

The Government's dossiers

460. **The main vehicle for the Government's use of intelligence in the public presentation of policy was the dossier of September 2002 and accompanying Ministerial statements**. (The dossier of February 2003 has been fully dealt with in the ISC Report and we make no further comment on it here, except to endorse the conclusion accepted by the Government that the procedures followed in producing it were unsatisfactory and should not be repeated.)

461. **The dossier broke new ground in three ways: the JIC had never previously produced a public document; no Government case for any international action had previously been made to the British public through explicitly drawing on a JIC publication; and the authority of the British intelligence community, and the JIC in particular, had never been used in such a public way**.

462. **The dossier was not intended to make the case for a particular course of action in relation to Iraq. It *was* intended by the Government to inform domestic and international understanding of the need for stronger action (though not necessarily military action) - the general direction in which Government policy had been moving since the early months of 2002, away from containment to a more proactive approach to enforcing Iraqi disarmament**. The Government's wish to give its case greater objectivity and credibility led to the Government's decision to commission the JIC to produce the dossier and to make public the JIC's authorship of it. The Chairman of the JIC accepted responsibility for its production with the intention of ensuring that it did not go beyond the judgements which the JIC had reached. He and the JIC therefore took on the ownership of it.

463. **The Government wanted an unclassified document on which it could draw in its *advocacy* of its policy. The JIC sought to offer a dispassionate *assessment* of intelligence and other material on Iraqi nuclear, biological, chemical and ballistic missile programmes. The JIC, with commendable motives, took responsibility for the dossier, in order that its content should properly reflect the judgements of the intelligence community. They did their utmost to ensure this standard was met. But this will have put a strain on them in seeking to maintain their normal standards of neutral and objective assessment.**

464. **Strenuous efforts were made to ensure that no individual statements were made in the dossier which went beyond the judgements of the JIC. But, in translating material from JIC assessments into the dossier, warnings were lost about the limited intelligence base on which some aspects of these assessments were being made.** The Government would have seen these warnings in the original JIC assessments and taken them into account in reading them. But the public, through reading the dossier, would not have known of them. The dossier did contain a chapter on the role of intelligence. But the **language in the dossier may have left with readers the impression that there was fuller and firmer intelligence behind the judgements than was the case: our view, having reviewed all of the material, is that judgements in the dossier went to (although not beyond) the outer limits of the intelligence available.** The Prime Minister's description, in his statement to the House of Commons on the day of publication of the dossier, of the picture painted by the intelligence services in the dossier as "*extensive, detailed and authoritative*" may have reinforced this impression.

465. **We conclude that it was a serious weakness that the JIC's warnings on the limitations of the intelligence underlying its judgements were not made sufficiently clear in the dossier.**

466. **We understand why the Government felt it had to meet the mounting public and Parliamentary demand for information. We also recognise that there is a real dilemma between giving the public an authoritative account of the intelligence picture and protecting the objectivity of the JIC from the pressures imposed by providing information for public debate. It is difficult to resolve these requirements. We conclude, with the benefit of hindsight, that making public that the JIC had authorship of the dossier was a mistaken judgement, though we do not criticise the JIC for taking responsibility for clearance of the intelligence content of the document. However, in the particular circumstances, the publication of such a document in the name and with the authority of the JIC had the result that more weight was placed on the intelligence than it could bear. The consequence also was to put the JIC and its Chairman into an area of public controversy and arrangements must be made for the future which avoid putting the JIC and its Chairman in a similar position.**

467. We recognise that there will be a dilemma if intelligence-derived material is in future to be put into the public domain. If future documents are published solely in the name of the Government, it is inevitable that Ministers will be asked if the JIC has endorsed the intelligence assessments inside them. But **we believe that there are other options that should be examined for the ownership of drafting, for gaining the JIC's endorsement of the intelligence material and assessments that are quoted and for subsequent 'branding'. One is for the government of the day to draft a document, to gain the JIC's endorsement of the intelligence material inside it and then to publish it acknowledging that it draws on intelligence but without ascribing it to the JIC. Or the Government, if it**

wishes to seek the JIC's credibility and authority, could publish a document with intelligence material and the JIC's endorsement of it shown separately. Or the JIC could prepare and publish itself a self-standing assessment, incorporating all of its normal caveats and warnings, leaving it to others to place that document within a broader policy context. This may make such documents less persuasive in making a policy case; but that is the price of using a JIC assessment. Our conclusion is that, between these options, the first is greatly preferable. Whichever route is chosen, JIC clearance of the intelligence content of any similar document will be essential**.

468. Furthermore, **we conclude that, if intelligence is to be used more widely by governments in public debate in future, those doing so must be careful to explain its uses and limitations. It will be essential, too, that clearer and more effective dividing lines between assessment and advocacy are established when doing so**.

469. In reaching these conclusions, **we realise that our conclusions may provoke calls for the current Chairman of the JIC, Mr Scarlett, to withdraw from his appointment as the next Chief of SIS. We greatly hope that he will not do so. We have a high regard for his abilities and his record**. Once the Government had decided to produce a dossier based on intelligence, he and the JIC took on ownership of it with the excellent motive of ensuring that everything it said was consistent with JIC judgements. We have said above that it was a mistaken judgement for the dossier to be so closely associated with the JIC but it was a collective one for which the Chairman of the JIC should not bear personal responsibility.

Intelligence and the legality of the use of military force

470. As described in Section 5.7, **the part played by intelligence in determining the legality of the use of force was limited**. The criterion which the Attorney General advised the Government to apply was the degree of Iraq's compliance and co-operation with United Nations Security Council Resolution 1441.

471. The Government received on 18 December the JIC's initial assessment on the quality of Iraq's declaration of 7 December, called for under Resolution 1441, on the status of its prohibited programmes. The Government also received in the period between September 2002 and March 2003 a significant stream of intelligence reports about attempts by the Iraqi regime at concealment, as well as information about the results of UNMOVIC and IAEA inspections inside Iraq, captured in the reports provided to the United Nations Security Council.

472. Even so **we have noted that, despite its importance to the determination of whether Iraq was in further material breach of its obligations under Resolution 1441, the JIC made no further assessment of the Iraqi declaration beyond its *'Initial Assessment'*. We have also recorded our surprise that policy-makers and the intelligence community did not, as the generally negative results of UNMOVIC inspections became increasingly apparent, re-evaluate in early-2003 the quality of the intelligence**.

VALIDATION OF THE INTELLIGENCE

473. As we set out at the start of this Chapter, we sought in our Review to assess the intelligence on Iraqi capabilities to enable us to answer three broad questions:

a. What was the quality of the intelligence and other evidence, and the assessments made of it, about the **strategic intent** of the Iraqi regime to pursue nuclear, biological, chemical or ballistic missile programmes in contravention of its obligations under United Nations Security Council Resolution 687?

b. What was the quality of the intelligence or other evidence, and the assessments made of it, about Iraq seeking to sustain and develop its indigenous knowledge, skills and materiel base which would provide it with a **'break-out' capability** in each of those fields? Was there in particular good intelligence or other evidence of Iraq pursuing activities to extend and enhance those capabilities in contravention of its obligations under United Nations Security Council Resolutions?

c. What was the quality of the intelligence or other evidence, and the assessments made of it, about Iraqi **production** or **possession** of prohibited chemical and biological agents and weapons, nuclear materials and ballistic missiles?

474. **Even now it would be premature to reach conclusions about Iraq's prohibited weapons. Much potential evidence may have been destroyed in the looting and disorder that followed the cessation of hostilities. Other material may be hidden in the sand, including stocks of agent or weapons. We believe that it would be a rash person who asserted at this stage that evidence of Iraqi possession of stocks of biological or chemical agents, or even of banned missiles, does not exist or will never be found. But as a result of our Review, and taking into account the evidence which has been found by the ISG and de-briefing of Iraqi personnel, we have reached the conclusion that prior to the war the Iraqi regime:**

a. **Had the strategic intention of resuming the pursuit of prohibited weapons programmes, including if possible its nuclear weapons programme, when United Nations inspection regimes were relaxed and sanctions were eroded or lifted.**

b. In support of that goal, was carrying out illicit research and development, and procurement, activities, to seek to sustain its indigenous capabilities.

c. Was developing ballistic missiles with a range longer than permitted under relevant United Nations Security Council resolutions; but did not have significant - if any - stocks of chemical or biological weapons in a state fit for deployment, or developed plans for using them.

CHAPTER 6

IRAQ: SPECIFIC ISSUES

6.1 INTRODUCTION

475.   In this Chapter, we consider a number of detailed issues arising from the intelligence on Iraq's nuclear, biological, chemical and ballistic missile programmes that have attracted particular controversy or which illuminate our analysis of the quality of the intelligence and the effectiveness of the way in which it was handled.

6.2 LINKS BETWEEN AL QAIDA AND THE IRAQI REGIME

476.   We start with the intelligence available to the Joint Intelligence Committee (JIC), and the assessments made of it, on links between Al Qaida and the Iraqi regime, and of the availability to Al Qaida of chemical and biological weapons as a possible consequence.

THE 'POISON CELL' IN KURDISH NORTHERN IRAQ

477.   In the wake of the overthrow of the Taliban in Afghanistan, a number of Al Qaida refugees arrived in the Kurdish Autonomous Zone (KAZ) outside Baghdad's control.

478.   Between October 2002 and February 2003, the JIC described their presence and operations[1], including the production of various poisons, in three assessments.

479.   We conclude having read these assessments that **the JIC made it clear that the Al Qaida-linked facilities in the Kurdish Ansar al Islam area were involved in the production of chemical and biological agents, but that they were beyond the control of the Iraqi regime.**

480.   Fixed installations associated with Ansar al Islam were destroyed by air strikes in March 2003.

CO-OPERATION BETWEEN THE IRAQI REGIME AND AL QAIDA

481.   There was, however, other evidence of an association between the Iraqi regime and Al Qaida. Contacts between Al Qaida and the Iraqi Directorate General of Intelligence had dated back over four years. *"Fragmentary and uncorroborated"* intelligence reports suggested that in 1998 there were contacts between Al Qaida and Iraqi intelligence. Those reports described Al Qaida seeking toxic chemicals as well as other conventional terrorist equipment. Some accounts suggested that Iraqi chemical experts may have been in Afghanistan during 2000. But in November 2001, the JIC concluded that:

> *... there is no evidence that these contacts led to practical co-operation; we judge it unlikely because of mutual mistrust.*
>
> [JIC, 28 November 2001]

---

[1] A photograph of one of their facilities was used to illustrate Secretary of State Powell's speech to the United Nations Security Council on 5 February 2003.

482.   Following the expulsion of Al Qaida from Afghanistan and their arrival in northern Iraq, Abu Musab al Zarqawi (a senior Al Qaida figure) was relatively free to travel within Iraq proper and to stay in Baghdad for some time. Several of his colleagues visited him there. In October 2002, the JIC said that:

> *Although Saddam's attitude to Al Qaida has not always been consistent, he has generally rejected suggestions of cooperation. Intelligence nonetheless indicates that . . . meetings have taken place between senior Iraqi representatives and senior Al Qaida operatives. Some reports also suggest that Iraq may have trained some Al Qaida terrorists since 1998. Al Qaida has shown interest in gaining chemical and biological (CB) expertise from Iraq, but we do not know whether any such training was provided. We have no intelligence of current cooperation between Iraq and Al Qaida and do not believe that Al Qaida plans to conduct terrorist attacks under Iraqi direction.*

[JIC, 10 October 2002]

483.   By March 2003, the JIC was able to add further information that al Zarqawi's activities might be of military significance:

> *Reporting since [February] suggests that senior Al Qaida associate Abu Musab al Zarqawi has established sleeper cells in Baghdad, to be activated during a US occupation of the city. These cells apparently intend to attack US targets using car bombs and other weapons. (It is also possible that they have received CB materials from terrorists in the KAZ.) Al Qaida-associated terrorists continued to arrive in Baghdad in early March.*

[JIC, 12 March 2003]

484.   We conclude that **the JIC made clear that, although there were contacts between the Iraqi regime and Al Qaida, there was no evidence of co-operation.** It did warn of the possibility of terrorist attacks on coalition forces in Baghdad.

6.3 OPERATION MASS APPEAL

485.   In November 2003, the former United Nations weapons inspector Scott Ritter was reported to have told journalists that, in the late-1990s, the Secret Intelligence Service (SIS) ran "Operation Mass Appeal" – an alleged disinformation campaign to disseminate "*single source data of dubious quality*" about Iraq, in order to "*shake up public opinion*".

486.   Mr Ritter was quoted as follows:

> *I was brought into the operation in 1997 because at the UN . . . I sat on a body of data which was not actionable, but was sufficiently sexy that if it could appear in the press could make Iraq look like in a bad way.*

> *I was approached by MI6 to provide that data, I met with the Mass Appeal operatives both in New York and London on several occasions. This data was provided and this data did find its way into the international media.*

It was intelligence data that dealt with Iraq's efforts to procure WMDs, with Iraq's efforts to conceal WMDs. It was all single source data of dubious quality, which lacked veracity.

They took this information and peddled it off to the media, internationally and domestically, allowing inaccurate intelligence data to appear on the front pages.

The government, both here in the UK and the US, would feed off these media reports, continuing the perception that Iraq was a nation ruled by a leader with an addiction to WMDs.

[BBC News, 12 November 2003]

487.	Mr Ritter was reported as saying that he was prepared to reveal details before a public inquiry.

488.	We took evidence from Mr Ritter, including on Operation Mass Appeal. Mr Ritter said that Operation Mass Appeal was already up and running when SIS approached him in December 1997. He was asked if there was material on Iraq's weapons programmes on which the United Nations Special Commission (UNSCOM) could not act, but which might be made public through media outlets in a range of countries. Mr Ritter said that Mr Richard Butler, the then Executive Chairman of UNSCOM, agreed that UNSCOM should co-operate with the UK in this way and that two reports relating to prohibited trade between Iraq and two other countries were passed to the UK the same month. UNSCOM's involvement then fell into abeyance until May 1998 when contact resumed. Mr Ritter said that he met SIS officers again in June 1998 to discuss Operation Mass Appeal for the last time. He resigned from UNSCOM soon after that.

489.	We have examined relevant SIS papers. These confirm that **there were two meetings between British Government officials and UNSCOM representatives, including Mr Ritter, in May and June 1998 at which there were discussions about how to make public the discovery of traces of the nerve agent VX on missile warheads after this fact had been reported to the United Nations Security Council. (Iraq had previously denied weaponising VX.) Operation Mass Appeal was set up for this specific purpose and did not exist before May 1998. In the event, before Operation Mass Appeal could proceed, the UNSCOM report was leaked to the press in Washington. Because of this, Operation Mass Appeal was abandoned.**

6.4 URANIUM FROM AFRICA

490.	There has been significant controversy surrounding the reliability of Government statements about Iraqi attempts to buy uranium from Africa. We have therefore studied this issue in detail.

491.	Natural uranium is the necessary starting point for all nuclear developments (whether for weapons or civil power). In the late 1970s, Iraq obtained large quantities of uranium ore from Niger, Portugal and Brazil. By the mid-1980s, however, Iraq had become self-sufficient in uranium ore, which was a by-product of indigenous phosphate mines at

Akashat and purifying plants at Al Qaim and Al Jazira which extracted and purified the uranium ore for subsequent use in nuclear enrichment processes.

492. In the course of the first Gulf war, the facilities involved in this indigenous route were severely damaged. Subsequently, the International Atomic Energy Agency (IAEA) supervised the dismantlement of all the facilities that Iraq had built to process, enrich and fabricate uranium, and removed all potentially fissile material. Some unprocessed uranium ore was left in country, but under IAEA safeguards and subject to regular inspections. Iraq would therefore have had to seek imports of uranium or uranium ore if it wished to restart its nuclear programme covertly.

493. In early 1999, Iraqi officials visited a number of African countries, including Niger. The visit[2] was detected by intelligence, and some details were subsequently confirmed by Iraq. The purpose of the visit was not immediately known. But uranium ore accounts for almost three-quarters of Niger's exports. Putting this together with past Iraqi purchases of uranium ore from Niger, the limitations faced by the Iraq regime on access to indigenous uranium ore and other evidence of Iraq seeking to restart its nuclear programme, the JIC judged that Iraqi purchase of uranium ore could have been the subject of discussions and noted in an assessment in December 2000 that:

> . . . unconfirmed intelligence indicates Iraqi interest in acquiring uranium.

> [JIC, 1 December 2000]

494. There was further and separate intelligence that in 1999 the Iraqi regime had also made inquiries about the purchase of uranium ore in the Democratic Republic of Congo. In this case, there was some evidence that by 2002 an agreement for a sale had been reached.

495. During 2002, the UK received further intelligence from additional sources which identified the purpose of the visit to Niger as having been to negotiate the purchase of uranium ore, though there was disagreement as to whether a sale had been agreed and uranium shipped.

496. This evidence underlay the statement in the Executive Summary of the Government's dossier of September 2002 that:

> As a result of the intelligence we judge that Iraq has:
>
> . . .
>
> • tried covertly to acquire technology and materials which could be used in the production of nuclear weapons;
>
> • sought significant quantities of uranium from Africa, despite having no active civil nuclear power programme that could require it . . .

and in Chapter 3 of Part 1 of the Government's dossier that:

> The main conclusions are that:

---

[2] This visit was separate from the Iraqi-Nigerien discussions, in the margins of the mid-1999 Organisation of African Unity meeting in Algiers, attested to by Ambassador Wilson in his book "The Politics of Truth" (Carroll & Graf, NY 2004, p28).

- *Saddam continues to attach great importance to the possession of weapons of mass destruction and ballistic missiles which he regards as being the basis for Iraq's regional power. He is determined to retain these capabilities;*

. . .

- *Iraq continues to work on developing nuclear weapons, in breach of its obligations under the Non-Proliferation Treaty and in breach of UNSCR 687. Uranium has been sought from Africa that has no civil nuclear application in Iraq.*

and:

Iraq's known holdings of processed uranium are under IAEA supervision. But there is intelligence that Iraq has sought the supply of significant quantities of uranium from Africa. Iraq has no active civil nuclear power programme or nuclear power plants and therefore has no legitimate reason to acquire uranium.

497. In preparing the dossier, the UK consulted the US. The CIA advised caution about any suggestion that Iraq had succeeded in acquiring uranium from Africa, but agreed that there was evidence that it had been sought.

498. The range of evidence described above underlay the relevant passage in the Prime Minister's statement in the House of Commons on 24 September 2002 that:

In addition, we know that Saddam has been trying to buy significant quantities of uranium from Africa, although we do not know whether he has been successful.

499. We conclude that, on the basis of the intelligence assessments at the time, covering both Niger and the Democratic Republic of Congo, the statements on Iraqi attempts to buy uranium from Africa in the Government's dossier, and by the Prime Minister in the House of Commons, were well-founded. By extension, we conclude also that the statement in President Bush's State of the Union Address of 28 January 2003 that:

The British Government has learned that Saddam Hussein recently sought significant quantities of uranium from Africa.

was well-founded.

500. We also note that, because the intelligence evidence was inconclusive, neither the Government's dossier nor the Prime Minister went on to say that a deal between the Governments of Iraq and Niger for the supply of uranium had been signed, or uranium shipped.

501. We have been told that it was not until early 2003 that the British Government became aware that the US (and other states) had received from a journalistic source a number of documents alleged to cover the Iraqi procurement of uranium from Niger. Those documents were passed to the IAEA, which in its update report to the United Nations Security Council in March 2003 determined that the papers were forgeries:

The investigation was centred on documents provided by a number of States that pointed to an agreement between Niger and Iraq for the sale of uranium to Iraq between 1999 and 2001. The IAEA has discussed these reports with the Governments of Iraq and Niger, both of which have denied that any such activity took place. For its part, Iraq has provided the IAEA with a comprehensive explanation of its relations with Niger, and has described a visit by an Iraqi official to a number of African countries, including Niger, in February 1999, which Iraq thought might have given rise to the reports. The IAEA was able to review correspondence coming from various bodies of the Government of Niger, and to compare the form, format, contents and signatures of that correspondence with those of the alleged procurement-related documentation. Based on thorough analysis, the IAEA has concluded, with the concurrence of outside experts, that these documents, which formed the basis for the reports of recent uranium transactions between Iraq and Niger, are in fact not authentic. We have therefore concluded that these specific allegations are unfounded.

[IAEA GOV/INF/2003/10 Annex of 7 March 2003]

502.   We have asked the IAEA what were their grounds for concluding that the visit paid by an Iraqi official to Africa was not for the purpose of acquiring uranium. The IAEA said:

. . . the Director General explained in his report dated 7 March 2004 [sic] to the UN Security Council that Iraq "described the visit by an Iraqi official to a number of African countries, including Niger, in February 1999, which Iraq thought might have given rise to the reports". On a number of occasions in early 2003, including in a letter dated 1 February 2003, the IAEA requested Iraq to provide details of all meetings held between Iraqi officials and officials from Niger around the year 2000. The Director of Iraq's National Monitoring Directorate responded in a letter of 7 February 2003 to the Director of the IAEA's Iraq Nuclear Verification Office. (It should be noted that at the time of Iraq's response Iraq had not been provided by the IAEA with any details contained in documents alleging the existence of a uranium contract.)

The Iraqi response referred to above explained that, on 8 February 1999, Mr. Wissam Al Zahawie, Iraq's then Ambassador to the Holy See, as part of a trip to four African countries, visited Niger as an envoy of the then President of Iraq to Mr. Ibrahim Bare, the then President of Niger, in order to deliver an official invitation for a visit to Iraq, planned for 20 to 30 April 1999. (N.B. Mr. Bare passed away on 9 April 1999.) According to the Iraqi information, no such presidential visit from Niger to Iraq took place before 2003.

The Iraqi authorities provided the IAEA with excerpts from Mr. Al Zahawie's travel report to Niger. These excerpts support the above explanation by the Ambassador regarding the purpose of his visit to Niger and do not contain any references to discussions about uranium supply from Niger.

In order to further clarify the matter, the IAEA interviewed Mr. Al Zahawie on 12 February 2003. The information provided by the Ambassador about details about his 1999 trip to Africa also supported the information obtained previously by the

Agency on this visit. The demeanour of the Ambassador and the general tone of the interview did not suggest that he was under particular pressure to hide or fabricate information.

Notwithstanding the information summarized above, and in view of the fact that the IAEA so far has not obtained any other related information than the forged documents, the IAEA is not in the position to demonstrate that Iraq never sought to import uranium in the past. This is the reason why the IAEA only concluded that it had "no indication that Iraq attempted to import uranium since 1990" but it would "follow up any additional evidence, if it emerges, relevant to efforts by Iraq to illicitly import nuclear materials". So far no such additional information has been obtained by the Agency.

503. **From our examination of the intelligence and other material on Iraqi attempts to buy uranium from Africa, we have concluded that:**

    a. **It is accepted by all parties that Iraqi officials visited Niger in 1999.**

    b. **The British Government had intelligence from several different sources indicating that this visit was for the purpose of acquiring uranium. Since uranium constitutes almost three-quarters of Niger's exports, the intelligence was credible.**

    c. **The evidence was not conclusive that Iraq actually <u>purchased</u>, as opposed to having <u>sought</u>, uranium and the British Government did not claim this.**

    d. **The forged documents were not available to the British Government at the time its assessment was made, and so the fact of the forgery does not undermine it.**

6.5 THE 45-MINUTE CLAIM

504. The Government's dossier of September 2002 contained the claim based on an intelligence report that some chemical and biological weapons could be deployed by Iraq within 45 minutes of an order to use them. Much public attention has been given to the Prime Minister's statement that he was not aware until after the war that this report should have been interpreted as referring to battlefield weapons.

505. If this report was regarded as having operational significance, and if in particular it had been regarded as covering ballistic missiles (as was reported in some newspapers), this would indeed have been surprising. If, however, it referred to forward-deployed battlefield munitions, the time period given would not have been surprising or worth drawing to the Prime Minister's attention. But it was unclear, both in the JIC assessment of 9 September and in the Government's dossier, which of the two it was.

Attention has also focused on the alleged scepticism of the then US Director of Central Intelligence, Mr George Tenet, about the report, which he is quoted in Mr Bob Woodward's book, "Plan of Attack[3]", as calling the *"they-can-attack-in-45-minutes shit"*.

We asked the Chief of SIS, if Mr Tenet had ever mentioned his scepticism to him. He said:

> *There's no record of them having commented negatively on the report and nor does the desk officer at the time recall any come-back from the CIA.*

We asked Mr Tenet directly for a comment but no reply had been received by the time that he resigned from office.

506. As the Intelligence and Security Committee (ISC) have already reported[4], the underlying intelligence report referred to an average period of 20 minutes, with a maximum of 45 minutes, for 'BCW munitions' to be moved into place for an attack. It was taken into the JIC assessment of 9 September through the inclusion of a sentence which noted that:

> *Intelligence also indicates that chemical and biological munitions could be with military units and ready for firing within 20-45 minutes.*
>
> [JIC, 9 September 2002]

507. The intelligence report itself was vague and ambiguous. The time period given was the sort of period which a military expert would expect; in fact it is somewhat longer than a well-organised military unit might aspire to. For those who interpreted it as referring to battlefield munitions, therefore, its significance was that it appeared to confirm that Iraq had both forward-deployed chemical and biological munitions and the necessary command and control arrangements in place to use them, rather than the period of time within which they could be deployed.

508. The ISC commented in their report that members of the Assessments Staff stated in evidence to that Committee that they, and the people they had consulted, did not know what munitions the report was referring to or their status, nor did they know from where and to where the munitions might be moved. But they also noted that they had reached a judgement that the report was referring to the time needed to move chemical and biological battlefield munitions from where they were held in forward-deployed storage sites to pre-designated military units. The Committee went on to say that the omission from the dossier of that judgement and the context it provided allowed speculation as to the exact meaning of the report and was unhelpful to an understanding of the issue.

509. We agree with this comment. We take the view that, in this instance, the JIC should have included that judgement in its assessment of 9 September 2002 and in the dossier. Alternatively, and as suggested by one witness who gave evidence to us, a more accurate representation by the Assessments Staff of the report would have highlighted the uncertainties in the intelligence by saying:

> *A source has claimed some weapons may be deployable within 45 minutes of an order to use them, but the exact nature of the weapons, the agents involved and the context of their use is not clear.*

510. The first media report of the '45 minute' story was carried in an exchange on the BBC *Today* programme about the dossier on the morning of its publication:

---

3 Simon & Schuster, London, 2004, page 190.
4 "Iraqi Weapons of Mass Destruction – Intelligence and Assessments." Cm 5972. September 2003.

Q. . . . if you were to choose a paragraph as the most dramatic that you've read this morning what is it?

A. Well to be honest it's not that kind of document. It's, it's actually rather sensibly cautious and measured in tone on the whole. There are, as I say a couple of, of sexy lines designed to make headlines for the tabloids like the fact that he can deploy within 45 minutes if the weapons were ready and that he could reach the British bases on Cyprus . . .

[BBC Today programme, 0855, 24 September 2002]

It was followed by stories in London and regional newspapers during the day, and by national newspapers the next day[5].

511.   We conclude that **the JIC should not have included the '45 minute' report in its assessment and in the Government's dossier without stating what it was believed to refer to. The fact that the reference in the classified assessment was repeated in the dossier later led to suspicions that it had been included because of its eye-catching character.**

512.   We have been informed by SIS that the validity of the intelligence report on which the 45-minute claim was based has come into question. Post-war source validation by SIS, described more fully at Chapter 5, has thrown doubt on the reliability of one of the links in the reporting chain affecting this intelligence report.

6.6   MOBILE BIOLOGICAL WEAPONS LABORATORIES

513.   There are two strands to this story. The first concerns intelligence about mobile equipment that, if it exists, has not yet been found. The intelligence on which this strand is based is being validated; some aspects of it are now unsafe. The second relates to trailers discovered by US forces post-war. We cover both strands below.

INTELLIGENCE ON MOBILE BIOLOGICAL AGENT PRODUCTION FACILITIES

514.   In January 1999, UNSCOM's final report noted that Iraq had *"once considered"* mobile biological agent production facilities. In early 2000, on the basis of intelligence from a new source, received via a liaison service, the JIC reported that:

Iraq seems to be exploring the use of mobile facilities to give its BW activities greater security.

and that, according to the source:

. . . Iraq had started to produce biological agent in 'mobile production centres'.

[JIC, 19 April 2000]

---

[5] We wrote to some 60 Editors of national and regional print and broadcast media to ask them if they had been briefed by representatives of the Government about the dossier immediately prior to its publication or whether, post-publication, they were guided to report particular aspects, such as the '45 minute' story. All of those who replied said that they had not been guided to particular parts of the dossier prior to its publication. There was some evidence from the replies that some journalists had had their attention drawn after its publication to passages in the Prime Minister's Foreword. Some Editors noted that the '45 minute' story attracted attention because it was of itself an eyecatching item in a document containing much that was either not new or rather technical in nature.

515. The JIC continued:

> There are reportedly 6 mobile production centres, with one under construction. As of March 1999, three of these were fully functional and work was under way to enable the production of 5 unspecified BW agents. At one of these sites, some 20-30 tonnes of BW primary product were reportedly manufactured over four months.
>
> [JIC, 19 April 2000]

516. This picture remained essentially constant for the next two years. By March 2002, the JIC was recording that the source had described seven such facilities in total, six road-based and one rail-based. The JIC continued to note that the intelligence was uncorroborated but did record that it was technically credible.

517. In September 2002, new intelligence from a reliable and established source quoting a new sub source provided a degree of corroboration for the original source's reporting. The new informant reported on the existence of mobile fermentation systems, designed for the military and allegedly for the production of single cell protein (a dietary supplement suitable for animal feed as well as human consumption) but having characteristics consistent with the production of biological agents. The informant was suspicious about the true purpose of the systems, although he did not connect them with biological warfare.

518. In its assessment in September 2002, the JIC noted that intelligence indicated that:

> . . . Iraq has developed for the military, fermentation systems which are capable of being mounted on road-trailers or rail cars. These could produce BW agent.
>
> [JIC, 9 September 2002]

519. This was the background to the account of mobile biological agent production facilities in the Government's dossier. The dossier said in the Executive Summary:

> As a result of the intelligence we judge that Iraq has:
>
> - developed mobile laboratories for military use, corroborating earlier reports about the mobile production of biological warfare agents.

and in Part 1 Chapter 3:

> There was intelligence that Iraq was starting to produce biological warfare agents in mobile production facilities. Planning for the project had begun in 1995 under Dr Rihab Taha, known to have been a central player in the pre-Gulf War programme. . . .
>
> UNSCOM established that Iraq considered the use of mobile biological agent production facilities. In the past two years evidence from defectors has indicated the existence of such facilities. Recent intelligence confirms that the Iraqi military have developed mobile facilities. These would help Iraq conceal and protect biological agent production from military attack or UN inspection.

520. In the subsequent debate in the House of Commons on 24 September 2002, the Prime Minister said:

. . .the UN inspection regime discovered that Iraq was trying to acquire mobile biological weapons facilities, which of course are easier to conceal. Present intelligence confirms that it has now got such facilities.

521. The United States National Intelligence Estimate issued in October 2002 drew similar conclusions about Iraqi ownership of mobile biological agent production facilities, as did Secretary of State Powell in his presentation to the United Nations Security Council on 5 February 2003. It subsequently emerged that the intelligence from one of the US sources, a defector associated with the Iraqi National Congress, had already been retracted by the time the National Intelligence Estimate was issued. This source was not, however, relied on by the UK.

522. Separately, Iraq made two declarations to UNMOVIC of a number of mobile facilities, none of which was judged by UNMOVIC to be related to the production of biological agent.

523. Although there was evidence of increased activity at facilities formerly associated with Iraq's biological warfare programme, there was no reliable intelligence during this period of an Iraqi biological agent production capability other than the mobile facilities. All JIC assessments about the actual <u>production</u> of biological warfare agents were based on intelligence about the mobile facilities.

VALIDATION

524. No evidence has been found to support the existence of the mobile facilities described by the liaison source. Some of the sites identified in the source's intelligence as being connected with the mobile facilities have been investigated. In May 2003, UNMOVIC's Thirteenth Quarterly Report to the UN Security Council contained the following paragraph on "Information provided by supporting Governments on mobile facilities":

UNMOVIC inspected a number of sites throughout Iraq based on intelligence information made available to it. In addition, other sites were inspected as a result of follow-up actions. Site inspections were aimed to investigate in detail the infrastructural signature necessary for the alleged function of such sites, eg, the presence of suitable support services for chemical and biological weapons mobile production facilities during production runs. Inspection results and analysis of detailed forensic sampling of the facilities did not reveal evidence of any past involvement of those sites in proscribed chemical and biological weapons mobile production activities.

[UNMOVIC Quarterly Report to the Security Council, 30 May 2003]

525. UNMOVIC also noted that:

No evidence of proscribed activities was observed during random checks of transport trucks.

[UNMOVIC Quarterly Report to the Security Council, 30 May 2003]

526. We were told that the ISG visited nearly all sites in the Baghdad area said to be associated with a mobile biological agent production programme, as well as all existing reported hide sites outside Baghdad. In addition, they conducted debriefings of the majority of

personnel that had either been directly named in refugees' reporting, had been associated with the source or were linked to sites that became part of the investigation. The information they gathered differs from the original reporting passed to SIS. This includes denials of the existence of the programme from personnel allegedly involved and discrepancies between the source's description of two of the sites and that observed by inspection by the ISG.

527.   SIS did not have direct access to the main source of this intelligence until well after the war. We describe at Chapter 5 the doubts which have arisen about the reliability of some aspects of the reporting received by SIS. We have been told in particular that an important technical detail was incorrect in the reports passed to SIS. If correctly reported, these would have shown that the product of the mobile laboratories would have been in a slurry form which has a shorter storage life than dried agent and would not have been suitable for stockpiling. The conclusion must be that the main grounds for the assessment that Iraq held recently-produced stocks of biological agent no longer exist.

MOBILE FACILITIES DISCOVERED POST-WAR

528.   In April 2003, US forces recovered two trailers, which are being examined by the ISG.

529.   We have been told that the current view of the UK intelligence community is that the trailers could be used as an inefficient system for either hydrogen or biological agent production and that there is insufficient evidence to draw any firm conclusions. It is generally accepted, however, that they are not the subjects of the intelligence provided by the liaison source.

530.   **We consider that it was reasonable for the JIC to include in its assessments of March and September 2002 a reference to intelligence reports on Iraq's seeking mobile biological agent production facilities. But it has emerged that the intelligence from the source, if it had been correctly reported, would not have been consistent with a judgement that Iraq had, on the basis of recent production, stocks of biological agent. If SIS had had direct access to the source from 2000 onwards, and hence correct intelligence reporting, the main evidence for JIC judgements on Iraq's stocks of recently-produced biological agent, as opposed to a break-out capacity, would not have existed.**

6.7 ALUMINIUM TUBES

531.   From the late 1990s onwards, the British Government had intelligence that Iraq was seeking to procure aluminium tubes. This intelligence was validated by the seizure of a shipment of Chinese-origin tubes destined for Iraq in June 2001. It has been a matter of uncertainty whether the tubes were evidence of Iraq's attempts to re-constitute a nuclear programme.

BACKGROUND

532.   Of the two fissile materials suitable for the production of a nuclear weapon, plutonium and highly enriched uranium (HEU), Iraq had no access to plutonium after the bombing in 1981

by Israel of the Osirak reactor. Thereafter, Iraq's efforts to create a nuclear weapon focused on HEU. HEU can be derived from natural uranium by enriching it in gas centrifuges, which contain rotor tubes spun at high speeds.

533. After the first Gulf war, inspections by the IAEA revealed that Iraq was closer to the development of a nuclear weapon than either the IAEA or western intelligence had suspected. Following its activities in Iraq in the 1990s, however, the IAEA concluded in October 1997 that:

> ... there were no indications of Iraq having:
>
> - produced a nuclear weapon;
>
> - produced more than a few grams of weapon-usable nuclear material (HEU or separated plutonium) through its indigenous processes;
>
> - otherwise acquired weapons-usable nuclear material; or
>
> - retained any physical capability for the production of amounts of weapons-usable nuclear material of any practical significance.
>
> [IAEA Bulletin, 44/2/2002, summarising S/1997/779]

THE EMERGING INTELLIGENCE PICTURE

534. In May 2001, the JIC reported:

> More recent intelligence indicates efforts by Iraq since 1998 to procure items that could be used in a uranium enrichment programme using centrifuges. These include:
>
> - attempts to procure production scale quantities of aluminium pipes of specifications similar to those that can be used for a first generation centrifuge; ...
>
> [JIC, 10 May 2001]

535. The intelligence on Iraq's efforts to procure aluminium tubes was substantial. A series of reports in mid-2001 described the progress of the particular shipment of Chinese-origin tubes that was eventually seized, in part, in Jordan. The seizure did not deter the Iraqis who, if anything, increased their efforts to acquire the tubes from a wider network of potential suppliers and intermediaries around the world. By November 2001, there was intelligence that their requirement had increased to 100,000 tubes.

536. That Iraq wanted aluminium tubes was therefore never in doubt. Nor was it in doubt that they were made of a proscribed material. But the purpose for which the tubes were sought was not established. We were assured that advice was obtained not only from the Defence Intelligence Staff (DIS) but also from a world expert on nuclear technology who had formerly worked at British Nuclear Fuels Limited. Even so, this did not solve the puzzle. It was clear from an early date that, on the basis of the specifications of the tubes Iraq was seeking to acquire, they would have required substantial re-engineering to make them suitable for gas centrifuge use, including reducing them in length, and machining

metal off the inside and outside. This was paradoxical, since Iraq had laid down very fine tolerances for the tubes.

537. The JIC, in March 2002, was careful in its description of the seized tubes:

A shipment stopped in Jordan was inspected by the IAEA, who accepted, that with some modifications, the aluminium would be suitable for use in centrifuges. But we have no definitive intelligence that the aluminium was destined for a nuclear programme.

[JIC, 15 March 2002]

538. The Government's dossier of September 2002 said:

Intelligence shows that the present Iraqi programme is almost certainly seeking an indigenous ability to enrich uranium to the level needed for a nuclear weapon. It indicates that the approach is based on gas centrifuge uranium enrichment, one of the routes Iraq was following for producing fissile material before the Gulf War . . .

Iraq has also made repeated attempts covertly to acquire a very large quantity (60,000 or more) of specialised aluminium tubes. The specialised aluminium in question is subject to international export controls because of its potential application in the construction of gas centrifuges used to enrich uranium, although there is no definitive intelligence that it is destined for a nuclear programme.

539. The JIC both reported the IAEA's caution on the need for modifications and reflected the uncertainty about the purpose to which the tubes might be put. The dossier repeated the JIC's language on this latter point. But we consider that the omission from the dossier of the fact that the tubes would need substantial re-engineering before they could be used materially strengthened the impression that they were suitable for gas centrifuge use.

540. There was, from the outset, an alternative explanation available for the aluminium tubes. Their potential for use as rocket motor casings was mentioned in intelligence reporting as early as summer 2001. One of the earliest intelligence reports recorded that Iraq had been seeking tubes of the same precise specification from Switzerland *"probably for the Iraqi Air Force"*. Other reports also suggested possible conventional military uses for the tubes. Combined with the known engineering obstacles to the use of the tubes as centrifuge rotors, this uncertainty contributed to the JIC's unwillingness to conclude that the tubes had a definite nuclear application.

541. On 11 April 2003, the IAEA reported to the Security Council as follows:

The IAEA conducted a thorough investigation of Iraq's attempts to purchase large quantities of [high-strength aluminium] tubes. As previously reported, Iraq has maintained that these aluminium tubes were sought for rocket production. Extensive field investigation and document analysis have failed to uncover any evidence that Iraq intended to use these tubes for any project other than the reverse engineering of rockets.

[Fifteenth Consolidated Report of the Director General of the IAEA, 11 April 2003]

542. Earlier, it had reported that:

> . . . the IAEA has learned that the original tolerances for the 81 mm tubes were set prior to 1987, and were based on physical measurements taken from a small number of imported rockets in Iraq's possession. . . .

> Based on available evidence, the IAEA team has concluded that Iraq's efforts to import these aluminium tubes were not likely to have been related to the manufacture of centrifuges and, moreover, that it was highly unlikely that Iraq could have achieved the considerable re-design needed to use them in a revived centrifuge programme. However, this issue will continue to be scrutinised and investigated.

[IAEA, 'The Status of Nuclear Inspections in Iraq: An Update', 7 March 2003]

The IAEA summarised these findings as follows:

> There is no indication that Iraq has attempted to import aluminium tubes for use in centrifuge enrichment. Moreover, even had Iraq pursued such a plan, it would have encountered practical difficulties in manufacturing centrifuges out of the aluminium tubes in question.

[IAEA, 'The Status of Nuclear Inspections in Iraq: An Update', 7 March 2003]

543. We have heard from the ISG that they have *"found no indications that the high-strength 81 mm aluminium tubes Iraq has sought since 1999 were intended as gas centrifuge rotors in a uranium enrichment programme"*. The ISG has not uncovered design drawings for a gas centrifuge with an 81 mm rotor nor procurement or production of other necessary equipment, material, machinery, or centrifuge parts - such as end caps, magnetic suspension bearings, motor stators, and vacuum casings. Captured documents and interviews with Iraqi scientists and engineers have all indicated that the aluminium tubes were used to make 81 mm tactical battlefield rockets. The ISG is continuing to investigate whether there was high-level Iraqi intent to divert post-1999 tubes from the rocket programme to gas centrifuge use.

544. Nevertheless, there remain unanswered questions about the use of the aluminium tubes for rocket casings. There is consensus among rocket experts that steel would be a more suitable material for such casings and that the manufacturing tolerances are far more precise than would be justified for such a use. But we were informed that at least one US rocket uses casings made from the same high-strength aluminium. The tubes are of the same dimensions and material as a stockpile of well over 50,000 tubes declared by Iraq to the United Nations and the IAEA in 1996 and connected to production of Iraq's 81 mm Nasser multiple rocket launcher (which appears to have been based on the Italian 81 mm Medusa rocket system). Iraq's rocket production plant had, according to Iraqi records, used almost twice as many such tubes between 1989 and 1996.

545. **The evidence we received on aluminium tubes was overwhelmingly that they were intended for rockets rather than a centrifuge. We found this convincing. Despite this, we conclude that the JIC was right to consider carefully the possibility that the tubes were evidence of a resumed nuclear programme, and that it properly reflected the doubts about the use of the tubes in the caution of its assessments. But in transferring its**

judgements to the dossier, the JIC omitted the important information about the need for substantial re-engineering of the aluminium tubes to make them suitable for use as gas centrifuge rotors. This omission had the effect of materially strengthening the impression that they may have been intended for a gas centrifuge and hence for a nuclear programme.

6.8 PLAGUE AND DUSTY MUSTARD

PLAGUE

546.   In November 1990, the JIC reported that:

> *According to the new intelligence, Iraq possesses the BW agents pneumonic plague and anthrax and has weaponised them . . . Weapons are ready for immediate use. . . .*
>
> *The report that Iraq has weaponised anthrax is consistent with our earlier assessment that it might have done so. But we have no collateral for the claim that it has developed plague to a similar extent. Plague was, however, one of the agents included in the list of those that Iraq had studied or on which it had information. . . . We believe that Iraq has the facilities to produce plague in sufficient quantities for weaponisation.*

[JIC, 9 November 1990]

547.   Slightly later in November 1990, the DIS said that plague seedstock was now *"probably available"* to Iraq.

548.   These judgements were based on several intelligence reports from a single informant described as *"a new source of unestablished reliability"*. In the heightened state of concern pre-war, and because the source was felt to be in a position to comment authoritatively, the British Government decided to inoculate UK forces against plague.

549.   After the first Gulf war, some apparently corroborative intelligence was obtained from two further sources. There were inconsistencies in the knowledge of one of these and of the original source that could have led to questioning of their access to information on the subject.   But, in August 1993 the JIC said:

> *Iraq has admitted to the UN that it conducted research into BW agents from 1986 to 1990, but claims never to have produced agent in quantity nor to have possessed biological weapons. We have information that this claim is untrue and assess that Iraq produced BW weapons containing anthrax and plague . . . Stocks of agents and weapons have probably been hidden, together with key items of equipment.*

[JIC, 25 August 1993]

550.   In August 1995, after Iraq had finally admitted weaponisation of some biological agents following the defection of Hussein Kamil, the JIC noted that:

> *We have convincing intelligence of a BW programme which started in the 1970s and strong indications that it produced and weaponised anthrax, botulinum toxin, and*

probably plague. With the exception of plague, Iraq previously admitted doing research on these and other agents but steadfastly denied the work was for an offensive programme. UNSCOM, although suspicious, could find no clear evidence to the contrary. . . . In a 'full, final and complete declaration' given to UNSCOM in August 1995, Iraq admitted to a major BW programme under which it had produced huge quantities of anthrax and botulinum toxin, but implausibly denied it had ever considered weaponisation. . . . In the last few days Iraq has admitted to UNSCOM that agent was produced at additional sites, field-testing of weapons took place in 1989, and that bombs and missile warheads were filled with anthrax and botulinum toxin in December 1990. . . . Many questions remain on the BW programme; Iraq has not, for example, admitted any work on plague.

[JIC, 24 August 1995]

551.   In June 1996, the JIC said:

Iraq has not yet admitted to work on plague and has played down its success in developing BW aerosol delivery systems.

[JIC, 12 June 1996]

552.   In September 1997, the JIC commented:

Iraq claimed, however, that it had terminated the [BW] programme and destroyed its arsenal before UN inspections began in 1991. These admissions, while assessed to be largely accurate, are incomplete. We assess that Iraq has withheld information on key elements of its programme: reliable intelligence has described work on plague and suspicions persist of work on other pox viruses.

[JIC, 3 September 1997]

553.   In March 2002, the JIC reported as follows:

We . . . judge that Iraq currently has available, either from pre Gulf war stocks or more recent production, anthrax spores, botulinum toxin, aflatoxin and possibly plague . . .

The following biological agents could be produced within days, if not already: Anthrax spores, botulinum toxin, aflatoxin and possibly plague.

[JIC, 15 March 2002]

554.   Plague seems to have been included in this list mainly on the basis of reporting from a much earlier period. The judgement that Iraq could *"possibly"* produce plague within days was stronger than was justified by more recent intelligence. UNSCOM's final report in January 1999 made no mention of plague. One intelligence report, issued in 1999 and re-issued in 2003, commented that cats, reportedly being used by Iraq in animal experiments, exhibited a susceptibility to plague that was similar to humans. But the report also noted that the informant was unaware of any Iraqi work on plague as a biological warfare agent. Comments on the report itself concluded prudently:

We do not currently have any evidence that plague forms part of the Iraq BW programme.

555. In August 2002 and again in March 2003, the DIS assessed that plague was *"probably available"* to Iraq. We note that this judgement was stronger than that of the JIC. It is understandable that intelligence assessments made in the period immediately before a conflict should reflect worst case assumptions, but we have seen no intelligence that would support this stronger judgement. We were told that, in the absence of new and plausible information categorically ruling out the original 1990 reporting, it was not possible to <u>exclude</u> plague from Iraq's biological warfare inventory.

556. In October 2002, the JIC said:

> *We judge that Iraq is self-sufficient in its BW programme and currently has available, either from pre-Gulf War stocks or more recent production, anthrax spores, botulinum toxin, aflatoxin, and possibly plague and ricin.*

[JIC, 28 October 2002]

557. The Government's dossier of September 2002 mentioned plague only once, in an historical context:

> *Iraq created forged documents to account for bacterial growth media, imported in the late 1980s, specifically for the production of anthrax, botulinum toxin and probably plague.*

558. We note that the dossier did not mention a <u>current</u> threat from plague, because the JIC concluded that the intelligence on plague was not sufficiently firm.

559. No evidence of Iraqi possession or production of plague has been found since the war.

DUSTY MUSTARD

560. In the approach to the first Gulf war, several JIC assessments noted that Iraq had developed and used, in the Iran-Iraq war, a mustard agent in 'dusty' form. UK experts were able to examine a munition filled with 'dusty mustard' from the Iran/Iraq war.

561. Over the following two years, JIC assessments mentioned 'dusty mustard' four times, usually in the context of Iraqi failure to declare the agent or failure by UNSCOM inspectors to find it. After February 1993, the subject disappeared from JIC history. As far as we can determine, UNSCOM did not find any evidence of 'dusty mustard', although in April 2002 Robert D Walpole, Special Assistant to the US Director of Central Intelligence for Persian Gulf War Illnesses, reported that:

> *UNSCOM information shows no research or production of dusty agents in the years prior to the war, although a hand-written note found by UNSCOM inspectors indicated that an Iraqi was considering the idea in the late 1980s.*

562. **Plague and 'dusty mustard' were just two of the many biological and chemical threats on which the intelligence community had to keep watch in the period before the first Gulf war, and subsequently.**

563. **The intelligence on their availability to Iraq in 1990 and 1991 rested on a small number of reports and the evidence derived from examination of a**

munition. **There were grounds for scepticism both about the reports' sources and their quality. Nevertheless, we conclude that the Government was right in 1990 and 1991 to act on a precautionary basis.**

564. **We find it harder to understand the treatment of the intelligence in the ensuing period. Dusty mustard disappears from JIC assessments from 1993 onwards. By contrast, although little new intelligence was received, and most of that was historical or unconvincing, plague continued to be mentioned in JIC assessments up to March 2003. Those fluctuated in the certainty of judgements about Iraqi possession of plague between *"possibly"* and *"probably"*.**

565. **We conclude that, in the case of plague, JIC assessments reflected historic evidence, and intelligence of dubious reliability, reinforced by suspicion of Iraq, rather than up-to-date evidence.**

6.9 DR JONES'S DISSENT

566. Dr Brian Jones, the then Head of the Nuclear, Biological, Chemical Technical Intelligence branch in the DIS, was on leave when the process of drafting the Government's dossier began. On his return to work on 18 September (that is, six days before publication of the dossier), his staff expressed to him a range of concerns about the strength of the judgements being made in the dossier, some of which they believed were not supported by the intelligence. Dr Jones shared a number of his staffs' concerns and recorded his concerns in a minute to his management on 19 September[6].

567. It is clear that Dr Jones saw the action that he had taken in registering his dissent as being unusual. We heard from the then Chief of Defence Intelligence, however, that:

> I saw it as part of the day-to-day process.

568. It is not our intention in this report to revisit issues already addressed by Lord Hutton. But we believe that the episode raises three broader issues about the use of the available intelligence material in the Government's dossier, and about the handling of sensitive intelligence more generally, which merit consideration here.

USE OF THE AVAILABLE INTELLIGENCE MATERIAL

569. Dr Jones raised concerns about the treatment of the intelligence containing the '45 minute' report. In his minute, Dr Jones said that:

> We have a number of questions in our minds relating to the intelligence on the military plans for the use of chemical and biological weapons, particularly about the times mentioned[7] and the failure to differentiate between the two types of weapons.

570. We conclude that **Dr Jones was right to raise concerns about the manner of expression of the '45 minute' report in the dossier given the vagueness of the underlying intelligence.**

---

[6] Submitted to Lord Hutton's Inquiry as MOD/22/0001.
[7] Dr Jones told us that he used guarded language in his minute because of its low classification.

571.   Dr Jones also raised concerns about the certainty of language used in the dossier on Iraqi production and possession of chemical agents.   In his minute, Dr Jones said that:

> *We have not seen intelligence which we believe 'shows' that Iraq has continued to produce CW agent in 1998-2002, although our judgement is that it has probably done so.*

572.   We have commented separately in Chapter 5 on the way in which the dossier did not reflect the limitations of some aspects of the intelligence on which it drew. We conclude that **Dr Jones was right to raise concerns about the certainty of language used in the dossier on Iraqi production and possession of chemical agents.**

THE HANDLING OF INTELLIGENCE

573.   Dr Jones was not shown one particularly sensitive human intelligence report which said that production of biological and chemical agent had been accelerated by the Iraqi Government, including through the building of further facilities throughout Iraq. Dr Jones's managers told him that they regarded this report as justifying the certainty of language in the dossier about Iraqi production of chemical weapons. We have looked into this point in some detail.

574.   The intelligence report came from a new source on trial. It was issued on 11 September 2002. SIS had what at the time appeared to be well-founded hopes that this source would become a major asset. In particular, the source had indicated to SIS that he would be able to provide substantial and critical additional intelligence in the near future. The Chief of SIS has told us that SIS were concerned to minimise knowledge of the existence of the source during what they expected to be an initial, very sensitive, period of development. The source's intelligence about chemical weapons production was therefore distributed to an extremely limited circle of senior readers.

575.   We understand SIS's concern to give maximum protection to their source in those particular, and transitional, circumstances. We were told that in-house SIS technical experts took a preliminary and provisional view that the report should be issued, as being from *"A new source on trial"*. But the exclusion of Dr Jones and his staff from readership of the original report meant that this intelligence was not seen by the few people in the UK intelligence community able to form all-round, professional technical judgements on its reliability and significance. In the event, SIS withdrew the intelligence from this source as being unreliable in July 2003.

576.   **We recognise that circumstances arise in which it is right for senior officials to take a broad view that differs from the opinions of those with expertise on points of detail. We do not, however, consider that the report held back from Dr Jones and his staff (which Dr Jones' superiors regarded as justifying the certainty of the language in the dossier) was one to which such considerations should have applied.** The judgement reached by the JIC in this case should have been able to depend on detailed, expert analysis of the intelligence. In the event, the JIC had no reason to know that that had not happened.

577. **It was understandable that SIS should have wanted to give greater than normal protection to the human intelligence source on this occasion. But a problem arose because it was kept from the relevant DIS analysts who had a wider perspective. It would have been more appropriate for senior managers in the DIS and SIS to have made arrangements for the intelligence to be shown to DIS experts rather than their making their own judgements on its significance.** The fact that it was not shown to them resulted in a stronger assessment in the dossier in relation to Iraqi chemical weapons production than was justified by the available intelligence. It also deprived SIS of key expertise that would have helped them to assess the reliability of their new source. We have not been presented with any evidence that persuades us that there was an insuperable obstacle to allowing expert-level DIS access to the intelligence.

578. The Chief of SIS told us that, because he had been aware of the report on 10 September, he had mentioned it to the Prime Minister's Foreign Affairs Adviser (Sir David Manning) at a meeting on 10 September and followed this up by arranging for the report to be sent to Sir David. As it happened, the Chief of SIS had a meeting with the Prime Minister on 12 September to brief him on SIS operations in respect of Iraq. At this meeting, he briefed the Prime Minister on each of SIS's main sources including the new source on trial. He told us that he had underlined to the Prime Minister the potential importance of the new source and what SIS understood his access to be; but also said that the case was developmental and that the source remained unproven. Nevertheless, it may be that, in the context of the intense interest at that moment in the status of Iraq's prohibited weapons programmes, and in particular continuing work on the dossier, this concurrence of events caused more weight to be given to this unvalidated new source than would normally have been the case.

6.10 OIL SUPPLIES

579. It has frequently been alleged that the real motivation behind the decision to go to war in Iraq was a desire to control Iraq's oil supplies. This issue does not fall within our terms of reference and we did not take evidence specifically on it. We did, however, review JIC assessments on the security of oil supplies issued in the period 2000-2003, in which such a motivation did not feature. We also think it improbable that such an objective or motivation, if it existed, would not have been apparent in the large volume and wide range of policy and intelligence papers that we examined. **We saw no evidence that a motive of the British Government for initiating military action was securing continuing access to oil supplies.**

CHAPTER 7

CONCLUSIONS ON BROADER ISSUES

7.1 GENERAL CONCLUSIONS ABOUT INTELLIGENCE AND ITS USE

580. In this Chapter, we set out some general conclusions about the gathering, evaluation and use of intelligence, in the light of our examination of the material in preceding Chapters.

OTHER CASES

581. As the Intelligence and Security Committee have observed[1]:

Most of the hard work that the Agencies do every year will never be made public.

582. Much that is in Chapter 2 can be told only because the outcomes described there are now publicly known. Nevertheless, the material we have published for the first time in this Report illustrates the contribution of intelligence reports and assessments to the handling of each of these cases over recent years. Intelligence has been validated to an impressive extent by what has been subsequently revealed and has played a crucial part in enabling developing threats to international security and stability to be identified and countered. For obvious reasons, we have not discussed the sources of the intelligence but we have examined them. The cases demonstrate a high degree of co-operation not only between the agencies but also with liaison services, and with the departments who have been enabled to act effectively on the intelligence.

INTERNATIONAL CO-OPERATION

583. We believe it to be right, therefore, to start this Chapter with our views on the importance of international co-operation in this field. While there may be differences between countries over policy issues, not least towards the Middle East, there is agreement among the great majority of countries over the need to tackle the risks posed by destabilising nuclear, biological and chemical weapons programmes, to limit proliferation and to prevent terrorists from increasing their arsenal of destruction by the acquisition of vastly more powerful weapons.

584. **We note that much of what was reliably known about Iraq's unconventional weapons programmes in the mid- and late-1990s was obtained through the reports of the UN Special Commission (UNSCOM) and of the International Atomic Energy Agency (IAEA). These international agencies now appear to have been more effective than was realised at the time in dismantling and inhibiting Iraq's prohibited weapons programmes. The value of such international organisations needs to be recognised and built on for the future, supported by the contribution of intelligence from national agencies.**

---

[1] Intelligence and Security Committee Annual Report 2003-2004. Cm 6240. June 2004.

CO-ORDINATION OF COUNTER-PROLIFERATION ACTIVITY

585.　It is clear that, in the continuing struggle against proliferation, it will be essential to continue to bring to bear all sources of intelligence in a co-ordinated way. We have noted in our general Conclusions on Chapter 2 that success in the cases we studied came through close collaboration between all involved to piece together the intelligence picture, with teams able to have shared access to all available intelligence. We welcome the arrangements for bringing together all sources of expertise on terrorism into the Joint Terrorism Analysis Centre. We have considered whether to recommend a similar organisation to deal with counter-proliferation. The difference between counter-terrorism and counter-proliferation is that a large part of the former is a problem of analysing and dealing with day-to-day threats while the latter is longer-term. We do not therefore consider that it would be justified or helpful to bring experts out of their parent organisations and to co-locate them. Moreover, we are impressed with the growing co-operation between departments and agencies and the exploitation of technical expertise through cross-postings and secondments. However, **we consider that it would be helpful through day-to-day processes and the use of new information systems to create a 'virtual' network bringing together the various sources of expertise in Government on proliferation and on activity to tackle it, who would be known to each other and could consult each other easily**.

7.2 INTELLIGENCE MACHINERY

THE DEFENCE INTELLIGENCE STAFF

586.　Much of the Government's expertise on technical issues relating to nuclear, biological and chemical weapons and ballistic missiles rests in the Defence Intelligence Staff (DIS). This expertise is used to produce all-source analysis which underpins the intelligence community's understanding on weapons programmes. Unlike the agencies, the DIS is not free-standing and, because its focus must be concentrated on the department it serves, it has in the past perhaps been seen as rather separate from the rest of the intelligence community, although it would be wrong to exaggerate this. We have considered whether to recommend that the DIS should be brought out of the Ministry of Defence (MOD) and become a separate agency with a similar relationship to the MOD as the Secret Intelligence Service (SIS) have to the Foreign and Commonwealth Office (FCO).

587.　Because the DIS is so crucial to the MOD in everything from strategic planning through equipment acquisition to the conduct of military operations, we do not believe that this would be helpful. But **we consider that further steps are needed to integrate the relevant work of the DIS more closely with the rest of the intelligence community. We welcome the arrangements now being made to give the Joint Intelligence Committee more leverage through the Intelligence Requirements process to ensure that the DIS serves wider national priorities as well as it does defence priorities and has the resources which the rest of the intelligence community needs to support its activities. If that involved increasing the Secret Intelligence Account by a sum to be at**

the Security and Intelligence Co-ordinator's disposal to commission such resources, we would support that.

588.   The question of whether there should have been better machinery for bringing to the attention of the Joint Intelligence Committee (JIC) dissenting opinions in the DIS arose in relation to the Government's dossier of September 2002. But the same point applies to JIC assessments. The Intelligence and Security Committee have recommended that if individuals in the intelligence community formally record concerns in relation to assessments these concerns should be brought to the attention of the JIC Chairman.

589.   The Government has said that it is keeping the situation under review, and that DIS standing instructions exist for the notification to the Chief of Defence Intelligence and his deputy of dissenting views on JIC issues. **We recommend consideration of the provision of proper channels for the expression of dissent within the DIS through the extension of the remit of the Staff Counsellor, who provides a confidential outlet for conscientious objection or dissent within the intelligence agencies, to cover DIS civilian staff and the Assessments Staff.**

590.   We have another recommendation in relation to the DIS. During the lead-up to the Iraq war, neither the Chief of Defence Intelligence nor his deputy were intelligence specialists. **We recognise the case for the Chief of Defence Intelligence to be a serving officer so that he is fully meshed into military planning. But we consider that the Deputy should, unless there are good reasons to the contrary at the time when a particular appointment is made, be an intelligence specialist.**

THE JOINT INTELLIGENCE COMMITTEE

591.   A good deal of our attention has inevitably been focussed on the JIC and its operations. Its role in co-ordinating the intelligence community and producing objective intelligence assessments is widely admired, including by all members of our Committee. We conclude that it is vital to maintain and reinforce its independence.

592.   As regards the JIC itself, two questions we have asked ourselves are whether, as a result of the additions to its membership described in Chapter 1, it has become too big, and whether its objectivity is in danger of being compromised by the presence of more policy heavy-weights than in the past.

593.   On the first question, the changed nature of the security challenges faced by the UK in the 21st century has inevitably led to intelligence having a wider application in policy-making. That in turn has resulted in more departments with only an occasional interest in the JIC's work being added to its membership. If all those members were to attend on each occasion, JIC meetings would certainly become unwieldy. But we understand that they do not. Provided that this is the case, it seems desirable that those departments which may have an interest in, and use for, intelligence should attend as necessary when items affecting their business are discussed.

594. The policy presence on the JIC has been increased in recent years. The posts of Director General (Defence and Intelligence) in the FCO and Policy Director in the MOD are members and it is desirable that they should remain so that the JIC can be well-informed about the policy interests of those departments.

595. The Intelligence Co-ordinator, the Prime Minister's Foreign Affairs Adviser and the head of the Cabinet Office Defence and Overseas Secretariat have also been members, and in fact all have chaired the JIC at various times. The posts of Prime Minister's Foreign Affairs Adviser and Head of the Defence and Overseas Secretariat have now been combined into a single post which is held at Permanent Secretary level. So, now, is the post of Security and Intelligence Co-ordinator.

596. These are two of the leading policy advisers in the field covered by the JIC. Nevertheless, since we have been assured by all witnesses that the tradition of the JIC has prevented policy imperatives from dominating objective assessment in the JIC's deliberations, **we recommend no change in the JIC's membership** on this account.

597. That brings us to the Chairmanship. We welcome the fact that the Chairmanship is now a single, independent post, not combined with other posts as sometimes in the past. Nevertheless, without any implied criticism of the present or past Chairmen, it seems wrong in principle that the Chairman of the JIC should be outranked not only by the heads of the agencies but also by two other heavyweight Permanent Secretaries on his Committee. Lord Franks stressed the need for the Chairman to be both full-time and independent. **We see a strong case for the post of Chairman of the JIC being held by someone with experience of dealing with Ministers in a very senior role, and who is demonstrably beyond influence, and thus probably in his last post**.

THE ASSESSMENTS STAFF

598. We have noted in Chapters 2, 3 and 5 the skill and objectivity of the Assessments Staff. But we are conscious that the resources of the Assessments Staff are very slight in relation to those of the collecting agencies. Moreover, for the most part the Assessments Staff is made up of officials from departments on short-term secondments. When the Assessments Staff were set up in 1968, it was envisaged that they would have a permanent staff but the shortage of opportunities for advancement has made that impracticable.

599. The Assessments Staff do a remarkable job, given their limited role, in pulling together objective assessments. But they have limited scope for employing formal techniques of challenge. These would clearly not be appropriate in every case but might well be desirable for major issues when the 'prevailing wisdom' risks becoming too conventional. Their limited role also means that much of the task of assessing the influence of informants' circumstances on the nature and quality of their reporting falls to the intelligence agencies, and is vulnerable to agencies championing their own sources.

600. The cost of the Assessments Staff is minimal in relation to the amounts the nation spends on the collection of intelligence. It is a false economy to skimp on the machinery through

which expensively-collected intelligence passes to decision-makers. **We recommend that the Security and Intelligence Co-ordinator reviews the size of the Assessments Staff, and in particular considers whether they have available the volume and range of resources to ask the questions which need to be asked in fully assessing intelligence reports and in thinking radically. We recommend also that this review should include considering whether there should be a specialism of analysis with a career structure and room for advancement, allowing the Assessments Staff to include some career members. We understand that the Intelligence and Security Committee are planning to look at this issue**.

601. In that connection, we note that the Cabinet Office used to have high-powered, though part-time, scientific advice available, for example through Lord Cherwell, Lord Zuckerman and Dr Frank Panton. Several witnesses told us that, in their view, this is no longer necessary because there are arrangements for close co-operation with the Government's Chief Scientific Adviser. We welcome this but note that the advantage of the former arrangement was that the individuals were on the spot and could, when necessary, challenge conventional wisdom. We conclude that **it may be worth considering the appointment of a distinguished scientist to undertake a part-time role as adviser to the Cabinet Office**.

7.3 INTELLIGENCE ASSESSMENTS

THE LANGUAGE OF JIC ASSESSMENTS

602. A recurring issue – but one which the experience of intelligence on Iraq raises again – is whether JIC assessments are drafted and presented in a way which best helps readers to pick up the range of uncertainty attaching to intelligence assessments.

603. Over the years, various approaches have been taken to this problem. The view currently taken by the witnesses we interviewed is that Ministers and other readers are not helped by assessments which are expressed in language of "on the one hand" and "on the other", and which thus leave the reader with no conclusion. So the general convention is that the JIC should produce its best assessment in the form of 'Key Judgements' drawn up in the light of the evidence. Such assessments often include warnings that the evidence is thin (and the word 'Judgement' is itself a signal to the reader that it is not a statement of fact). But it is not the current JIC convention to express degrees of confidence in the judgement or to include alternative or minority hypotheses. The consequence is that the need to reach consensus may result in nuanced language. Subtleties such as "the intelligence indicates" rather than "the intelligence shows" may escape the untutored or busy reader. We also came across instances where Key Judgements unhelpfully omitted qualifications about the limitations of the intelligence which were elsewhere in the text.

604. We would not think it desirable that any convention should be binding, and different treatments may be suitable for different subjects. But we note that the US Government does from time to time attach degrees of confidence and notes of dissent to its National Intelligence Estimates. These may help to prevent readers from attaching more certainty

to judgements than is justified and intended. We conclude that **the JIC has been right not to reach a judgement when the evidence is insubstantial. We believe that the JIC should, where there are significant limitations in the intelligence, state these clearly alongside its Key Judgements. While not arguing for a particular approach to the language of JIC assessments and the way in which alternative or minority hypotheses, or uncertainty, are expressed, we recommend that the intelligence community review their conventions again to see if there would be advantage in refreshing them**.

JIC ASSESSMENTS

605. There are other aspects of JIC assessments on which our Review causes us to offer observations:

    a. It should continue to be made clear on the face of the circulated document for what purpose an assessment is being produced.

    b. It is reasonable for assessments requested by the MOD for planning purposes relating to potential military activity to consider worst case scenarios. The burden of proof in such cases may reasonably be lower than in normal circumstances and assessments may reasonably be made on a more precautionary basis. But JIC assessments that take this approach should state that fact explicitly. So should assessments and analysis derived from them, then and subsequently. Care should be taken to ensure that worst case analysis is not carried forward into assessments except those (like assessments of enemy capabilities) which warrant such an approach.

    c. JIC assessments should make clear what the JIC does not know in areas where gaps and uncertainties are material to the assessment.

    d. Assessments should not give undue weight to intelligence reports over wider analysis of historical, psychological or geopolitical factors.

    e. All reasonably sustainable hypotheses should not be dismissed finally until there is sufficient information to do so.

    f. Challenge should be an accepted and routine part of the assessment process as well as an occasional formal exercise, built into the system.

    g. Consideration should be given from time to time to occasional external peer review, particularly on technical issues.

    h. The JIC should continue to conduct regular lessons-learned processes. We have observed in the context of Iraq the truism that under-estimates of a problem tend to get highlighted and over-estimates forgotten on the basis that the latter are less damaging. Attention needs to be paid to misjudgements in both directions.

7.4 MACHINERY OF GOVERNMENT

606. We received evidence from two former Cabinet members, one of the present and one of a previous administration, who expressed their concern about the informal nature of much

of the Government's decision-making process, and the relative lack of use of established Cabinet Committee machinery.

607. Two changes which occurred over this period had implications for the application of intelligence to collective ministerial decision-making. One was the splitting of the Cabinet Secretary's responsibilities through the creation of the post of Security and Intelligence Co-ordinator. The latter is able to devote the majority of his time to security and intelligence issues in a way that the Cabinet Secretary, with all the many other calls on his time, could not. It was represented to us that this change was particularly necessary after the terrorist attacks of 11 September 2001. However, the effect is that the Cabinet Secretary is no longer so directly involved in the chain through which intelligence reaches the Prime Minister. It follows that the Cabinet Secretary, who attends the Cabinet and maintains the machinery to support their decision-making, is less directly involved personally in advising the Prime Minister on security and intelligence issues. By the same token, the Security and Intelligence Co-ordinator does not attend Cabinet and is not part of the Cabinet Secretariat supporting Cabinet Ministers in discharging their collective responsibilities in defence and overseas policy matters. We understand that the Intelligence and Security Committee will shortly review how this arrangement has worked.

608. The second change was that two key posts at the top of the Cabinet Secretariat, those of Head of the Defence and Overseas Secretariat and Head of the European Affairs Secretariat, were combined with the posts of the Prime Minister's advisers on Foreign Affairs and on European Affairs respectively. We believe that the effect of the changes has been to weight their responsibility to the Prime Minister more heavily than their responsibility through the Cabinet Secretary to the Cabinet as a whole. It is right to acknowledge that the view of the present post-holders is that the arrangement works well, in particular in connecting the work of the Cabinet Secretariat to that of the Prime Minister's office. We should also record that it was clear from the departmental policy papers we read that there was very close co-operation between officials in the Prime Minister's office and in the FCO in policy-making on Iraq. It is nonetheless a shift which acts to concentrate detailed knowledge and effective decision-making in fewer minds at the top.

609. In the year before the war, the Cabinet discussed policy towards Iraq as a specific agenda item 24 times. It also arose in the course of discussions on other business. Cabinet members were offered and many received briefings on the intelligence picture on Iraq. There was therefore no lack of discussion on Iraq; and we have been informed that it was substantive. The Ministerial Committee on Defence and Overseas Policy did not meet. By contrast, over the period from April 2002 to the start of military action, some 25 meetings attended by the small number of key Ministers, officials and military officers most closely involved provided the framework of discussion and decision-making within Government.

610. One inescapable consequence of this was to limit wider collective discussion and consideration by the Cabinet to the frequent but unscripted occasions when the Prime Minister, Foreign Secretary and Defence Secretary briefed the Cabinet orally. Excellent quality papers were written by officials, but these were not discussed in Cabinet or in Cabinet Committee. Without papers circulated in advance, it remains possible but is obviously much more difficult for members of the Cabinet outside the small circle directly

involved to bring their political judgement and experience to bear on the major decisions for which the Cabinet as a whole must carry responsibility. The absence of papers on the Cabinet agenda so that Ministers could obtain briefings in advance from the Cabinet Office, their own departments or from the intelligence agencies plainly reduced their ability to prepare properly for such discussions, while the changes to key posts at the head of the Cabinet Secretariat lessened the support of the machinery of government for the collective responsibility of the Cabinet in the vital matter of war and peace.

611. **We do not suggest that there is or should be an ideal or unchangeable system of collective Government, still less that procedures are in aggregate any less effective now than in earlier times. However, we are concerned that the informality and circumscribed character of the Government's procedures which we saw in the context of policy-making towards Iraq risks reducing the scope for informed collective political judgement. Such risks are particularly significant in a field like the subject of our Review, where hard facts are inherently difficult to come by and the quality of judgement is accordingly all the more important.**

CHAPTER 8

SUMMARY OF CONCLUSIONS

This summary follows the order of the Chapters of our Report. It comprises the passages we have highlighted in each Section and is intended to convey the gist of our Conclusions. However, we emphasise the importance of reading the Sections of the Report in full since the picture of the sources, assessment and use of intelligence is necessarily complicated and our Conclusions need to be read in context in order to be fully understood.

CHAPTER 2 – COUNTRIES OF CONCERN OTHER THAN IRAQ AND GLOBAL TRADE

1.   All four of the case studies we discuss (AQ Khan, Libya, Iran, North Korea) were to a greater or lesser extent success stories. To a degree, that was inevitable – we chose those cases where intelligence about nuclear, biological, chemical and ballistic missile programmes and proliferation activities can be discussed precisely because it has contributed to disclosure of those activities. But that should not detract from what has clearly been an impressive performance by the intelligence community and policy-makers in each case, and overall. (Paragraph 107)

2.   A number of common threads have become clear from our examination of each case. The first and most obvious is the powerful effect of exploiting the linkages where they exist between suppliers (AQ Khan; North Korea) and buyers (Iran; Libya; others) for counter-proliferation activity. It is in the nature of proliferation that what can be discovered about a supplier leads to information about the customer, and *vice versa*. The second thread flows from this – the powerful multiplier effect of effective international (in many cases, multinational) collaboration. Third, this is painstaking work, involving the piecing together over extended timescales of often fragmentary information. There are the surprises and 'lucky breaks'. But they often come from the foundation of knowledge developed over several years. It requires close collaboration between all involved, in agencies and departments, to build the jigsaw, with teams able to have access to available intelligence and to make the most of each clue. It also depends on continuity of shared purpose amongst collectors and analysts, and between the intelligence and policy communities, in gathering, assessing and using intelligence in tackling proliferation and nuclear, biological and chemical weapons programmes which are destabilising in security terms. (Paragraphs 108/109)

CHAPTER 3 – TERRORISM

3.   All of the UK intelligence agencies are developing new techniques, and we have seen clear evidence that they are co-operating at all levels. (Paragraph 133)

4.   JTAC has now been operating for over a year and has proved a success. (Paragraph 134)

5.   International counter-terrorism collaboration has also been significantly enhanced in the past six or seven years. Though we understand that other countries have not yet achieved

the same level of inter-departmental synthesis, considerable developments have taken place. Staff of the UK intelligence and security agencies are today in much wider contact with their opposite numbers throughout the world. We note these initiatives, but remain concerned that the procedures of the international community are still not sufficiently aligned to match the threat. (Paragraph 136)

CHAPTER 4 – COUNTER-PROLIFERATION MACHINERY

6. Intelligence performs an important role in many aspects of the Government's counter-proliferation work. It helps to identify proliferating countries, organisations and individuals through JIC assessments, DIS proliferation studies and operational intelligence. It can help to interdict or disrupt the activities of proliferators either nationally or in co-operation with other countries. It can support diplomatic activity by revealing states' attitudes to counter-proliferation or by informing the assessments of international partners. It can also support inspection, monitoring and verification regimes and on occasions military action. Intelligence can play an important part in enforcing export controls, particularly in relation to 'dual-use' goods and technologies. (Paragraphs 149/150)

CHAPTER 5 – IRAQ

THE POLICY CONTEXT

7. The developing policy context of the previous four years [see paragraphs 210–217] and especially the impact of the events of 11 September 2001, formed the backdrop for changes in policy towards Iraq in early 2002. The Government's conclusion in the spring of 2002 that stronger action (although not necessarily military action) needed to be taken to enforce Iraqi disarmament was not based on any new development in the current intelligence picture on Iraq. (Paragraph 427)

8. When the Government concluded that action going beyond the previous policy of containment needed to be taken, there were many grounds for concern arising from Iraq's past record and behaviour. There was a clear view that, to be successful, any new action to enforce Iraqi compliance with its disarmament obligations would need to be backed with the credible threat of force. But there was no recent intelligence that would itself have given rise to a conclusion that Iraq was of more immediate concern than the activities of some other countries. (Paragraph 427)

9. The Government, as well as being influenced by the concerns of the US Government, saw a need for immediate action on Iraq because of the wider historical and international context, especially Iraq's perceived continuing challenge to the authority of the United Nations. The Government also saw in the United Nations and a decade of Security Council Resolutions a basis for action through the United Nations to enforce Iraqi compliance with its disarmament obligations. (Paragraph 428)

10. The Government considered in March 2002 two options for achieving the goal of Iraqi disarmament - a toughening of the existing containment policy; and regime change by military means. Ministers were advised that, if regime change was the chosen policy, only

the use of overriding force in a ground campaign would achieve the removal of Saddam Hussein and Iraq's re-integration with the international community. Officials noted that regime change of itself had no basis in international law; and that any offensive military action against Iraq could only be justified if Iraq were held to be in breach of its disarmament obligations under United Nations Security Council Resolution 687 or some new resolution. Officials also noted that for the five Permanent Members of the Security Council and the majority of the 15 members of the Council to take the view that Iraq was in breach of its obligations under Resolution 687, they would need to be convinced that Iraq was in breach of its obligations; that such proof would need to be incontrovertible and of large-scale activity; but that the intelligence then available was insufficiently robust to meet that criterion. (Paragraph 429)

11.   Intelligence on Iraqi nuclear, biological, chemical and ballistic missile programmes was used in support of the execution of this policy to inform planning for a military campaign; to inform domestic and international opinion, in support of the Government's advocacy of its changing policy towards Iraq; and to obtain and provide information to United Nations inspectors. (Paragraph 431)

12.   Iraq was not the only issue on which the intelligence agencies, the JIC and the departments concerned were working during this period. Other matters, including terrorism and the activities of other countries of concern, were requiring intensive day-to-day observation and action. (Paragraph 432)

THE SOURCES OF INTELLIGENCE

13.   Between 1991 and 1998, the bulk of information used in assessing the status of Iraq's biological, chemical and ballistic missile programmes was derived from UNSCOM reports. (Paragraph 433)

14.   After the departure of the United Nations inspectors in December 1998, information sources were sparse, particularly on Iraq's chemical and biological weapons programmes. (Paragraph 433)

15.   The number of primary human intelligence sources remained few. Other intelligence sources provided valuable information on other activity, including overseas procurement activity. They did not generally provide confirmation of the intelligence received from human sources, but did contribute to the picture of the continuing intention of the Iraqi regime to pursue its prohibited weapons programmes. (Paragraphs 434/435)

16.   Validation of human intelligence sources after the war has thrown doubt on a high proportion of those sources and of their reports, and hence on the quality of the intelligence assessments received by Ministers and officials in the period from summer 2002 to the outbreak of hostilities. Of the main human intelligence sources:

        a.   One SIS main source reported authoritatively on some issues, but on others was passing on what he had heard within his circle.

        b.   Reporting from a sub-source to a second SIS main source that was important to JIC assessments on Iraqi possession of chemical and biological weapons must be open to doubt.

c.   Reports from a third SIS main source have been withdrawn as unreliable.

d.   Reports from two further SIS main sources continue to be regarded as reliable, although it is notable that their reports were less worrying than the rest about Iraqi chemical and biological weapons capabilities.

e.   Reports received from a liaison service on Iraqi production of biological agent were seriously flawed, so that the grounds for JIC assessments drawing on those reports that Iraq had recently-produced stocks of biological agent no longer exist. (Paragraph 436)

17.   We do not believe that over-reliance on dissident and emigré sources was a major cause of subsequent weaknesses in the human intelligence relied on by the UK. (Paragraph 438)

18.   One reason for the number of agents whose reports turned out to be unreliable or questionable may be the length of the reporting chains. Another reason may be that agents who were known to be reliable were asked to report on issues going well beyond their usual territory. A third reason may be that, because of the scarcity of sources and the urgent requirement for intelligence, more credence was given to untried agents than would normally be the case. (Paragraphs 440–442)

19.   A major underlying reason for the problems that have arisen was the difficulty of achieving reliable human intelligence on Iraq. However, even taking into account the difficulty of recruiting and running reliable agents on Iraqi issues, we conclude that part of the reason for the serious doubt being cast over a high proportion of human intelligence reports on Iraq arises from weaknesses in the effective application by SIS of its validation procedures and in their proper resourcing. Our Review has shown the vital importance of effective scrutiny and validation of human intelligence sources and of their reporting to the preparation of accurate JIC assessments and high-quality advice to Ministers. We urge the Chief of SIS to ensure that this task is properly resourced and organised to achieve that result, and we think that it would be appropriate if the Intelligence and Security Committee were to monitor this. (Paragraphs 443–445)

ASSESSMENT

20.   In general, we found that the original intelligence material was correctly reported in JIC assessments. An exception was the '45 minute' report. But this sort of example was rare. (Paragraph 449)

21.   We should record in particular that we have found no evidence of deliberate distortion or of culpable negligence. (Paragraph 449)

22.   We found no evidence of JIC assessments and the judgements inside them being pulled in any particular direction to meet the policy concerns of senior officials on the JIC. (Paragraph 450)

23.   We conclude in general that the intelligence community made good use of the technical expertise available to the Government. (Paragraph 451)

24.   We accept the need for careful handling of human intelligence reports to sustain the security of sources. We have, however, seen evidence of difficulties that arose from the

unduly strict 'compartmentalisation' of intelligence. It was wrong that a report which was of significance in the drafting of a document of the importance of the dossier was not shown to key experts in the DIS who could have commented on the validity and credibility of the report. We conclude that arrangements should always be sought to ensure that the need for protection of sources should not prevent the exposure of reports on technical matters to the most expert available analysis. (Paragraphs 452)

25.   We were impressed by the quality of intelligence assessments on Iraq's nuclear capabilities. (Paragraphs 453)

26.   Partly because of inherent difficulties in assessing chemical and biological programmes, JIC assessments on Iraq's chemical and biological weapons programmes were less assured. The most significant is the 'dual use' issue – because chemical and biological weapons programmes can draw heavily on 'dual use' materials, it is easier for a proliferating state to keep its programmes covert. (Paragraph 454/455)

27.   There were also Iraq-specific factors. The intelligence community will have had in mind that Iraq had not only owned but used its chemical weapons in the past. It will inevitably have been influenced by the way in which the Iraqi regime was engaged in a sustained programme to try to deceive United Nations inspectors. Most of the intelligence reports on which assessments were being made were inferential. The Assessments Staff and JIC were not fully aware of the access and background of key informants, and could not therefore read their material against the background of an understanding of their motivations. The broad conclusions of the UK intelligence community (although not some particular details) were widely-shared by other countries. (Paragraphs 456/457)

28.   We detected a tendency for assessments to be coloured by over-reaction to previous errors. As a result, there was a risk of over-cautious or worst case estimates, shorn of their caveats, becoming the 'prevailing wisdom'. The JIC may, in some assessments, also have misread the nature of Iraqi governmental and social structures. (Paragraph 458/459)

29.   We emphasise the importance of the Assessments Staff and the JIC having access to a wide range of information, especially in circumstances (e.g. where the UK is likely to become involved in national reconstruction and institution-building) where information on political and social issues will be vital. (Paragraph 459)

THE USE OF INTELLIGENCE

30.   The main vehicle for the Government's use of intelligence in the public presentation of policy was the dossier of September 2002 and accompanying Ministerial statements. The dossier broke new ground in three ways: the JIC had never previously produced a public document; no Government case for any international action had previously been made to the British public through explicitly drawing on a JIC publication; and the authority of the British intelligence community, and the JIC in particular, had never been used in such a public way. (Paragraph 460/461)

31.   The dossier was not intended to make the case for a particular course of action in relation to Iraq. It *was* intended by the Government to inform domestic and international understanding of the need for stronger action (though not necessarily military action) – the

general direction in which Government policy had been moving since the early months of 2002, away from containment to a more proactive approach to enforcing Iraqi disarmament. (Paragraph 462)

32. The Government wanted an unclassified document on which it could draw in its *advocacy* of its policy. The JIC sought to offer a dispassionate *assessment* of intelligence and other material on Iraqi nuclear, biological, chemical and ballistic missile programmes. The JIC, with commendable motives, took responsibility for the dossier, in order that its content should properly reflect the judgements of the intelligence community. They did their utmost to ensure this standard was met. But this will have put a strain on them in seeking to maintain their normal standards of neutral and objective assessment. (Paragraph 463)

33. Strenuous efforts were made to ensure that no individual statements were made in the dossier which went beyond the judgements of the JIC. But, in translating material from JIC assessments into the dossier, warnings were lost about the limited intelligence base on which some aspects of these assessments were being made. Language in the dossier may have left with readers the impression that there was fuller and firmer intelligence behind the judgements than was the case: our view, having reviewed all of the material, is that judgements in the dossier went to (although not beyond) the outer limits of the intelligence available. (Paragraph 464)

34. We conclude that it was a serious weakness that the JIC's warnings on the limitations of the intelligence underlying its judgements were not made sufficiently clear in the dossier. (Paragraph 465)

35. We understand why the Government felt it had to meet the mounting public and Parliamentary demand for information. We also recognise that there is a real dilemma between giving the public an authoritative account of the intelligence picture and protecting the objectivity of the JIC from the pressures imposed by providing information for public debate. It is difficult to resolve these requirements. We conclude, with the benefit of hindsight, that making public that the JIC had authorship of the dossier was a mistaken judgement, though we do not criticise the JIC for taking responsibility for clearance of the intelligence content of the document. However, in the particular circumstances, the publication of such a document in the name and with the authority of the JIC had the result that more weight was placed on the intelligence than it could bear. The consequence also was to put the JIC and its Chairman into an area of public controversy and arrangements must be made for the future which avoid putting the JIC and its Chairman in a similar position. (Paragraph 466)

36. We believe that there are other options that should be examined for the ownership of drafting, for gaining the JIC's endorsement of the intelligence material and assessments that are quoted and for subsequent 'branding'. One is for the government of the day to draft a document, to gain the JIC's endorsement of the intelligence material inside it and then to publish it acknowledging that it draws on intelligence but without ascribing it to the JIC. Or the Government, if it wishes to seek the JIC's credibility and authority, could publish a document with intelligence material and the JIC's endorsement of it shown separately. Or the JIC could prepare and publish itself a self-standing assessment, incorporating all of its normal caveats and warnings, leaving it to others to place that

document within a broader policy context. This may make such documents less persuasive in making a policy case; but that is the price of using a JIC assessment. Our conclusion is that, between these options, the first is greatly preferable. Whichever route is chosen, JIC clearance of the intelligence content of any similar document will be essential. (Paragraph 467)

37. We conclude that, if intelligence is to be used more widely by governments in public debate in future, those doing so must be careful to explain its uses and limitations. It will be essential, too, that clearer and more effective dividing lines between assessment and advocacy are established when doing so. (Paragraph 468)

38. We realise that our conclusions may provoke calls for the current Chairman of the JIC, Mr Scarlett, to withdraw from his appointment as the next Chief of SIS. We greatly hope that he will not do so. We have a high regard for his abilities and his record. (Paragraph 469)

39. The part played by intelligence in determining the legality of the use of force was limited. (Paragraph 470)

40. We have noted that, despite its importance to the determination of whether Iraq was in further material breach of its obligations under Resolution 1441, the JIC made no further assessment of the Iraqi declaration beyond its 'Initial Assessment' provided on 18 December. We have also recorded our surprise that policy-makers and the intelligence community did not, as the generally negative results of UNMOVIC inspections became increasingly apparent, re-evaluate in early 2003 the quality of the intelligence. (Paragraph 472)

VALIDATION OF THE INTELLIGENCE

41. Even now it would be premature to reach conclusions about Iraq's prohibited weapons. Much potential evidence may have been destroyed in the looting and disorder that followed the cessation of hostilities. Other material may be hidden in the sand, including stocks of agent or weapons. We believe that it would be a rash person who asserted at this stage that evidence of Iraqi possession of stocks of biological or chemical agents, or even of banned missiles, does not exist or will never be found. But as a result of our Review, and taking into account the evidence which has been found by the ISG and de-briefing of Iraqi personnel, we have reached the conclusion that prior to the war the Iraqi regime:

   a. Had the strategic intention of resuming the pursuit of prohibited weapons programmes, including if possible its nuclear weapons programme, when United Nations inspection regimes were relaxed and sanctions were eroded or lifted.

   b. In support of that goal, was carrying out illicit research and development, and procurement, activities, to seek to sustain its indigenous capabilities.

   c. Was developing ballistic missiles with a range longer than permitted under relevant United Nations Security Council resolutions; but did not have significant – if any – stocks of chemical or biological weapons in a state fit for deployment, or developed plans for using them. (Paragraph 474)

CHAPTER 6 – IRAQ: SPECIFIC ISSUES

LINKS BETWEEN AL QAIDA AND THE IRAQI REGIME

42. The JIC made it clear that the Al Qaida-linked facilities in the Kurdish Ansar al Islam area were involved in the production of chemical and biological agents, but that they were beyond the control of the Iraqi regime. (Paragraph 479)

43. The JIC made clear that, although there were contacts between the Iraqi regime and Al Qaida, there was no evidence of co-operation. (Paragraph 484)

OPERATION MASS APPEAL

44. There were two meetings between British Government officials and UNSCOM representatives, including Mr Ritter, in May and June 1998 at which there were discussions about how to make public the discovery of traces of the nerve agent VX on missile warheads after this fact had been reported to the United Nations Security Council. (Iraq had previously denied weaponising VX.) Operation Mass Appeal was set up for this specific purpose and did not exist before May 1998. In the event, before Operation Mass Appeal could proceed, the UNSCOM report was leaked to the press in Washington. Because of this, Operation Mass Appeal was abandoned. (Paragraph 489)

URANIUM FROM AFRICA

45. From our examination of the intelligence and other material on Iraqi attempts to buy uranium from Africa, we have concluded that:

   a.   It is accepted by all parties that Iraqi officials visited Niger in 1999.

   b.   The British Government had intelligence from several different sources indicating that this visit was for the purpose of acquiring uranium. Since uranium constitutes almost three-quarters of Niger's exports, the intelligence was credible.

   c.   The evidence was not conclusive that Iraq actually purchased, as opposed to having sought, uranium and the British Government did not claim this.

   d.   The forged documents were not available to the British Government at the time its assessment was made, and so the fact of the forgery does not undermine it. (Paragraph 503)

THE '45 MINUTE' CLAIM

46. The JIC should not have included the '45 minute' report in its assessment and in the Government's dossier without stating what it was believed to refer to. The fact that the

reference in the classified assessment was repeated in the dossier later led to suspicions that it had been included because of its eye-catching character. (Paragraph 511)

MOBILE BIOLOGICAL WEAPONS LABORATORIES

47.　We consider that it was reasonable for the JIC to include in its assessments of March and September 2002 a reference to intelligence reports on Iraq's seeking mobile biological agent production facilities. But it has emerged that the intelligence from the source, if it had been correctly reported, would not have been consistent with a judgement that Iraq had, on the basis of recent production, stocks of biological agent. If SIS had had direct access to the source from 2000 onwards, and hence correct intelligence reporting, the main evidence for JIC judgements on Iraq's stocks of recently-produced biological agent, as opposed to a break-out capacity, would not have existed. (Paragraph 530)

ALUMINIUM TUBES

48.　The evidence we received on aluminium tubes was overwhelmingly that they were intended for rockets rather than a centrifuge. We found this convincing. Despite this, we conclude that the JIC was right to consider carefully the possibility that the tubes were evidence of a resumed nuclear programme, and that it properly reflected the doubts about the use of the tubes in the caution of its assessments. But in transferring its judgements to the dossier, the JIC omitted the important information about the need for substantial re-engineering of the aluminium tubes to make them suitable for use as gas centrifuge rotors. This omission had the effect of materially strengthening the impression that they may have been intended for a gas centrifuge and hence for a nuclear programme. (Paragraph 545)

PLAGUE AND DUSTY MUSTARD

49.　Plague and 'dusty mustard' were just two of the many biological and chemical threats on which the intelligence community had to keep watch in the period before the first Gulf war, and subsequently. (Paragraph 562)

50.　The intelligence on their availability to Iraq in 1990 and 1991 rested on a small number of reports and the evidence derived from examination of a munition. There were grounds for scepticism both about the reports' sources and their quality. Nevertheless, we conclude that the Government was right in 1990 and 1991 to act on a precautionary basis. (Paragraph 563)

51.　We find it harder to understand the treatment of the intelligence in the ensuing period. 'Dusty mustard' disappears from JIC assessments from 1993 onwards. By contrast, although little new intelligence was received, and most of that was historical or unconvincing, plague continued to be mentioned in JIC assessments up to March 2003. Those fluctuated in the certainty of judgements about Iraqi possession of plague between "possibly" and "probably". (Paragraph 564)

52.　We conclude that, in the case of plague, JIC assessments reflected historic evidence, and intelligence of dubious reliability, reinforced by suspicion of Iraq, rather than up-to-date evidence. (Paragraph 565)

DR JONES'S DISSENT

53.   Dr Jones was right to raise concerns about the manner of expression of the '45 minute' report in the dossier given the vagueness of the underlying intelligence. (Paragraph 570)

54.   Dr Jones was right to raise concerns about the certainty of language used in the dossier on Iraqi production and possession of chemical agents. (Paragraph 572)

55.   We recognise that circumstances arise in which it is right for senior officials to take a broad view that differs from the opinions of those with expertise on points of detail. We do not, however, consider that the report held back from Dr Jones and his staff (which Dr Jones' superiors regarded as justifying the certainty of the language in the dossier) was one to which such considerations should have applied. It was understandable that SIS should have wanted to give greater than normal protection to the human intelligence source on this occasion. But a problem arose because it was kept from the relevant DIS analysts who had a wider perspective. It would have been more appropriate for senior managers in the DIS and SIS to have made arrangements for the intelligence to be shown to DIS experts rather than their making their own judgements on its significance. (Paragraph 576/577)

OIL SUPPLIES

56.   We saw no evidence that a motive of the British Government for initiating military action was securing continuing access to oil supplies. (Paragraph 579)

CHAPTER 7 – CONCLUSIONS ON BROADER ISSUES

INTERNATIONAL CO-OPERATION

57.   We note that much of what was reliably known about Iraq's unconventional weapons programmes in the mid- and late-1990s was obtained through the reports of the UN Special Commission (UNSCOM) and of the International Atomic Energy Agency (IAEA). These international agencies now appear to have been more effective than was realised at the time in dismantling and inhibiting Iraq's prohibited weapons programmes. The value of such international organisations needs to be recognised and built on for the future, supported by the contribution of intelligence from national agencies. (Paragraph 584)

CO-ORDINATION OF COUNTER-PROLIFERATION ACTIVITY

58.   We consider that it would be helpful through day-to-day processes and the use of new information systems to create a 'virtual' network bringing together the various sources of expertise in Government on proliferation and on activity to tackle it, who would be known to each other and could consult each other easily. (Paragraph 585)

THE DEFENCE INTELLIGENCE STAFF

59.   We consider that further steps are needed to integrate the relevant work of the DIS more closely with the rest of the intelligence community. We welcome the arrangements now being made to give the Joint Intelligence Committee more leverage through the

Intelligence Requirements process to ensure that the DIS serves wider national priorities as well as it does defence priorities and has the resources which the rest of the intelligence community needs to support its activities. If that involved increasing the Secret Intelligence Account by a sum to be at the Security and Intelligence Co-ordinator's disposal to commission such resources, we would support that. (Paragraph 587)

60.   We recommend consideration of the provision of proper channels for the expression of dissent within the DIS through the extension of the remit of the Staff Counsellor, who provides a confidential outlet for conscientious objection or dissent within the intelligence agencies, to cover DIS civilian staff and the Assessments Staff. (Paragraph 589)

61.   We recognise the case for the Chief of Defence Intelligence to be a serving officer so that he is fully meshed into military planning. But we consider that the Deputy should, unless there are good reasons to the contrary at the time when a particular appointment is made, be an intelligence specialist. (Paragraph 590)

THE JOINT INTELLIGENCE COMMITTEE

62.   We recommend no change in the JIC's membership. (Paragraph 596)

63.   We see a strong case for the post of Chairman of the JIC being held by someone with experience of dealing with Ministers in a very senior role, and who is demonstrably beyond influence, and thus probably in his last post. (Paragraph 597)

THE ASSESSMENTS STAFF

64.   We recommend that the Security and Intelligence Co-ordinator reviews the size of the Assessments Staff, and in particular considers whether they have available the volume and range of resources to ask the questions which need to be asked in fully assessing intelligence reports and in thinking radically. We recommend also that this review should include considering whether there should be a specialism of analysis with a career structure and room for advancement, allowing the Assessments Staff to include some career members. We understand that the Intelligence and Security Committee are planning to look at this issue. (Paragraph 600)

65   It may be worth considering the appointment of a distinguished scientist to undertake a part-time role as adviser to the Cabinet Office. (Paragraph 601)

THE LANGUAGE OF JIC ASSESSMENTS

66.   The JIC has been right not to reach a judgement when the evidence is insubstantial. We believe that the JIC should, where there are significant limitations in the intelligence, state these clearly alongside its Key Judgements. While not arguing for a particular approach to the language of JIC assessments and the way in which alternative or minority hypotheses, or uncertainty, are expressed, we recommend that the intelligence community review their conventions again to see if there would be advantage in refreshing them. (Paragraph 604)

MACHINERY OF GOVERNMENT

67.   We do not suggest that there is or should be an ideal or unchangeable system of collective Government, still less that procedures are in aggregate any less effective now than in earlier times. However, we are concerned that the informality and circumscribed character of the Government's procedures which we saw in the context of policy-making towards Iraq risks reducing the scope for informed collective political judgement. Such risks are particularly significant in a field like the subject of our Review, where hard facts are inherently difficult to come by and the quality of judgement is accordingly all the more important. (Paragraph 611)

ANNEX A

LIST OF WITNESSES

Ministers

Rt Hon Tony Blair MP - Prime Minister
Rt Hon Jack Straw MP - Foreign Secretary
Rt Hon Geoff Hoon MP - Defence Secretary
Rt Hon Lord Goldsmith, QC - Attorney General

Officials

(i) **10 Downing Street and the Cabinet Office**

Jonathan Powell
Tim Dowse
Sir David Omand
John Scarlett
Sir Andrew Turnbull

(ii) **Foreign and Commonwealth Office**

William Ehrman
Sir Jeremy Greenstock
Sir David Manning
Sir Peter Ricketts
Stephen Wright

(iii) **Ministry of Defence**

Admiral Lord Michael Boyce
Air Marshal Joe French
Julian Miller
Lieutenant General Andrew Ridgway
Sir Kevin Tebbit
Simon Webb
and four members of the Defence Intelligence Staff

(iv) **Members of the intelligence community**

Sir Richard Dearlove
Eliza Manningham-Buller
Dr David Pepper
and one member of GCHQ, and two members of the Secret Intelligence Service

International Organisations

Dr Hans Blix

Former Chairs of the Joint Intelligence Committee

Sir Roderic Braithwaite
Sir Colin Budd
Rt Hon Sir Percy Cradock
Sir Paul Lever
Dame Pauline Neville Jones
The Hon Sir Michael Pakenham

Other witnesses

Dr John Chipman
Michael Herman
Dr Brian Jones
John Kampfner
Dr David Kay
Rt Hon Lord Owen
Dr Gary Samore
Elizabeth Wilmshurst
and two further witnesses who asked for their identities to be protected.

We also had meetings with Rt Hon Lord Hutton, Rt Hon David Blunkett MP, Rt Hon Michael Howard MP, Rt Hon Robin Cook MP, Rt Hon Clare Short MP, Sir Michael Jay and Sir Nigel Sheinwald.

INTELLIGENCE ASSESSMENT AND PRESENTATION: FROM MARCH TO SEPTEMBER 2002

15 March 2002	21 August 2002	9 September 2002	24 September 2002	24 September 2002
JIC(02)059: THE STATUS OF IRAQI WMD PROGRAMMES (15 March 2002) (substantial extracts)

Key Judgements

I. Iraq **retains up to 20 Al Hussein ballistic missiles**, produced prior to the Gulf War, with a range of 650km and capable of hitting Israel. The location and condition of these is unknown, but there is sufficient engineering expertise to make them operational.

II. Iraq has begun development of **medium range ballistic missiles over 1000km** that could target countries throughout the Middle East and Gulf Region, but will **not be able to produce such a missile before 2007** provided sanctions remain effective.

III. Iraq **is pursuing a nuclear weapons programme. But it will not be able to indigenously produce a nuclear weapon while sanctions** remain in place, unless suitable fissile material is purchased from abroad.

IV. Iraq **may retain some stocks of chemical agents**. Following a decision to do so, Iraq could produce:

• significant quantities **of mustard within weeks**;

• significant quantities of **sarin and VX within months**, and in the case of VX may have already done so.

V. Iraq currently **has available**, either from pre Gulf War stocks or more recent production, a number of **biological agents**. Iraq could | JIC(02)181: IRAQ: SADDAM'S DIPLOMATIC AND MILITARY OPTIONS (21 August 2002) (relevant extracts)

Key Judgements

V. Early on in any conflict Saddam would order missile attacks on Israel, coalition forces and regional States providing the US with bases.

...Secondary goals will be to preserve and enhance his WMD capability.

...As we have | JIC(02)202: IRAQI USE OF CHEMICAL AND BIOLOGICAL WEAPONS – POSSIBLE SCENARIOS (9 September 2002) (substantial extracts)

Key Judgements

I. Iraq has a chemical and biological weapons capability and Saddam is prepared to use it.

II. Faced with the likelihood of military defeat and being removed from power, Saddam is unlikely to be deterred from using chemical and biological weapons by any diplomatic or military means.

III. The use of chemical and biological weapons prior to any military attack would boost support for US-led action and is unlikely.

IV. Saddam is prepared to order missile strikes against Israel, with chemical or biological warheads, in order to widen the war once hostilities begin.

V. Saddam could order the use of CBW weapons in order to deny space and territory to Coalition forces, or to cause casualties, slow any advance, and sap US morale.

VI. If not previously employed, Saddam will order the indiscriminate use of whatever CBW weapons remain available late in a ground campaign | EXTRACTS FROM THE GOVERNMENT DOSSIER (24 September 2002)

Executive Summary

1. Under Saddam Hussein Iraq developed chemical and biological weapons, acquired missiles allowing it to attack neighbouring countries with these weapons and persistently tried to develop a nuclear bomb. Saddam has used chemical weapons, both against Iran and against his own people. Following the Gulf War, Iraq had to admit to all this. And in the ceasefire of 1991 Saddam agreed unconditionally to give up his weapons of mass destruction.

2. Much information about Iraq's weapons of mass destruction is already in the public domain from UN reports and from Iraqi defectors. This points clearly to Iraq's continuing possession, after 1991, of chemical and biological agents and weapons produced before the Gulf War. It shows that Iraq has refurbished sites formerly associated with the production of chemical and biological agents. And it indicates that Iraq remains able to manufacture these agents, and to use bombs, shells, artillery rockets and ballistic missiles to deliver them.

3. An independent and well-researched overview of this public evidence was provided by the International Institute for Strategic Studies (IISS) on 9 September. The IISS report also suggested that Iraq could assemble nuclear weapons within months of obtaining fissile material from foreign sources.

4. As well as the public evidence, however, significant additional information is available to the Government from secret intelligence sources, described in more detail in this paper. This intelligence cannot tell us about everything. However, it provides a fuller picture of Iraqi plans and capabilities. It shows that Saddam Hussein attaches great importance to possessing weapons of mass destruction which he regards as the basis for Iraq's regional power. It shows that he does not regard them only as weapons of last resort. He is ready to use them, including against his own population, and is determined to retain them, in breach of United Nations Security Council Resolutions (UNSCR).

5. Intelligence also shows that Iraq is preparing plans to conceal evidence of these weapons, including incriminating documents, from renewed inspections. And it confirms that despite sanctions and the policy of containment, Saddam has continued to make progress with his illicit weapons programmes.

6. As a result of the intelligence we judge that Iraq has:

• Continued to produce chemical and biological agents; | FOREWORD TO THE GOVERNMENT DOSSIER (signed by the Prime Minister)

The document published today is based, in large part, on the work of the Joint Intelligence Committee (JIC). The JIC is at the heart of the British intelligence machinery. It is chaired by the Cabinet Office and made up of the heads of the UK's three Intelligence and Security Agencies, the Chief of Defence Intelligence, and senior officials from key government departments. For over 60 years the JIC has provided regular assessments to successive Prime Ministers and senior colleagues on a wide range of foreign policy and international security issues.

Its work, like the material it analyses, is largely secret. It is unprecedented for the Government to publish this kind of document. But in light of the debate about Iraq and Weapons of Mass Destruction (WMD), I wanted to share with the British public the reasons why I believe this issue to be a current and serious threat to the UK national interest.

In recent months, I have been increasingly alarmed by the evidence from inside Iraq that despite sanctions, despite the damage done to his capability in the past, despite the UN Security Council Resolutions expressly outlawing it, and despite his denials, Saddam Hussein is continuing to develop WMD, and with them the ability to inflict real damage upon the region, and the stability of the world.

Gathering intelligence inside Iraq is |

NOTE: Redactions are not indicated

15 March 2002	21 August 2002	9 September 2002	24 September 2002	24 September 2002
produce more of these biological agents within days. VI. A decision to begin CBW production would probably go undetected. VII. Iraq can deliver CBW weapons by a variety of means including ballistic missiles. **Iraq's CBW production capability is designed to survive** a military attack and UN inspections. Intelligence on Iraq's weapons of mass destruction (WMD) and ballistic missile programmes is sporadic and patchy. Iraq is also well practised in the art of deception, such as concealment and exaggeration. A complete picture of the various programmes is therefore difficult. But it is clear that Iraq continues to pursue a policy of acquiring WMD and their delivery means. Intelligence indicates that planning to reconstitute some of its programmes began in 1995. WMD programmes were then given a further boost in 1998 with the withdrawal of UNSCOM inspectors. **Ballistic Missiles** Iraq has rebuilt much of the military production infrastructure associated with the missile programme damaged in the Gulf War and the few high profile sites targeted in Operation Desert Fox in 1998. New infrastructure is being built, with a particular focus on improving the support to the solid propellant missile programme. Since the Gulf War, Iraq has been openly developing **short-range ballistic missiles (SRBM)** up to a range of 150km, which are permitted under UN Security Council Resolution 687. Intelligence indicates that:	previously judged, even if inspectors were allowed to return, Iraq would embark on a renewed policy of frustration, involving denial, deception, obstruction and delay. ... Saddam could: • Threaten the use of WMD against regional states. **Missiles and WMD** We judge that Saddam would probably order **missile attacks** on Israel and the coalition early on in a conflict in an attempt to attract Israeli retaliation and thus widen the war, split the coalition and arouse popular opinion in the Arab States. Such missiles could be armed with chemical or biological warfare (CBW) agents. Saddam might be deterred, at least initially, by the threat of Israeli nuclear retaliation. Other factors would be the limited number of long range missiles Iraq would have available (we	or as a final act of vengeance. But such an order would depend on the availability of delivery means and the willingness of commanders to obey. Recent intelligence casts light on Iraq's holdings of weapons of mass destruction and on its doctrine for using them. Intelligence remains limited and Saddam's own unpredictability complicates judgements about Iraqi use of these weapons. Much of this paper is necessarily based on judgement and assessment. Iraq used chemical weapons on a large scale during the Iran/Iraq War. Use on the same scale now would require large quantities of chemical weapons and survivable delivery means in the face of overwhelming US air superiority. Iraq did not use chemical weapons during the Gulf War. Intelligence suggests that Iraq may have used the biological agent, aflatoxin, against the Shia population in 1991. We do not believe that Iraq possesses nuclear weapons and there is no intelligence that Iraq is currently interested in radiological dispersal devices. **Chemical and biological capabilities** Based on intelligence on the nature of Iraqi CBW weapons, known delivery means, continuing procurement activity, and experience from previous	• Military plans for the use of chemical and biological weapons, including against its own Shia population. Some of these weapons are deployable within 45 minutes of an order to use them; • Command and control arrangements in place to use chemical and biological weapons. Authority ultimately resides with Saddam Hussein. (There is intelligence that he may have delegated this authority to his son Qusai); • Developed mobile laboratories for military use, corroborating earlier reports about the mobile production of biological warfare agents; • Pursued illegal programmes to procure controlled materials of potential use in the production of chemical and biological weapons programmes; • Tried covertly to acquire technology and materials which could be used in the production of nuclear weapons; • Sought significant quantities of uranium from Africa, despite having no active civil nuclear power programme that could require it; • Recalled specialists to work on its nuclear programme; • Illegally retained up to 20 al-Hussein missiles, with a range of 650km, capable of carrying chemical or biological warheads; • Started deploying its al-Samoud liquid propellant missile, and has used the absence of weapons inspectors to work on extending its range to at least 200km, which is beyond the limit of 150km imposed by the United Nations; • Started producing the solid-propellant Ababil-100, and is making efforts to extend its range to at least 200km, which is beyond the limit of 150km imposed by the United Nations; • Constructed a new engine test stand for the development of missiles capable of reaching the UK Sovereign Base Areas in Cyprus and NATO members (Greece and Turkey), as well as all Iraq's Gulf neighbours and Israel; • Pursued illegal programmes to procure materials for use in its illegal development of long range missiles; • Learnt lessons from previous UN weapons inspections and has already begun to conceal sensitive equipment and documentation in advance of the return of inspectors.	not easy. Saddam's is one of the most secretive and dictatorial regimes in the world. So I believe people will understand why the Agencies cannot be specific about the sources, which have formed the judgements in this document, and why we cannot publish everything we know. We cannot, of course, publish the detailed raw intelligence. I and other Ministers have been briefed in detail on the intelligence and are satisfied as to its authority. I also want to pay tribute to our Intelligence and Security Services for the often extraordinary work that they do. What I believe the assessed intelligence has established beyond doubt is that Saddam has continued to produce chemical and biological weapons, that he continues in his efforts to develop nuclear weapons, and that he has been able to extend the range of his ballistic missile programme. I also believe that, as stated in the document, Saddam will now do his utmost to try to conceal his weapons from UN inspectors. The picture presented to me by the JIC in recent months has become more not less worrying. It is clear that, despite sanctions, the policy of containment has not worked sufficiently well to prevent Saddam from developing these weapons. I am in no doubt that the threat is serious and current, that he has made progress on WMD, and that he has to be stopped. Saddam has used chemical weapons, not only against an enemy state, but against his own people. Intelligence reports make clear that he sees the building up of his WMD capability, and the belief overseas

NOTE: Redactions are not indicated

15 March 2002	21 August 2002	9 September 2002	24 September 2002	24 September 2002
• the 150km range liquid propellant **Al Samoud** missile has been extensively flight-tested. Intelligence indicates that Iraq has produced at least 50 Al Samouds, including those test fired, and preparations are underway to deploy some of these to military units. Iraq has reportedly succeeded in developing a number of 200km range variants of Al Samoud, although it is unclear if these are for operational use or research and development for longer-range systems. A small number of transporter-erector-launchers (TELs) have been seen, although others may exist; • the solid propellant **Ababil-100** has also been tested, and has reached ranges up to 150km. We judge that this system is likely to become operational as an SRBM within 2 years. It might enter service earlier as an artillery rocket. Intelligence indicates that Iraq has plans to extend the range of the Ababil-100 to 250km. *Immediate missile capability* *We judge that Iraq has the following missiles available for immediate use:* *Some Al Samoud (up to 150km)* *Up to 20 Al Hussein (650km)* *There are a limited number of launchers available.* *Both missiles could deliver basic chemical and biological warheads.* We judge Iraq has also retained some **20 Al Hussein missiles** (650km range stretched SCUD), the type fired at Israel and Saudi Arabia during the Gulf War. We do not know the location of these missiles or their state of readiness, but judge that the engineering expertise available would	assess he has retained 12-20 650km range Al Hussein missiles) and the need, in the case of attacking coalition forces in Kuwait, to deploy short range missiles (we assessed in March that at least 50 150km range al-Samoud missiles had been produced; more produced since then) into the 'no drive zone'. Although a pre-emptive missile attack on Israel would offer many of the same advantages, we judge this would be less likely because it would show Iraq had been lying about its retention of long range missiles prohibited by the UN, providing a justification for US action. Although we have little intelligence on Iraq's CBW doctrine, and know little about Iraq's CBW work since late 1998, we judge it likely that Saddam would order the use of CBW against	conflicts, we judge that: • Iraq currently has available, either from pre Gulf War stocks or more recent production, a number of biological warfare (BW) and chemical warfare (CW) agents and weapons; • following a decision to do so, Iraq could produce significant quantities of mustard agent within weeks; significant quantities of the nerve agents sarin and VX within months (and in the case of VX Iraq may have already done so). Production of sarin and VX would be heavily dependent on hidden stocks of precursors, the size of which are unknown; • Iraq could produce more biological agents within days. At the time of the Gulf War Iraq had developed the lethal BW agents anthrax, botulinum toxin and aflatoxin. Iraq was also researching a number of other agents including some non-lethal (incapacitating) agents; even if stocks of chemical and biological weapons are limited, they would allow for focused strikes against key military targets or for strategic purposes (such as a strike against Israel or Kuwait); • Iraq could deliver CW and BW agents by a variety of means including free fall bombs, airborne sprays, artillery shells, mortar	7. These judgements reflect the views of the Joint Intelligence Committee (JIC). More details on the judgements and on the development of the JIC's assessments since 1998 are set out in Part 1 of this paper. **PART 1** **IRAQ'S CHEMICAL, BIOLOGICAL, NUCLEAR AND BALLISTIC MISSILE PROGRAMMES** **CHAPTER 1: The Role of Intelligence (extract)** 1. Since UN inspectors were withdrawn from Iraq in 1998, there has been little overt information on Iraq's chemical, biological, nuclear and ballistic missile programmes. Much of the publicly available information about Iraqi capabilities and intentions is dated. But we also have available a range of secret intelligence about these programmes and Saddam Hussein's intentions. This comes principally from the United Kingdom's intelligence and analysis agencies – the Secret Intelligence Service (SIS), the Government Communications Headquarters (GCHQ), the Security Service, and the Defence Intelligence Staff (DIS). We also have access to intelligence from close allies. 2. Intelligence rarely offers a complete account of activities which are designed to remain concealed. The nature of Saddam's regime makes Iraq a difficult target for the intelligence services. Intelligence, however, has provided important insights into Iraqi programmes and Iraqi military thinking. Taken together with what is already known from other sources, this intelligence builds our understanding of Iraq's capabilities and adds significantly to the analysis already in the public domain. But intelligence sources need to be protected, and this limits the detail that can be made available. 3. Iraq's capabilities have been regularly reviewed by the Joint Intelligence Committee (JIC), which has provided advice to the Prime Minister and his senior colleagues on the developing assessment, drawing on all available sources. Part 1 of this paper includes some of the most significant views reached by the JIC between 1999 and 2002. **CHAPTER 2: Iraq's Programmes, 1971–1998 (extract)** [This historical chapter covers past Iraqi research into chemical and biological warfare; what quantities of agent Iraq had produced by the early 1990s; its use of chemical weapons during the Iran/Iraq war,	that he would use these weapons, as vital to his strategic interests, and in particular his goal of regional domination. And the document discloses that his military planning allows for some of the WMD to be ready within 45 minutes of an order to use them. I am quite clear that Saddam will go to extreme lengths, indeed has already done so, to hide these weapons and avoid giving them up. In today's inter-dependent world, a major regional conflict does not stay confined to the region in question. Faced with someone who has shown himself capable of using WMD, I believe the international community has to stand up for itself and ensure its authority is upheld. The threat posed to international peace and security, when WMD are in the hands of a brutal and aggressive regime like Saddam's, is real. Unless we face up to the threat, not only do we risk undermining the authority of the UN, whose resolutions he defies, but more importantly and in the longer term, we place at risk the lives and prosperity of our own people. The case I make is that the UN Resolutions demanding he stops his WMD programme are being flouted; that since the inspectors left four years ago he has continued with this programme; that the inspectors must be allowed back in to do their job properly; and that if he refuses, or if he makes it impossible for them to do their job, as he has done in the past, the international community will have to act. I believe that faced with the

NOTE: Redactions are not indicated

15 March 2002	21 August 2002	9 September 2002	24 September 2002	24 September 2002
allow these missiles to be effectively maintained. Iraq is seeking to develop new, **larger liquid and solid propellant missiles,** contrary to UN limits. Recent intelligence indicates personnel associated with the Al Samoud programme have now been tasked to concentrate on designing liquid propellant systems with ranges of 2000-3000km. New intelligence indicates the main focus may be on the development of a SCUD derivative, which we judge has an intended range of around 1200km. Work on an engine for this system began in 1998, involving personnel who had been reviewing the details of previous Al Hussein production since 1995, although by the end of the year 2000 they were still experiencing technical problems. Additional personnel were probably assigned to other parts of the programme during 2000. A large static test stand capable of testing liquid propellant engines bigger than the SCUD engine has been under construction since mid-2000, probably in support of this programme. Work on large motor cases for longer-range solid propellant systems has been noted over the last 2-3 years. Providing sanctions remain effective, Iraq is **unlikely to be able to produce a longer-range missile before 2007.** Despite retaining engineers with expertise in missile design and production, **UN sanctions and the work of the inspectors** have caused significant problems for Iraq's missile industry in acquiring components and production technology, in particular for improving guidance and control systems and therefore missile accuracy. Iraq is actively seeking to procure materials for its missile programme.	coalition forces at some point, probably after coalition attacks had begun. Iraqi CBW use would become increasingly likely the closer coalition forces came to Baghdad. Military targets might include troop concentrations or important fixed targets in rear areas such as ports and airfields. **Alternative scenarios and at the death** It is also possible that Saddam might pursue an extreme course of action at an earlier stage than we have envisaged . . . In particular, unorthodox options might include: • The early or pre-emptive use of **CBW.** Because of the time lag between infection and incapacitation, there is some incentive to use biological weapons early. Coalition forces would also be most geographically concentrated	bombs and battlefield rockets; • Iraq told UNSCOM in the 1990s that it filled 25 warheads with anthrax, botulinum toxin and aflatoxin for its Al Hussein ballistic missile (range 650km). Iraq also admitted it had developed 50 chemical warheads for Al Hussein. We judge Iraq retains up to 20 Al Husseins and a limited number of launchers; • Iraq is also developing short-range systems Al Samoud/Ababil 100 ballistic missiles (range 150km plus) – One intelligence report suggests that Iraq has "lost" the capability to develop warheads capable of effectively disseminating chemical and biological agent and that it would take six months to overcome the "technical difficulties". However, both these missile systems are currently being deployed with military units and an emergency operational capability with conventional warheads is probably available; • Iraq may have other toxins, chemical and biological agents that we do not know about; • the effectiveness of any CBW attack would depend on the method of delivery, concentration of the target, dissemination efficiency, meteorological conditions and the	including against its own (Kurdish) citizens; the progress of its nuclear programme by 1991; its ballistic missile programmes; its use of such missiles during the first Gulf war; and Iraq's admission to UNSCOM of having had chemical and biological warheads available for its ballistic missiles.] 13. Based on the UNSCOM report to the UN Security Council in January 1999 and earlier UNSCOM reports, we assess that when the UN inspectors left Iraq they were unable to account for: • up to 360 tonnes of bulk chemical warfare agent, including 1.5 tonnes of VX nerve agent; • up to 3,000 tonnes of precursor chemicals, including approximately 300 tonnes which, in the Iraqi chemical warfare programme, were unique to the production of VX; • growth media procured for biological agent production (enough to produce over three times the 8,500 litres of anthrax spores Iraq admits to having manufactured); • over 30,000 special munitions for delivery of chemical and biological agents. 14. The departure of UNSCOM meant that the international community was unable to establish the truth behind these large discrepancies and greatly diminished its ability to monitor and assess Iraq's continuing attempts to reconstitute its programmes. **CHAPTER 3: The Current Position: 1998–2002 (extract)** 1. This chapter sets out what we know of Saddam Hussein's chemical, biological, nuclear and ballistic missile programmes, drawing on all the available evidence. While it takes account of the results from UN inspections and other publicly available information, it also draws heavily on the latest intelligence about Iraqi efforts to develop their programmes and capabilities since 1998. The **main conclusions** are that: • Iraq has a useable chemical and biological weapons capability, in breach of UNSCR 687, which has included recent production of chemical and biological agents; • Saddam continues to attach great importance to the possession of weapons of mass destruction and ballistic missiles which he regards as being the basis for Iraq's regional power. He is determined to retain these capabilities; • Iraq can deliver chemical and biological agents using an extensive range of artillery shells, free-fall bcmbs, sprayers and ballistic missiles;	information available to me, the UK Government has been right to support the demands that this issue be confronted and dealt with. We must ensure that he does not get to use the weapons he has, or get hold of the weapons he wants. **HOUSE OF COMMONS, TUESDAY 24 SEPTEMBER 2002** <u>The Prime Minister:</u> Mr Speaker, thank you for recalling Parliament to debate the best way to deal with the issue of the present leadership of Iraq and weapons of mass destruction. Today we published a 50-page dossier, detailing the history of Iraq's weapons of mass destruction programme, its breach of United Nations resolutions, and its attempts to rebuild that illegal programme. I have placed a copy in the Library. At the end of the Gulf war, the full extent of Saddam's chemical, biological and nuclear weapons programmes became clear. As a result, the United Nations passed a series of resolutions, demanding that Iraq disarm itself of such weapons and establishing a regime of weapons inspections and monitoring to do the task. The inspectors were to be given unconditional and unrestricted access to all and any Iraqi sites. All this is accepted fact. In addition, it is fact, documented by UN inspectors, that Iraq almost immediately began to obstruct the inspections. Visits were delayed; on occasions, inspectors threatened; matériel was moved; special sites, shut to the inspectors, were unilaterally designated by Iraq. The work of the inspectors continued, but against a background of increasing obstruction and non-compliance.

15 March 2002	21 August 2002	9 September 2002	24 September 2002	24 September 2002
Chemical and Biological Warfare (CBW) We continue to judge that Iraq has an offensive chemical warfare (CW) programme, although there is very little intelligence relating to it. From the evidence available to us, we believe Iraq retains some production equipment, and some small stocks of CW agent precursors, and may have hidden small quantities of agents and weapons. Anomalies in Iraqi declarations to UNSCOM suggest stocks could be much larger. Given the size and scope of Iraq's pre Gulf War programme, little or no research and development work would need to be carried out. Intelligence on production facilities is scarce; the reconstructed former precursor production facility near Habbaniyah in itself is insufficient to support large-scale CW agent production. Other industrial chemical facilities could be used in support of a chemical weapons programme, but we have no intelligence to suggest that they are currently being used in that role. Intelligence has indicated an Iraqi interest in transportable production facilities for chemical weapons, but these could produce only small amounts of agent and we judge it more likely that the mobile units are for filling munitions rather than producing agent. We assess that following a decision to do so, Iraq could produce: • **Significant quantities of mustard within weeks,** using hidden stocks of precursors and with support from Iraq's chemical industry. • **Significant quantities of nerve agent within months,** mainly sarin and VX. This would be heavily dependent on hidden stocks of precursors. There has been one uncorroborated report that Iraq filled some artillery rocket munitions with VX in the period 1996-1998, and	directly before or at the onset of a military campaign. He might also consider: • **CBW terrorism**: although Saddam probably lacks the capability to deploy a sophisticated device, he could cause widespread panic. Should he feel his fate is sealed, Saddam's judgement might change to 'bring the temple down' on his enemies no matter what the cost to the country as a whole. We judge that at this stage, Saddam would order the unrestrained use of CBW against coalition forces, supporting regional states and Israel, although he would face practical problems of command and control, the loyalty of his commanders, logistics problems and the availability of chemical or biological agents in sufficient quantities to be	availability of suitable defensive counter measures. Other recent intelligence indicates that: • production of chemical and biological weapons is taking place; • Saddam attaches great importance to having CBW, is committed to using CBW if he can and is aware of the implications of doing so. Saddam wants it to dominate his neighbours and deter his enemies who he considers are unimpressed by his weakened conventional military capability; • Iraq has learned from the Gulf War the importance of mobile systems that are much harder to hit than large static sites. Consequently Iraq has developed for the military, fermentation systems which are capable of being mounted on road-trailers or rail cars. These could produce BW agent; • Iraq has probably dispersed its special weapons, including its CBW weapons. Intelligence also indicates that chemical and biological munitions could be with military units and ready for firing within 20-45 minutes. **Intentions for use** Intelligence indicates that Saddam has already taken the decision that all	• Iraq continues to work on developing nuclear weapons, in breach of its obligations under the Non-Proliferation Treaty and in breach of UNSCR 687. Uranium has been sought from Africa that has no civil nuclear application in Iraq; • Iraq possesses extended-range versions of the SCUD ballistic missile in breach of UNSCR 687 which are capable of reaching Cyprus, Eastern Turkey, Tehran and Israel. It is also developing longer-range ballistic missiles; • Iraq's current military planning specifically envisages the use of chemical and biological weapons; • Iraq's military forces are able to use chemical and biological weapons, with command, control and logistical arrangements in place. The Iraqi military are able to deploy these weapons within 45 minutes of a decision to do so; • Iraq has learnt lessons from previous UN weapons inspections and is already taking steps to conceal and disperse sensitive equipment and documentation in advance of the return of inspectors; • Iraq's chemical, biological, nuclear and ballistic missiles programmes are well-funded. **CHEMICAL AND BIOLOGICAL WEAPONS** 4. In the last six months the JIC has confirmed its earlier judgements on Iraqi chemical and biological warfare capabilities and assessed that Iraq has the means to deliver chemical and biological weapons. **Recent intelligence** 5. Subsequently, intelligence has become available from reliable sources which complements and adds to previous intelligence and confirms the JIC assessment that Iraq has chemical and biological weapons. The intelligence also shows that the Iraqi leadership has been discussing a number of issues related to these weapons. This intelligence covers: • **Confirmation that chemical and biological weapons play an important role in Iraqi military thinking:** intelligence shows that Saddam attaches great importance to the possession of chemical and biological weapons which he regards as being the basis for Iraqi regional power. He believes that respect for Iraq rests on its possession of these weapons and the missiles capable of delivering them. Intelligence indicates that Saddam is determined to retain this capability and recognises that Iraqi political weight would be diminished if Iraq's military power rested solely on its conventional military forces.	Indeed, Iraq denied that its biological weapons programme existed until forced to acknowledge it after high-ranking defectors disclosed its existence in 1995. Eventually, in 1997, the UN inspectors declared that they were unable to fulfil their task. A year of negotiation and further obstruction occurred until finally, in late 1998, the UN team was forced to withdraw. As the dossier sets out, we estimate on the basis of the UN's work that there were up to 360 tonnes of bulk chemical warfare agents, including 1.5 tonnes of VX nerve agent; up to 3,000 tonnes of precursor chemicals; growth media sufficient to produce 26,000 litres of anthrax spores; and over 30,000 special munitions for delivery of chemical and biological agents. All of this was missing and unaccounted for. Military action by the United States and United Kingdom followed and a certain amount of infrastructure for Iraq's weapons of mass destruction and missile capability was destroyed, setting the Iraqi programme back, but not ending it. From late 1998 onwards, therefore, the sole inhibition on Saddam's WMD programme was the sanctions regime. Iraq was forbidden to use the revenue from its oil except for certain specified non-military purposes. The sanctions regime, however, was also subject to illegal trading and abuse. Because of concerns about its inadequacy—and the impact on the Iraqi people—we made several attempts to refine it, culminating in a new UN resolution in May of this year. But it was only partially effective. Around $3 billion of money is illegally taken by Saddam every

NOTE: Redactions are not indicated

15 March 2002	21 August 2002	9 September 2002	24 September 2002	24 September 2002
another that a team of chemists was formed in 1998 to produce 5 tons of VX. The source was told this had been completed by the end of 1998; • Incapacitants including the mental incapacitant Agent 15. Iraq's military forces used chemical weapons during the Iran-Iraq War. Intelligence indicates command, control and logistical arrangements are in place. *Immediate CBW capability* *The following chemical agents could be produced within weeks, if not already: Mustard, sarin and VX;* *The following biological agents could be produced within days, if not already: Anthrax spores, botulinum toxin, aflatoxin and possibly plague* *These could be delivered by a variety of means, including ballistic missiles and special forces.* Iraq was forced by UNSCOM discoveries and the defection of Hussein Kamil to admit to having had a **biological warfare (BW) programme**. BW work at the time of the Gulf War. BW work continued throughout the period of UNSCOM inspections and intelligence indicates that this programme continues. Key figures from the pre-Gulf War programme are reported to be involved. Research and development is assessed to continue under cover of a number of legitimate institutes and possibly in a number of covert facilities. We judge that Iraq could produce significant quantities of BW agents within days of a decision to do so. There is no intelligence on any BW agent production facilities, but one source indicates that Iraq may have	effective and the means to deliver them.	resources, including CBW, be used to defend the regime from attack. One report states that Saddam would not use CBW during the initial air phase of any military campaign but would use CBW once a ground invasion of Iraq has begun. Faced with the likelihood of military defeat and being removed from power, we judge that it is unlikely there would be any way to deter Saddam from using CBW. We judge that several factors could influence the timing of a decision by Saddam to authorise the use of CBW weapons; • the availability of stocks of CW and BW agents; • the survivability of his delivery means. Many are vulnerable. Once a military campaign is underway the pressure will increase to use certain assets before they are destroyed; • the survivability of command and control mechanisms. The method and timing of such decision making is unknown. Intelligence indicates that Saddam's son Qusai may already have been given authority to order the use of CBW. Authorising front line units to use chemical and biological weapons could become more difficult once fighting begins. Saddam may therefore specify in advance of a	• **Iraqi attempts to retain its existing banned weapons systems:** Iraq is already taking steps to prevent UN weapons inspectors finding evidence of its chemical and biological weapons programme. Intelligence indicates that Saddam has learnt lessons from previous weapons inspections, has identified possible weak points in the inspections process and knows how to exploit them. Sensitive equipment and papers can easily be concealed and in some cases this is already happening. The possession of mobile biological agent production facilities will also aid concealment efforts. Saddam is determined not to lose the capabilities that he has been able to develop further in the four years since inspectors left. • **Saddam's willingness to use chemical and biological weapons:** intelligence indicates that as part of Iraq's military planning Saddam is willing to use chemical and biological weapons, including against his own Shia population. Intelligence indicates that the Iraqi military are able to deploy chemical or biological weapons within 45 minutes of an order to do so. **Chemical and biological agents: surviving stocks** 6. When confronted with questions about the unaccounted stocks, Iraq has claimed repeatedly that if it had retained any chemical agents from before the Gulf War they would have deteriorated sufficiently to render them harmless. But Iraq has admitted to UNSCOM to having the knowledge and capability to add stabiliser to nerve agent and other chemical warfare agents which would prevent such decomposition. In 1997 UNSCOM also examined some munitions which had been filled with mustard gas prior to 1991 and found that they remained very toxic and showed little sign of deterioration. 7. Iraq has claimed that all its biological agents and weapons have been destroyed. No convincing proof of any kind has been produced to support this claim. In particular, Iraq could not explain large discrepancies between the amount of growth media (nutrients required for the specialised growth of agent) it procured before 1991 and the amounts of agent it admits to having manufactured. The discrepancy is enough to produce more than three times the amount of anthrax allegedly manufactured. **Chemical agent: production capabilities** 8. Intelligence shows that Iraq has continued to produce chemical agent. 9. Other dual-use facilities, which are capable of being used to support the production of chemical agent and precursors, have been rebuilt and re-equipped. New chemical facilities have been built, some with illegal	year now, double the figure for the year 2000. Self-evidently, there is no proper accounting for this money. Because of concerns that a containment policy based on sanctions alone could not sufficiently inhibit Saddam's weapons programme, negotiations continued, even after 1998, to gain readmission for the UN inspectors. In 1999, a new UN resolution demanding their re-entry was passed and ignored. Further negotiations continued. Finally, after several months of discussion with Saddam's regime, in July this year, Kofi Annan, the UN Secretary-General, concluded that Saddam was not serious about readmitting the inspectors and ended the negotiations. All this is established fact. I set out the history in some detail because occasionally debate on this issue seems to treat it almost as if it had suddenly arisen, coming out of nowhere on a whim in the last few months of 2002. It is actually an 11-year history: a history of UN will flouted, of lies told by Saddam about the existence of his chemical, biological and nuclear weapons programmes, and of obstruction, defiance and denial. There is one common, consistent theme, however: the total determination of Saddam to maintain that programme; to risk war, international ostracism, sanctions and the isolation of the Iraqi economy to keep it. At any time, he could have let the inspectors back in and put the world to proof. At any time, he could have co-operated with the United Nations. Ten days ago, he made the offer unconditionally under threat of war. He could have done it at any

15 March 2002	21 August 2002	9 September 2002	24 September 2002	24 September 2002
developed **mobile production facilities**. A liaison source reports that: - the transportable production programme began in 1995; - 6 road based facilities, on trailers, and 1 rail based facility, on railway carriages, were constructed and by March 1999; three were operational; - the facilities were capable of making 5 different (unspecified/unknown) biological agents. Between November 1998 and March 1999 20-30 tons of BW agent was produced. Though not corroborated, we judge the reporting is technically credible. We do not know which types of agents are produced by these facilities, but judge that **Iraq currently has available, either from pre Gulf War stocks or more recent production, anthrax spores, botulinum toxin, aflatoxin and possibly plague.** The continued operation of the castor oil extraction plant at the former Habbaniyah chemical weapons site may provide the base for producing ricin, although there is no evidence that Iraq is currently doing so. Iraq's acknowledged to UNSCOM that it worked on a number of other BW agents including agents which would incapacitate, rather than kill, humans and on anti-crop and anti-livestock agents. Iraq almost certainly retains the capability to produce such agents. **Iraq is judged to be self-sufficient in the production of biological weapons.** Iraq has a variety of **delivery means** available for both chemical and biological weapons, some of which are		war the specific conditions in which commanders should use these weapons e.g. once coalition forces have crossed a particular geographical line; - the reliability of the units in question. Late in any military campaign commanders may not be prepared to use CBW weapons if they judge that Saddam is about to fall. **Possible scenarios: pre-emptive use before a conflict begins** The aim of a pre-emptive strike would be to incapacitate or kill Coalition troops in their concentration areas. Intelligence indicates that Saddam has identified Bahrain, Jordan, Qatar, Israel and Kuwait as targets. Turkey could also be at risk. Both chemical and biological weapons could be used; biological agents could be particularly effective against such force concentrations. But the use of CBW weapons carries serious risks and Saddam will weigh up their military utility against the political costs. Use of CBW weapons would expose the lies and deception about Iraq's WMD capabilities, undermining Iraqi diplomatic efforts and helping build support for rapid and effective US action. Saddam might also consider using non-lethal agents in a deniable manner; whilst it would be difficult to quickly establish a clear attribution of responsibility,	foreign assistance, and are probably fully operational or ready for production. These include the Ibn Sina Company at Tarmiyah, which is a chemical research centre. It undertakes research, development and production of chemicals previously imported but not now available and which are needed for Iraq's civil industry. The Director General of the research centre is Hikmat Na'im al-Jalu who prior to the Gulf War worked in Iraq's nuclear weapons programme and after the war was responsible for preserving Iraq's chemical expertise. 10. Parts of the al-Qa'qa' chemical complex damaged in the Gulf War have also been repaired and are operational. Of particular concern are elements of the phosgene production plant at al-Qa'qa'. These were severely damaged during the Gulf War, and dismantled under UNSCOM supervision, but have since been rebuilt. While phosgene does have industrial uses it can also be used by itself as a chemical agent or as a precursor for nerve agent. 11. Iraq has retained the expertise for chemical warfare research, agent production and weaponisation. Most of the personnel previously involved in the programme remain in country. While UNSCOM found a number of technical manuals (so called 'cook books') for the production of chemical agents and critical precursors, Iraq's claim to have unilaterally destroyed the bulk of the documentation cannot be confirmed and is almost certainly untrue. Recent intelligence indicates that Iraq is still discussing methods of concealing such documentation in order to ensure that it is not discovered by any future UN inspections. **The Problem of Dual-Use Facilities** Almost all components and supplies used in weapons of mass destruction and ballistic missile programmes are dual-use. For example, any major petrochemical or biotech industry, as well as public health organisations, will have legitimate need for most materials and equipment required to manufacture chemical and biological weapons. Without UN weapons inspectors it is very difficult therefore to be sure about the true nature of many of Iraq's facilities. For example, Iraq has built a large new chemical complex, Project Baiji, in the desert in north west Iraq at al-Sharquat. This site is a former uranium enrichment facility which was damaged during the Gulf War and rendered harmless under supervision of the IAEA. Part of the site has been rebuilt, with work starting in 1992, as a chemical production complex. Despite the site being far away from populated areas it is surrounded by a high wall with watch towers and guarded by armed guards. Intelligence reports indicate that it will produce nitric acid which can be used in explosives, missile fuel and in the purification of uranium.	time in the last 11 years, but he did not. Why? The dossier that we publish gives the answer. The reason is that his chemical, biological and nuclear weapons programme is not an historic left-over from 1998. The inspectors are not needed to clean up the old remains. His weapons of mass destruction programme is active, detailed and growing. The policy of containment is not working. The weapons of mass destruction programme is not shut down; it is up and running now. The dossier is based on the work of the British Joint Intelligence Committee. For over 60 years, beginning just before world war two, the JIC has provided intelligence assessments to British Prime Ministers. Normally, its work is obviously secret. Unusually, because it is important that we explain our concerns about Saddam to the British people, we have decided to disclose its assessments. I am aware, of course, that people will have to take elements of this on the good faith of our intelligence services, but this is what they are telling me, the British Prime Minister, and my senior colleagues. The intelligence picture that they paint is one accumulated over the last four years. It is extensive, detailed and authoritative. It concludes that Iraq has chemical and biological weapons, that Saddam has continued to produce them, that he has existing and active military plans for the use of chemical and biological weapons, which could be activated within 45 minutes, including against his own Shia population, and that he is actively trying to acquire nuclear

NOTE: Redactions are not indicated

15 March 2002	21 August 2002	9 September 2002	24 September 2002	24 September 2002
very basic. These include, free fall bombs, artillery shells, helicopter and aircraft borne sprayers and ballistic missile warheads, although the exact numbers are unknown. Iraq is also continuing with the L–29 remotely piloted vehicle programme, which could have chemical and biological weapons applications. Covert delivery also remains an option. Because of the shortage of some platforms, such as aircraft and helicopters, we judge that Iraq would not be able to conduct a sustained CBW campaign in the manner of the Iran-Iraq War, even if Iraq could produce enough CBW agents to do so. But a single major attack or a number of small attacks would be feasible. **Nuclear Weapons Programme** We judge that Iraq **does not possess a nuclear weapons capability**. We previously assessed that Iraq was within three years of producing a weapon when the Gulf War intervened. Its programme was effectively dismantled by the IAEA and subject to the monitoring process subsequently installed. Although there is very little intelligence we continue to judge that Iraq is pursuing a nuclear weapons programme. We assess the programme to be based on gas centrifuge **uranium enrichment**, which was the route Iraq was following for producing fissile material prior to the Gulf War. Recent intelligence indicates that nuclear scientists were recalled to work on a nuclear programme in the autumn of 1998, but we do not know if large scale development work has yet recommenced. Procurement of dual-use items over the last few years could be used in a uranium enrichment programme. There have been determined efforts to purchase high strength aluminium alloy, prohibited under the Nuclear Suppliers Group		Saddam could not be sure of the US reaction to an outbreak of a non-lethal disease. The early, widespread use of CBW or non-lethal agents would affect Coalition military planning; disruption of the build-up of personnel and material could delay operations. On balance however we judge that the political cost of using CBW weapons would outweigh the military advantages and that Saddam would probably not use CBW weapons pre-emptively. **Possible scenarios: use during the ground phase of a conflict** There is no intelligence on specific Iraqi plans for how CBW would be used in a conflict. Large numbers of chemical munitions would need to be used to make a major battlefield impact. BW could also be used although it is less effective as a tactical weapon against Coalition units than CW. But the use of even small quantities of chemical weapons would cause significant degradation in Coalition progress and might contribute to redressing Coalition conventional superiority on the battlefield. Iraq could make effective use of persistent chemical agents to shape the battlefield to Iraq's advantage by denying space and territory to Coalition forces. Booby-traps and improvised explosive devices could be used as	**Biological agent: production capabilities** 12. We know from intelligence that Iraq has continued to produce biological warfare agents. As with some chemical equipment, UNSCOM only destroyed equipment that could be directly linked to biological weapons production. Iraq also has its own engineering capability to design and construct biological agent associated fermenters, centrifuges, sprayer dryers and other equipment and is judged to be self-sufficient in the technology required to produce biological weapons. The experienced personnel who were active in the programme have largely remained in the country. Some dual-use equipment has also been purchased, but without monitoring by UN inspectors Iraq could have diverted it to their biological weapons programme. This newly purchased equipment and other equipment previously subject to monitoring could be used in a resurgent biological warfare programme. Facilities of concern include: • the Castor Oil Production Plant at Fallujah: this was damaged in UK/US air attacks in 1998 (Operation Desert Fox) but has been rebuilt. The residue from the castor bean pulp can be used in the production of the biological agent ricin; • the al-Dawrah Foot and Mouth Disease Vaccine Institute: which was involved in biological agent production and research before the Gulf War; • the Amariyah Sera and Vaccine Plant at Abu Ghraib: UNSCOM established that this facility was used to store biological agents, seed stocks and conduct biological warfare associated genetic research prior to the Gulf War. It has now expanded its storage capacity. 13. UNSCOM established that Iraq considered the use of mobile biological agent production facilities. In the past two years evidence from defectors has indicated the existence of such facilities. Recent intelligence confirms that the Iraqi military have developed mobile biological agent production facilities. These would help Iraq conceal and protect biological agent production from military attack or UN inspection. **Chemical and biological agents: delivery means** 14. Iraq has a variety of delivery means available for both chemical and biological agents. These include: • free-fall bombs: Iraq acknowledged to UNSCOM the deployment to two sites of free-fall bombs filled with biological agent during 1990–91. These bombs were filled with anthrax, botulinum toxin and aflatoxin. Iraq also acknowledged possession of four types of aerial bomb with various chemical agent fills including sulphur mustard, tabun, sarin and cyclosarin;	weapons capability. On chemical weapons, the dossier shows that Iraq continues to produce chemical agents for chemical weapons; has rebuilt previously destroyed production plants across Iraq; has bought dual-use chemical facilities; has retained the key personnel formerly engaged in the chemical weapons programme; and has a serious ongoing research programme into weapons production, all of it well funded. In respect of biological weapons, again, production of biological agents has continued; facilities formerly used for biological weapons have been rebuilt; equipment has been purchased for such a programme; and again, Saddam has retained the personnel who worked on it prior to 1991. In particular, the UN inspection regime discovered that Iraq was trying to acquire mobile biological weapons facilities, which of course are easier to conceal. Present intelligence confirms that it has now got such facilities. The biological agents that we believe Iraq can produce include anthrax, botulinum toxin, aflatoxin and ricin—all eventually result in excruciatingly painful death. As for nuclear weapons, Saddam's previous nuclear weapons programme was shut down by the inspectors, following disclosure by defectors of the full, but hidden, nature of it. The programme was based on gas centrifuge uranium enrichment. The known remaining stocks of uranium are now held under supervision by the International Atomic Energy Agency. But we now know the following: since

NOTE: Redactions are not indicated

15 March 2002	21 August 2002	9 September 2002	24 September 2002	24 September 2002
because of its application in uranium enrichment. A shipment stopped in Jordan was inspected by the IAEA, who accepted that, with some modifications, the aluminium would be suitable for use in centrifuges. But we have no definitive intelligence that the aluminium was destined for a nuclear programme. We continue to judge that: • while sanctions remain effective, Iraq cannot indigenously develop and produce nuclear weapons; • **if sanctions were removed or became ineffective, it would take at least five years to produce a nuclear weapon.** This timescale would shorten if fissile material was acquired from abroad. Iraq is capable of producing an **improvised nuclear device**, but it lacks suitable fissile material. **Dispersal of key equipment** Following 11 September 2001 Iraq temporarily dispersed key equipment from its missile production facilities, and is likely to do so again if it believes an attack is imminent. Recent intelligence indicates that Qusai Saddam Hussain has directed the Military Industrialisation Commission to ensure that all sensitive weapons and chemical technology was well hidden in case of further UN inspections. Dispersal makes the targeting of production equipment very difficult, but it also prevents any surge in production while dispersed.		chemical and biological weapons to inflict local losses in urban areas. It is also possible that Saddam would seek to use chemical and biological munitions against any internal uprising; intelligence indicates that he is prepared to deliberately target the Shia population. One report indicates that he would be more likely to use CBW against Western forces than on Arab countries. **Drawing Israel into the conflict** Launching a CBW attack against Israel could allow Saddam to present Iraq as the champion of the Palestinian cause and to undermine Arab support for the Coalition by sowing a wider Middle East conflict. One intelligence report suggests that if Saddam were to use CBW, his first target would be Israel. Another intelligence report suggests that Iraq believes Israel will respond with nuclear weapons if attacked with CBW or conventional warheads. It is not clear if Saddam is deterred by this threat or judges it to be unlikely. **Unconventional use of CBW** Although there is no intelligence to indicate that Iraq has considered using chemical and biological agents in terrorist attacks, we cannot rule out the possibility. Saddam could also remove his existing constraints on	• artillery shells and rockets: Iraq made extensive use of artillery munitions filled with chemical agents during the Iran-Iraq War. Mortars can also be used for chemical agent delivery. Iraq is known to have tested the use of shells and rockets filled with biological agents. Over 20,000 artillery munitions remain unaccounted for by UNSCOM; • helicopter and aircraft borne sprayers: Iraq carried out studies into aerosol dissemination of biological agent using these platforms prior to 1991. UNSCOM was unable to account for many of these devices. It is probable that Iraq retains a capability for aerosol dispersal of both chemical and biological agent over a large area; • al-Hussein ballistic missiles (range 650km): Iraq told UNSCOM that it filled 25 warheads with anthrax, botulinum toxin and aflatoxin. Iraq also developed chemical agent warheads for al-Hussein. Iraq admitted to producing 50 chemical warheads for al-Hussein which were intended for the delivery of a mixture of sarin and cyclosarin. However, technical analysis of warhead remnants has shown traces of VX degradation product which indicate that some additional warheads were made and filled with VX; • al-Samoud/Ababil-100 ballistic missiles (range 150km plus): it is unclear if chemical and biological warheads have been developed for these systems, but given the Iraqi experience on other missile systems, we judge that Iraq has the technical expertise for doing so; • L-29 remotely piloted vehicle programme (see figure 3): we know from intelligence that Iraq has attempted to modify the L-29 jet trainer to allow it to be used as an Unmanned Aerial Vehicle (UAV) which is potentially capable of delivering chemical and biological agents over a large area. **Chemical and biological warfare: command and control** 15. The authority to use chemical and biological weapons ultimately resides with Saddam but intelligence indicates that he may have also delegated this authority to his son Qusai. Special Security Organisation (SSO) and Special Republican Guard (SRG) units would be involved in the movement of any chemical and biological weapons to military units. The Iraqi military holds artillery and missile systems at Corps level throughout the Armed Forces and conducts regular training with them. The Directorate of Rocket Forces has operational control of strategic missile systems and some Multiple Launcher Rocket Systems. **Chemical and biological weapons: summary** 16. Intelligence shows that Iraq has covert chemical and biological weapons programmes, in breach of UN Security Council Resolution 687	the departure of the inspectors in 1998, Saddam has bought or attempted to buy specialised vacuum pumps of the design needed for the gas centrifuge cascade to enrich uranium; an entire magnet production line of the specification for use in the motors and top bearings of gas centrifuges; dual-use products, such as anhydrous hydrogen fluoride and fluoride gas, which can be used both in petrochemicals but also in gas centrifuge cascades; a filament winding machine, which can be used to manufacture carbon fibre gas centrifuge rotors; and he has attempted, covertly, to acquire 60,000 or more specialised aluminium tubes, which are subject to strict controls owing to their potential use in the construction of gas centrifuges. In addition, we know that Saddam has been trying to buy significant quantities of uranium from Africa, although we do not know whether he has been successful. Again, key personnel who used to work on the nuclear weapons programme are back in harness. Iraq may claim that this is for a civil nuclear power programme, but I would point out that it has no nuclear power plants. So that is the position in respect of the weapons — but of course, the weapons require ballistic missile capability. That, again, is subject to UN resolutions. Iraq is supposed only to have missile capability up to 150 km for conventional weaponry. Pages 27 to 31 of the dossier detail the evidence on that issue. It is clear that a significant number of longer-range missiles were effectively concealed from the previous inspectors and remain, including up to 20 extended-range Scud missiles; that in mid-2001 there was a step change in the

NOTE: Redactions are not indicated

171

15 March 2002	21 August 2002	9 September 2002	24 September 2002	24 September 2002
		dealing with Al Qaida (extremists are conducting low-level work on toxins in an area of northern Iraq outside Saddam's control). Al Qaida could carry out proxy attacks and would require little encouragement to do so. Saddam's intelligence agencies have some experience in the use of poisons and even small-scale attacks could have a significant psychological impact. Intelligence indicates that Saddam has specifically commissioned a team of scientists to devise novel means of deploying CBW. **Possible scenarios: at the death** In the last resort Saddam is likely to order the indiscriminate use of whatever chemical and biological weapons remain available to him, in a last attempt to cling on to power or to cause as much damage as possible in a final act of vengeance. If he has not already done so by this stage Saddam will launch CBW attacks on Israel. Implementation of such orders would depend on the delivery means still remaining, the survivability of the command chain and the willingness of commanders to obey.	and has continued to produce chemical and biological agents. Iraq has: • chemical and biological agents and weapons available, both from pre-Gulf War stocks and more recent production; • the capability to produce the chemical agents mustard gas, tabun, sarin, cyclosarin, and VX capable of producing mass casualties; • a biological agent production capability and can produce at least anthrax, botulinum toxin, aflatoxin and ricin. Iraq has also developed mobile facilities to produce biological agents; • a variety of delivery means available; • military forces, which maintain the capability to use these weapons with command, control and logistical arrangements in place. **NUCLEAR WEAPONS** **Joint Intelligence Committee (JIC) Assessments: 1999–2001** 17. Since 1999 the JIC has monitored Iraq's attempts to reconstitute its nuclear weapons programme. In mid-2001 the JIC assessed that Iraq had continued its nuclear research after 1998. The JIC drew attention to intelligence that Iraq had recalled its nuclear scientists to the programme in 1998. Since 1998 Iraq had been trying to procure items that could be for use in the construction of centrifuges for the enrichment of uranium. **Iraqi nuclear weapons expertise** 18. The IAEA dismantled the physical infrastructure of the Iraqi nuclear weapons programme, including the dedicated facilities and equipment for uranium separation and enrichment, and for weapon development and production, and removed the remaining highly enriched uranium. But Iraq retained, and retains, many of its experienced nuclear scientists and technicians who are specialised in the production of fissile material and weapons design. Intelligence indicates that Iraq also retains the accompanying programme documentation and data. 19. Intelligence shows that the present Iraqi programme is almost certainly seeking an indigenous ability to enrich uranium to the level needed for a nuclear weapon. It indicates that the approach is based on gas centrifuge uranium enrichment, one of the routes Iraq was following for producing fissile material before the Gulf War. But Iraq needs certain key equipment, including gas centrifuge components and components for the production of fissile material before a nuclear bomb could be developed. 20. Following the departure of weapons inspectors in 1998 there has	programme and, by this year, Iraq's development of weapons with a range of more than 1,000 km was well under way; and that hundreds of people are employed in that programme, facilities are being built and equipment procured—usually clandestinely. Sanctions and import controls have hindered the programme, but only slowed its progress. The capability being developed, incidentally, is for multi-purpose use, including with WMD warheads. That is the assessment, given to me, of the Joint Intelligence Committee. In addition, we have well founded intelligence to tell us that Saddam sees his WMD programme as vital to his survival and as a demonstration of his power and influence in the region. There will be some who will dismiss all this. Intelligence is not always right. For some of the material, there might be innocent explanations. There will be others who say rightly that, for example, on present going, it could be several years before Saddam acquires a usable nuclear weapon—though if he were able to purchase fissile matériel illegally, it would be only a year or two. But let me put it at its simplest: on this 11-year history, with this man Saddam; with this accumulated, detailed intelligence available; with what we know and what we can reasonably speculate, would the world be wise to leave the present situation undisturbed—to say that, despite 14 separate UN demands on the issue, all of which Saddam is in breach of, we should do nothing, and to conclude that we should trust, not to the good faith of the UN weapons inspectors, but to the good faith of the current Iraqi regime? I do not believe

NOTE: Redactions are not indicated

15 March 2002	21 August 2002	9 September 2002	24 September 2002	24 September 2002
			been an accumulation of intelligence indicating that Iraq is making concerted covert efforts to acquire dual-use technology and materials with nuclear applications. Iraq's known holdings of processed uranium are under IAEA supervision. But there is intelligence that Iraq has sought the supply of significant quantities of uranium from Africa. Iraq has no active civil nuclear power programme or nuclear power plants and therefore has no legitimate reason to acquire uranium. 21. Intelligence shows that other important procurement activity since 1998 has included attempts to purchase: • vacuum pumps which could be used to create and maintain pressures in a gas centrifuge cascade needed to enrich uranium; • an entire magnet production line of the correct specification for use in the motors and top bearings of gas centrifuges. It appears that Iraq is attempting to acquire a capability to produce them on its own rather than rely on foreign procurement; • Anhydrous Hydrogen Fluoride (AHF) and fluorine gas. AHF is commonly used in the petrochemical industry and Iraq frequently imports significant amounts, but it is also used in the process of converting uranium into uranium hexafluoride for use in gas centrifuge cascades; • one large filament winding machine which could be used to manufacture carbon fibre gas centrifuge rotors; • a large balancing machine which could be used in initial centrifuge balancing work. 22. Iraq has also made repeated attempts covertly to acquire a very large quantity (60,000 or more) of specialised aluminium tubes. The specialised aluminium in question is subject to international export controls because of its potential application in the construction of gas centrifuges used to enrich uranium, although there is no definitive intelligence that it is destined for a nuclear programme. **Nuclear weapons: timelines** 23. In early 2002, the JIC assessed that UN sanctions on Iraq were hindering the import of crucial goods for the production of fissile material. The JIC judged that while sanctions remain effective Iraq would not be able to produce a nuclear weapon. If they were removed or prove ineffective, it would take Iraq at least five years to produce sufficient fissile material for a weapon indigenously. However, we know that Iraq retains expertise and design data relating to nuclear weapons. We therefore judge that if Iraq obtained fissile material and other essential components from foreign sources the timeline for production of a nuclear	that that would be a responsible course to follow. Our case is simply this: not that we take military action come what may, but that the case for ensuring Iraqi disarmament, as the UN itself has stipulated, is overwhelming. I defy anyone, on the basis of this evidence, to say that that is an unreasonable demand for the international community to make when, after all, it is only the same demand that we have made for 11 years and that Saddam has rejected. People say, "But why Saddam?" I do not in the least dispute that there are other causes of concern on weapons of mass destruction. I said as much in this House on 14 September last year. However, two things about Saddam stand out. He has used these weapons in Iraq itself—thousands dying in those chemical weapons attacks—and in the Iran-Iraq war, started by him, in which 1 million people died; and his is a regime with no moderate elements to appeal to. Read the chapter on Saddam and human rights in this dossier. Read not just about the 1 million dead in the war with Iran, not just about the 100,000 Kurds brutally murdered in northern Iraq, not just about the 200,000 Shia Muslims driven from the marshlands in southern Iraq, and not just about the attempt to subjugate and brutalise the Kuwaitis in 1990 that led to the Gulf war. I say, "Read also about the routine butchering of political opponents, the prison 'cleansing' regimes in which thousands die, the torture chambers and the hideous penalties supervised by him and his family and detailed by Amnesty International." Read it all

15 March 2002	21 August 2002	9 September 2002	24 September 2002	24 September 2002
			weapon would be shortened and Iraq could produce a nuclear weapon in between one and two years. **BALLISTIC MISSILES** **Joint Intelligence Committee (JIC) Assessment: 1999–2002** 24. In mid-2001 the JIC drew attention to what it described as a "step-change" in progress on the Iraqi missile programme over the previous two years. It was clear from intelligence that the range of Iraqi missiles which was permitted by the UN and supposedly limited to 150kms was being extended and that work was under way on larger engines for longer-range missiles. 25. In early 2002 the JIC concluded that Iraq had begun to develop missiles with a range of over 1,000kms. The JIC assessed that if sanctions remained effective the Iraqis would not be able to produce such a missile before 2007. Sanctions and the earlier work of the inspectors had caused significant problems for Iraqi missile development. In the previous six months Iraqi foreign procurement efforts for the missile programme had been bolder. The JIC also assessed that Iraq retained up to 20 al-Hussein missiles from before the Gulf War. **The Iraqi ballistic missile programme since 1998** 26. Since the Gulf War, Iraq has been openly developing two short-range missiles up to a range of 150km, which are permitted under UN Security Council Resolution 687. The al-Samoud liquid propellant missile has been extensively tested and is being deployed to military units. Intelligence indicates that at least 50 have been produced. Intelligence also indicates that Iraq has worked on extending its range to at least 200km in breach of UN Security Council Resolution 687. Production of the solid propellant Ababil-100 is also underway, probably as an unguided rocket at this stage. There are also plans to extend its range to at least 200km. Compared to liquid propellant missiles, those powered by solid propellant offer greater ease of storage, handling and mobility. They are also quicker to take into and out of action and can stay at a high state of readiness for longer periods. 27. According to intelligence, Iraq has retained up to 20 al-Hussein missiles, in breach of UN Security Council Resolution 687. These missiles were either hidden from the UN as complete systems, or re-assembled using illegally retained engines and other components. We judge that the engineering expertise available would allow these missiles to be maintained effectively, although the fact that at least some require re-assembly makes it difficult to judge exactly how many could be available for use. They could be used with conventional, chemical or biological warheads and, with a range of up to 650km, are capable of	and, again, I defy anyone to say that this cruel and sadistic dictator should be allowed any possibility of getting his hands on chemical, biological and nuclear weapons of mass destruction. "Why now?" people ask. I agree that I cannot say that this month or next, even this year or next, Saddam will use his weapons. But I can say that if the international community, having made the call for disarmament, now, at this moment, at the point of decision, shrugs its shoulders and walks away, he will draw the conclusion that dictators faced with a weakening will always draw: that the international community will talk but not act, will use diplomacy but not force. We know, again from our history, that diplomacy not backed by the threat of force has never worked with dictators and never will. If we take this course and if we refuse to implement the will of the international community, Saddam will carry on, his efforts will intensify, his confidence will grow and, at some point in a future not too distant, the threat will turn into reality. The threat therefore is not imagined. The history of Saddam and weapons of mass destruction is not American or British propaganda. The history and the present threat are real. If people say, "Why should Britain care?", I answer, "Because there is no way this man, in this region above all regions, could begin a conflict using such weapons and the consequences not engulf the whole world, including this country." That, after all, is the reason the UN passed its resolutions. That is why it is right that the UN Security Council again makes its will and its unity clear and lays down a strong new UN resolution

174

NOTE: Redactions are not indicated

15 March 2002	21 August 2002	9 September 2002	24 September 2002	24 September 2002
			reaching a number of countries in the region including Cyprus, Turkey, Saudi Arabia, Iran and Israel. 28. Intelligence has confirmed that Iraq wants to extend the range of its missile systems to over 1000km, enabling it to threaten other regional neighbours. This work began in 1998, although efforts to regenerate the long-range ballistic missile programme probably began in 1995. Iraq's missile programmes employ hundreds of people. Satellite imagery has shown a new engine test stand being constructed, which is larger than the current one used for al-Samoud, and that formerly used for testing SCUD engines which was dismantled under UNSCOM supervision. This new stand will be capable of testing engines for medium range ballistic missiles (MRBMs) with ranges over 1000km, which are not permitted under UN Security Council Resolution 687. Such a facility would not be needed for systems that fall within the UN permitted range of 150km. The Iraqis have recently taken measures to conceal activities at this site. Iraq is also working to obtain improved guidance technology to increase missile accuracy. 29. The success of UN restrictions means the development of new longer-range missiles is likely to be a slow process. These restrictions impact particularly on the: • availability of foreign expertise; • conduct of test flights to ranges above 150km; • acquisition of guidance and control technology. 30. Saddam remains committed to developing longer-range missiles. Even if sanctions remain effective, Iraq might achieve a missile capability of over 1000km within 5 years. 31. Iraq has managed to rebuild much of the missile production infrastructure destroyed in the Gulf War and in Operation Desert Fox in 1998. New missile-related infrastructure is also under construction. Some aspects of this, including rocket propellant mixing and casting facilities at the al-Mamoun Plant, appear to replicate those linked to the prohibited Badr-2000 programme (with a planned range of 700–1000km) which were destroyed in the Gulf War or dismantled by UNSCOM. A new plant at al-Mamoun for indigenously producing ammonium perchlorate, which is a key ingredient in the production of solid propellant rocket motors, has also been constructed. This has been provided illicitly by NEC Engineers Private Limited, an Indian chemical engineering firm with extensive links in Iraq, including to other suspect facilities such as the Fallujah 2 chlorine plant. After an extensive investigation, the Indian authorities have recently suspended its export licence, although other individuals and companies are still illicitly procuring for Iraq.	and mandate. Then Saddam will have the choice: comply willingly or be forced to comply. That is why, alongside the diplomacy, there must be genuine preparedness and planning to take action if diplomacy fails. Let me be plain about our purpose. Of course there is no doubt that Iraq, the region and the whole world would be better off without Saddam. Iraq deserves to be led by someone who can abide by international law, not a murderous dictator; by someone who can bring Iraq back into the international community where it belongs, not leave it languishing as a pariah; by someone who can make the country rich and successful, not impoverished by Saddam's personal greed; and by someone who can lead a Government more representative of the country as a whole while maintaining absolutely Iraq's territorial integrity. We have no quarrel with the Iraqi people. Indeed, liberated from Saddam, they could make Iraq prosperous and a force for good in the middle east. So the ending of this regime would be the cause of regret for no one other than Saddam. But our purpose is disarmament. No one wants military conflict. The whole purpose of putting this before the UN is to demonstrate the united determination of the international community to resolve this in the way it should have been resolved years ago: through a proper process of disarmament under the UN. Disarmament of all weapons of mass destruction is the demand. One way or another, it must be acceded to.

15 March 2002	21 August 2002	9 September 2002	24 September 2002	24 September 2002
			32. Despite a UN embargo, Iraq has also made concerted efforts to acquire additional production technology, including machine tools and raw materials, in breach of UN Security Council Resolution 1051. The embargo has succeeded in blocking many of these attempts, such as requests to buy magnesium powder and ammonium chloride. But we know from intelligence that some items have found their way to the Iraqi ballistic missile programme. More will inevitably continue to do so. Intelligence makes it clear that Iraqi procurement agents and front companies in third countries are seeking illicitly to acquire propellant chemicals for Iraq's ballistic missiles. This includes production level quantities of near complete sets of solid propellant rocket motor ingredients such as aluminium powder, ammonium perchlorate and hydroxyl terminated polybutadiene. There have also been attempts to acquire large quantities of liquid propellant chemicals such as Unsymmetrical Dimethylhydrazine (UDMH) and diethylenetriamene. We judge these are intended to support production and deployment of the al-Samoud and development of longer-range systems.	

NOTE: Redactions are not indicated

ANNEX C

IRAQ: MILITARY CAMPAIGN OBJECTIVES

1. Our policy objectives were set out in Parliament on 7 January 2003. The prime objective remains to rid Iraq of its weapons of mass destruction and their associated programmes and means of delivery, including prohibited ballistic missiles, as set out in relevant United Nations Security Council Resolutions (UNSCRs).

2. In UNSCR 1441, the Security Council decided that Iraq was in material breach of its obligations under UNSCR 687 and other relevant resolutions. The Council gave Iraq a final opportunity to comply by co-operating with the enhanced inspection regime established by UNSCR 1441, but warned of the serious consequences of failing to do so. The evidence shows that Iraq has failed to comply with the terms of UNSCR 1441 and is now in further material breach of its obligations. In these circumstances, UNSCR 678 authorises the use of force to enforce Iraq's compliance with its disarmament obligations.

3. The obstacle to Iraq's compliance with its disarmament obligations under relevant UNSCRs is the current Iraqi regime, supported by the security forces under its control. The British Government has therefore concluded that military action is necessary to enforce Iraqi compliance and that it is therefore necessary that the current Iraqi regime be removed from power. All military action must be limited to what is necessary to achieve that end. The UK is contributing maritime, land and air forces as part of a US-led coalition.

4. **The UK's overall objective for the military campaign is to create the conditions in which Iraq disarms in accordance with its obligations under UNSCRs and remains so disarmed in the long term.** Tasks which flow from this objective are set out below.

5. In aiming to achieve this objective as swiftly as possible, every effort will be made to minimise civilian casualties and damage to essential economic infrastructure, and to minimise and address adverse humanitarian consequences. The main tasks of the coalition are to:

    a. overcome the resistance of Iraqi security forces;

    b. deny the Iraqi regime the use of weapons of mass destruction now and in the future;

    c. remove the Iraqi regime, given its clear and unyielding refusal to comply with the UN Security Council's demands;

    d. identify and secure the sites where weapons of mass destruction and their means of delivery are located;

    e. secure essential economic infrastructure, including for utilities and transport, from sabotage and wilful destruction by Iraq; and

    f. deter wider conflict both inside Iraq and in the region.

Military action will be conducted in conformity with international law, including the UN Charter and international humanitarian law.

6.   Our wider political objectives in support of the military campaign are to:

      a.   demonstrate to the Iraqi people that our quarrel is not with them and that their security and well-being is our concern;

      b.   work with the United Nations to lift sanctions affecting the supply of humanitarian and reconstruction goods, and to enable Iraq's own resources, including oil, to be available to meet the needs of the Iraqi people;

      c.   sustain the widest possible international and regional coalition in support of military action;

      d.   preserve wider regional security, including by maintaining the territorial integrity of Iraq and mitigating the humanitarian and other consequences of conflict for Iraq's neighbours;

      e.   help create conditions for a future, stable and law-abiding government of Iraq; and

      f.   further our policy of eliminating terrorism as a force in international affairs.

7.   In the wake of hostilities, the immediate military priorities for the coalition are to:

      a.   provide for the security of friendly forces;

      b.   contribute to the creation of a secure environment so that normal life can be restored;

      c.   work in support of humanitarian organisations to mitigate the consequences of hostilities and, in the absence of such civilian humanitarian capacity, provide relief where it is needed;

      d.   work with UNMOVIC/IAEA to rid Iraq of its weapons of mass destruction and their means of delivery;

      e.   facilitate remedial action where environmental damage has occurred;

      f.   enable the reconstruction and recommissioning of essential infrastructure for the political and economic development of Iraq, and the immediate benefit of the Iraqi people; and

      g.   lay plans for the reform of Iraq's security forces.

Wherever possible, these tasks will be carried out in cooperation with the United Nations.

8.   British military forces will withdraw as soon as practicable. We hope to see the early establishment of a transitional civilian administration. We will work with the international community to build the widest possible international and regional support for the reconstruction of Iraq and the move to representative government.

9.   It remains our wish to see Iraq become a stable, united and law abiding state, within its present borders, cooperating with the international community, no longer posing a threat to its neighbours or to international security, abiding by all its international obligations and providing effective representative government for its own people.

March 2003

ANNEX D

17 March 2003

Foreign &
Commonwealth
Office

London SW1A 2AH

from The Foreign Secretary

Dear Donald

<u>Iraq: Legal Position Concerning the Use of Force</u>

As you may be aware, the Attorney General, Lord Goldsmith, has this morning answered a Question in the Lords setting out his views of the legal basis for the use of force against Iraq.

I now enclose a copy of his Answer, together with a paper which gives the legal background in more detail, for the information of your Committee.

You will also wish to be aware that I am this morning publishing a Command Paper (CM5785) "Iraq - UN Documents of early March 2003". This supplements the Command Paper I published last month.

I am placing a copy of this letter and enclosures in the Library.

Yours ever
Jack

JACK STRAW

The Rt Hon Donald Anderson MP

Question: To ask HMG what is the Attorney General's view of the legal basis for the use of force against Iraq

Answer: The Attorney General (Lord Goldsmith):

Authority to use force against Iraq exists from the combined effect of resolutions 678, 687 and 1441. All of these resolutions were adopted under Chapter VII of the UN Charter which allows the use of force for the express purpose of restoring international peace and security:

1. In resolution 678 the Security Council authorised force against Iraq, to eject it from Kuwait and to restore peace and security in the area.

2. In resolution 687, which set out the ceasefire conditions after Operation Desert Storm, the Security Council imposed continuing obligations on Iraq to eliminate its weapons of mass destruction in order to restore international peace and security in the area. Resolution 687 suspended but did not terminate the authority to use force under resolution 678.

3. A material breach of resolution 687 revives the authority to use force under resolution 678.

4. In resolution 1441 the Security Council determined that Iraq has been and remains in material breach of resolution 687, because it has not fully complied with its obligations to disarm under that resolution.

5. The Security Council in resolution 1441 gave Iraq "a final opportunity to comply with its disarmament obligations" and warned Iraq of the "serious consequences" if it did not.

6. The Security Council also decided in resolution 1441 that, if Iraq failed at any time to comply with and cooperate fully in the implementation of resolution 1441, that would constitute a further material breach.

7. It is plain that Iraq has failed so to comply and therefore Iraq was at the time of resolution 1441 and continues to be in material breach.

8. Thus, the authority to use force under resolution 678 has revived and so continues today.

9. Resolution 1441 would in terms have provided that a further decision of the Security Council to sanction force was required if that had been intended. Thus, all that resolution 1441 requires is reporting to and discussion by the Security Council of Iraq's failures, but not an express further decision to authorise force.

I have lodged a copy of this answer, together with resolutions 678, 687 and 1441 in the Library of both Houses.

IRAQ: LEGAL BASIS FOR THE USE OF FORCE

Summary

1.   The legal basis for any military action against Iraq would be the authorisation which the Security Council, by its resolution 678 (1990), gave to Member States to use all necessary means to restore international peace and security in the area. That authorisation was suspended but not terminated by Security Council resolution (SCR) 687 (1991), and revived by SCR 1441 (2002). In SCR 1441, the Security Council has determined -

    (1)   that Iraq's possession of weapons of mass destruction (WMD) constitutes a threat to international peace and security;

    (2)   that Iraq has failed - in clear violation of its legal obligations - to disarm; and

    (3)   that, in consequence, Iraq is in material breach of the conditions for the ceasefire laid down by the Council in SCR 687 at the end of the hostilities in 1991, thus reviving the authorisation in SCR 678.

The extent of the authority to use force contained in SCR 678

2.   Chapter VII of the United Nations Charter gives the Security Council the power to authorise States to take such military action as may be necessary to maintain or restore international peace and security.

3.   In the case of Iraq, the Security Council took such a step following the Iraqi invasion of Kuwait. Paragraph 2 of SCR 678 authorised "Member States co-operating with the Government of Kuwait ... to use all necessary means to uphold and implement resolution 660 (1990) and all subsequent relevant resolutions and to restore international peace and security in the area." The phrase "all necessary means" was understood then (as it is now) as including the use of force.

4.   Following the liberation of Kuwait, the Security Council adopted SCR 687. This resolution set out the steps which the Council required Iraq to take in order

to restore international peace and security in the area. Iraq's acceptance of those requirements was the condition for the declaration of a formal ceasefire. Those steps included the destruction of all WMD under international supervision and the requirement that Iraq should not attempt to acquire such weapons or the means of their manufacture. As a means to achieving the disarmament required by the Security Council, SCR 687 also required Iraq to submit to extensive weapons inspection by UNSCOM (now UNMOVIC) and the IAEA. The Security Council was quite clear that these steps were essential to the restoration of international peace and security in the area.

5.   SCR 687 did not repeal the authorisation to use force in paragraph 2 of SCR 678. On the contrary, it confirmed that SCR 678 remained in force. The authorisation was suspended for so long as Iraq complied with the conditions of the ceasefire. But the authorisation could be revived if the Council determined that Iraq was acting in material breach of the requirements of SCR 687. Although almost twelve years have elapsed since SCR 687 was adopted, Iraq has never taken the steps required of it by the Council. Throughout that period the Council has repeatedly condemned Iraq for violations of SCR 687 and has adopted numerous resolutions on the subject. In 1993 and again in 1998 the coalition took military action under the revived authority of SCR 678 to deal with the threat to international peace and security posed by those violations.

6.   In relation to the action in 1993, the Minister of State at the Foreign and Commonwealth Office wrote: "The Security Council determined in its statements of 8 and 11 January that Iraq was in material breach of resolutions 687 and its related resolutions, and warned Iraq that serious consequences would ensue from continued failure to comply with its obligations. Resolution 687 lays down the terms for the formal ceasefire between the coalition states and Iraq at the end of the hostilities mandated by the Security Council in resolution 678. These terms are binding in themselves but have also been specifically accepted by Iraq as a condition for the formal ceasefire to come into effect. In the light of Iraq's continued breaches of Security Council resolution 687 and thus of the ceasefire terms, and the repeated warnings given by the Security Council and members of the coalition, their forces were entitled to take

necessary and proportionate action in order to ensure that Iraq complies with those terms."

7. On 14 January 1993, in relation to the UK/US military action the previous day, the then UN Secretary-General said: "The raid yesterday, and the forces which carried out the raid, have received a mandate from the Security Council, according to resolution 678, and the cause of the raid was the violation by Iraq of resolution 687 concerning the ceasefire. So, as Secretary-General of the United Nations, I can say that this action was taken and conforms to the resolutions of the Security Council and conforms to the Charter of the United Nations."

8. In relation to the military action undertaken in 1998, the then Parliamentary Under-Secretary of State (now Minister of State) at the Foreign and Commonwealth Office, Baroness Symons of Vernham Dean stated: "In our previous discussions in this House some of your Lordships asked about the legality of our action. Any action involving UK forces would be based on international law. The Charter of the United Nations allows for the use of force under the authority of the Security Council. The Security Council resolution adopted before the Gulf conflict authorised the use of force in order to restore international peace and security in the region. Iraq is in clear breach of Security Council resolution 687 which laid down the conditions for the ceasefire at the end of the conflict. Those conditions included a requirement on Iraq to eliminate its weapons of mass destruction under international supervision. Those conditions have been broken."

Security Council Resolution 1441 (2002)

9. It is against that legal background that United Kingdom and the United States brought to the Council the draft resolution which was eventually adopted unanimously as SCR 1441 on 8 November 2002. The preamble to that resolution again expressly referred to SCR 678, confirming once more that that resolution was still in force. It also recognised the threat that Iraq's non-compliance with Council resolutions posed to international peace and security; and it recalled that SCR 687 imposed obligations on Iraq as a necessary step for the achievement of its objective of restoring international peace and security. In paragraph 1 the Council went on to decide that Iraq "has been and remains in material breach" of its obligations under SCR 687 and other relevant resolutions. The use of the term "material breach" is of the utmost importance because the practice of the Security

Council during the 1990's shows that it was just such a finding of material breach by Iraq which served to revive the authorisation of force in SCR 678.

10. On this occasion, however, the Council decided (in paragraph 2 of SCR 1441) to offer Iraq "a final opportunity to comply with its disarmament obligations." Iraq was required to produce an accurate, full and complete declaration of all aspects of its prohibited programmes (paragraph 3), and to provide immediate and unrestricted access to UNMOVIC and IAEA (paragraph 5). Failure by Iraq to comply with the requirements of SCR 1441 was declared to be a further material breach of Iraq's obligations (paragraph 4), in addition to the continuing breach already identified in paragraph 1. In the event of a further breach (paragraph 4), or interference by Iraq with the inspectors or failure to comply with any of the disarmament obligations under any of the relevant resolutions (paragraph 11), the matter was to be reported to the Security Council. The Security Council was then to convene "to consider the situation and the need for full compliance with all of the relevant Council resolutions in order to secure international peace and security" (paragraph 12). The Council warned Iraq (paragraph 13) that "it will face serious consequences as a result of its continued violations of its obligations".

11. It is important to stress that SCR 1441 did not revive the 678 authorisation immediately on its adoption. There was no "automaticity". The resolution afforded Iraq a final opportunity to comply and it provided for any failure by Iraq to be "considered" by the Security Council (under paragraph 12 of the resolution). That paragraph does not, however, mean that no further action can be taken without a new resolution of the Council. Had that been the intention, it would have provided that the Council would <u>decide</u> what needed to be done to restore international peace and security, not that it would <u>consider</u> the matter. The choice of words was deliberate; a proposal that there should be a requirement for a decision by the Council, a position maintained by several Council members, was not adopted. Instead the members of the Council opted for the formula that the Council must consider the matter before any action is taken.

12. That consideration has taken place regularly since the adoption of SCR 1441. It is plain, including from UNMOVIC's statements to the Security Council, its Twelfth Quarterly Report and the so-called "Clusters Document", that Iraq has not complied as required with its disarmament obligations. Whatever other

differences there may have been in the Security Council, no member of the Council has questioned this conclusion. It therefore follows that Iraq has not taken the final opportunity offered to it and remains in material breach of the disarmament obligations which, for twelve years, the Council has insisted are essential for the restoration of peace and security. In these circumstances, the authorisation to use force contained in SCR 678 revives.

Foreign and Commonwealth Office
17 March 2003

IRAQI NON-COMPLIANCE WITH UNSCR 1441

15 March 2003

Background

Iraq has failed to comply fully with 14 previous UN resolutions related to WMD.

UNSCR 1441 is unambiguous:

- "Recognising the threat Iraq's non-compliance with Council resolutions and proliferation of weapons of mass destruction and long-range missiles poses to international peace and security" (PP3)

- "Decides that Iraq has been and remains in material breach of its obligations under relevant resolutions" (OP1).

  "Decides... to afford Iraq, by this resolution, a final opportunity to comply with its disarmament obligations under relevant resolutions of the Council" (OP2).

- "Decides that false statements or omissions in the declarations submitted by Iraq... and failure by Iraq at any time to comply with, and co-operate fully in the implementation of, this resolution shall constitute a further material breach of Iraq's obligations" (OP4)

The attached material assesses Iraqi progress in complying with relevant provisions of UNSCR 1441 with illustrative examples.

The Government of Iraq shall provide to UNMOVIC, the IAEA, and the Council, not later than 30 days from the date of this resolution, <u>a currently</u> <u>accurate, full, and complete declaration of all aspects of its programmes</u> to develop chemical, biological, and nuclear weapons, ballistic missiles, and other delivery systems...as well as all other chemical, biological, and nuclear programmes, including any which it claims are for purposes not related to weapon production or material" (OP3)

Not *met.* Although a 12,000-page document was submitted on 7 December, it did not contain new information to answer any of the outstanding questions relating to Iraqi disarmament. None of the issues identified in the UN's Butler or Amorim reports (1999) have been resolved.

Dr Blix, 27 January "Regrettably, the 12,000 page declaration, most of which is a reprint of earlier documents, does not seem to contain any new evidence that would eliminate the questions or reduce their number".

Dr Blix, 14 February "The declaration submitted by Iraq on 7 December, despite its large volume, missed the opportunity to provide the fresh material and evidence needed to respond to the open questions"

IAEA written report, 27 January "The Declaration contains numerous clarifications. It does not include, however, additional information related to the questions and concerns", outstanding since 1998.

Outstanding issues that were not resolved in Iraq's 7-8 December Declaration include:

- Failure to account adequately for SCUD-type missiles and components "suggests that these items may have been retained for a prohibited missile force" (UNMOVIC document, *Unresolved Disarmament Issues, 6 March*)

- Failure to explain why Iraq has built a missile test stand at Al Rafah that can accommodate missiles with over 4 times the thrust of the (prohibited) Al-Samoud 2 missile.

- Amount of mustard gas unaccounted for is at least 80 tonnes (in 550 shells and 450 aerial bombs) - but "based on a document recently received from Iraq, this quantity could be substantially higher" *(Unresolved Disarmament* issues, *6 March)*

- "Given Iraq's history of concealment with respect to its VX programme, it cannot be excluded that it has retained some capability with regard to VX" that could still be viable today. There are significant discrepancies in accounting for all key VX precursors. Iraq said it never weaponised VX - but UNSCOM found evidence to contradict this. *(Unresolved Disarmament Issues, 6 March)* It was not until 15 March - over three months after the specified date for the Declaration - that Iraq provided a further document which it claimed contained additional information (although this remains unconfirmed).

- "It seems highly probable that destruction of bulk agent, including anthrax, stated by Iraq to be at Al Hakam in July/August 1991, did not occur. Based on all the available evidence, the strong presumption is that about 10,000 litres of anthrax was not destroyed and may still exist". *(Unresolved Disarmament Issues, 6 March)*

- Failure to account for all of the aircraft associated with the L-29/Al-Bai'aa remotely piloted vehicle (RPV) programme. Furthermore, there is no explanation of 27 June 2002 RPV flight of 500kms (the proscribed limit is 150kms).

- Failure to account for material unaccounted for when UNSCOM were forced to withdraw from Iraq in 1998: for example, what happened to up to 3,000 tonnes of precursor chemicals, including 300 tonnes unique (in the Iraqi programme) to the production of VX nerve agent? UNSCOM estimated that quantities of undeclared growth media could have produced: 3-11,000 litres of botulinum toxin; 6-16,000 litres of anthrax, and 5,600 litres of clostridium perfringens. *(Amorim and Butler reports, 1999)*

- According to Dr El-Baradei *(IAEA written report, 27 January)* the Declaration "does not include, however, additional information related to the questions and concerns" outstanding since 1998. These were:

  - the uncertainty about the progress made in weapons design and centrifuge development due to the lack of relevant documentation

  - the extent of external assistance from which Iraq benefited

  - the lack of evidence that Iraq had abandoned definitively its nuclear programme.

Apart from failing to answer unresolved questions, the Declaration also contained some significant falsehoods:

- *Dr Blix, 27 January.* "Iraq did not declare a significant quantity, some 650 kg, of bacterial growth media, which was acknowledged as imported in Iraq's submission to the Amorim panel in February 1999. As part of its 7 December 2002 Declaration, Iraq resubmitted the Amorim panel document, but the table showing this particular import of media was not included. The absence of this table would appear to be deliberate as the pages of the resubmitted document were renumbered."

- The 7 December Declaration maintains that the Al-Samoud 2 missile has a maximum range of 150kms. UNMOVIC and a panel of international experts have established that the Al-Samoud 2 is a prohibited system, designed to have a range beyond the 150 kms limit imposed by the UN in 1991 - one variant having a range (based on separate Iraqi data) of just under 200kms. In addition, Iraq declared that the missile was still under development - however, as of February 2003 63 missiles had already been deployed with the Iraqi armed forces.

- The Declaration admits that 131 Volga missile engines had been imported, in contravention of sanctions. However, according to UNMOVIC Iraq actually imported at least 380 engines.

- The Declaration claims that its UAVs and cruise missiles adhere to UN restrictions. However, recent inspections have revealed a type of unmanned drone that was not referred to in the Declaration, and its range easily exceeds the UN proscribed limit of 150kms. There has never been full Iraqi disclosure on any of its UAVs.

- The Declaration also fails to account property for work on aircraft fuel drop tanks that were converted to deliver CBW agent. The UN found modified aircraft fuel tanks at the Khan Bani Sa'ad Airfield in December 2002. These tanks were stated to have been part of an indigenously manufactured agricultural spray system that was said to have been produced by the Iraqi Air Force *(Unresolved Disarmament Issues, 6 March)*

- According to an Iraqi document that UNMOVIC obtained separately from the Declaration, "13,000 chemical bombs were dropped by the Iraqi Air Force between 1983 and 1988, while Iraq has declared that 19,500 bombs were consumed during this period. Thus, there is a discrepancy of 6,500 bombs. The amount of chemical agent in these bombs would be in the order of about 1,000 tonnes. In the absence of evidence to the contrary, we must assume that these quantities are now unaccounted for." *(Dr Blix, 27 January)*

Iraq shall provide UNMOVIC and the IAEA "immediate, unimpeded. unrestricted, and private access to all officials and other persons whom UNMOVIC or the IAEA wish to interview in the mode or location of UNMOVIC's or the IAEA's choice pursuant to any aspect of their mandates" (OP5)

Not met. At first, none of the Iraqi personnel requested for interview by UNMOVIC agreed to be interviewed in private. At a meeting in Baghdad on 19-20 January, the Iraqi side committed itself to "encourage" private interviews. However, it was not until 6-7 February (i.e. just before Dr Blix and Dr El-Baradei's last visit to Baghdad) that three people agreed to be interviewed in private. But these interviews were with personnel volunteered by the Iraqi authorities, not with Scientists requested by UNMOVIC.

On 28 February, a further two scientists were interviewed in private. As of 14 March, UNMOVIC had asked 41 people to be interviewed, but only 12 had agreed to UNMOVIC's terms. The remainder of the interviews could not be carried out because of unacceptable restrictions (e.g. insistence on the presence of official Iraqi minders, or that the interviews be tape-recorded).

It was not until 26 February that the IAEA carried out its first private interview; as of 14 March, IAEA had only been able to carry out 3 private interviews.

We have reason to believe that the Iraqi authorities have intimidated interviewees; that rooms have been bugged; and that some potential interviewees have been kept away from the inspectors by the Iraqi authorities.

- *UNMOVIC written report, 28 February.* "the reality is that, so far, no persons not nominated by the Iraqi side have been willing to be interviewed without a tape recorder running or an Iraqi witness present"

- *Dr El-Baradei, 7 March:* "When wo first began to request private, unoscorted interviews, the Iraqi interviewees insisted on taping the interviews and keeping the recorded tapes"

"UNMOVIC and the IAEA may at their discretion <u>conduct interviews inside or outside of Iraq,</u> may facilitate the travel of those interviewed and family members outside of Iraq, and that, at the sole discretion of UNMOVIC and the IAEA, such interviews may occur without the presence of observers
from the Iraqi Government" (OP5)

<u>Not met.</u> No interviews have taken placed outside Iraq.

There is evidence that Iraqi scientists have been intimidated into refusing interviews outside Iraq. They - and their families - have been threatened with execution if they deviate from the official line.

"UNMOVIC and the IAEA shall have the right to be <u>provided by Iraq the names of all personnel currently and formerly associated with Iraq's chemical, biological, nuclear, and ballistic missile programmes</u> and the associated research, development, and production facilities" (OP7)

<u>Not met.</u> *Dr Blix, 27 January.* "Some 400 names for all biological and chemical weapons programmes as well as their missile programmes were provided by the Iraqi side. This can be compared to over 3,500 names of people associated with those past weapons programmes that UNSCOM either interviewed in the 1990s or knew from documents and other sources".

During February, Iraq supplied some additional names. However, the information provided is still inadequate. For example, according to UNMOVIC's document on *Unresolved Disarmament Issues, 6 March,* Iraq provided a list of people who worked in the entire chemical weapons programme - but Iraq's 132 names contrast with UNMOVIC's records, which show that "over 325 people were involved in chemical weapons research" at <u>one establishment alone.</u>

"UNMOVIC and the IAEA shall have the <u>free and unrestricted use and</u> <u>landing</u> <u>of fixed- and rotary-winged aircraft,</u> including manned and unmanned reconnaissance vehicles" (OP7)

<u>**Partially met**</u> **- belatedly, and under pressure**. Iraq initially hindered UNMOVIC helicopter flights. Dr Blix, 27 January: "Iraq had insisted on sending helicopters of their own to accompany ours. This would have raised a safety problem." The matter was resolved when UNMOVIC agreed to take Iraqi escorts in UNMOVIC's own helicopters.

Iraq also obstructed U2 reconnaissance flights over Iraq, placing unacceptable pre-conditions on the flights. Almost three months after inspections began, just before Dr Blix presented a report on Iraqi co-operation to the Security Council, Iraq finally relented. The first U2 flight took place on 17 February.

"UNMOVIC and the IAEA shall have the right at their sole discretion verifiably to <u>remove. destroy. or render harmless all prohibited weapons,</u> <u>subsystems, components, records, materials, and other related items,</u> and the right to impound or close any facilities or equipment** for the production **thereof" (OP7)

<u>**Not yet met.**</u> UNMOVIC has determined that the Al-Samoud 2 missile programme, as well as rocket motor casting chambers at Al-Mamoun, are prohibited under SCR687. This assessment has been confirmed by a panel of independent experts, who concluded that the (light) Al-Samoud 2 was designed to fly just under 200kms. In the case of the casting chambers, this equipment was previously destroyed by UNSCOM as being part of a prohibited weapons programme - but was subsequently rebuilt by Iraq.

UNMOVIC gave Iraq a deadline of 1 March to begin the destruction of these prohibited systems (missiles plus associated components/infrastructure, and casting chamber). At first, Iraq said that the Iraqi authorities intended "to study" the demand. Then the Iraqi authorities said that they agreed "in principle" to the destruction of the missiles, "despite our belief that the decision to destroy was unjust... and the timing of this request seems to us to be one with political aims" (letter to Dr Blix from Dr Al-Saadi, 27 January).

Destruction began on 1 March, but Iraq has threatened that it may stop the destruction process at any time. As of 14 March, Iraq had destroyed:

- 65 missiles (Iraq has declared production of 76 missiles, but UNMOVIC estimate there are around 120 missiles)

- 42 warheads (out of 118)

- 5 engines (out of an estimated 380)

- 2 missile launchers (out of 9)

"Decides further that _Iraq shall not take or threaten hostile acts_ directed against any representative or personnel of the United Nations" (OP8)

Partially met. Inspections have largely been incident-free. However, UNMOVIC has noted some "friction" during inspections, and occasional harassment. On several occasions inspectors have been met with demonstrations. _Dr Blix, 27 January._ "Demonstrations and outbursts of this kind are unlikely to occur in Iraq without initiative or encouragement from the authorities."

On several occasions Iraqi authorities have claimed that inspectors were spying.

"Demands further that _Iraq cooperate immediately. unconditionally, and actively_ with UNMOVIC and the IAEA" (OP9).

Not met. The questions outstanding since UNSCOM was forced to withdraw in 1998 have still not been answered. Nor have those issues raised by the Amorim panel, a group of international experts convened under UN auspices to identify outstanding Iraqi disarmament issues. Although Iraq has provided some documents, it is not answering any substantive questions.

On 6 March, UNMOVIC released a paper on _Unresolved Disarmament_ Issues - _Iraq's Proscribed Weapons Programmes._ The paper is a 173 page-long catalogue of Iraqi intransigence since 1991, detailing

- Some 29 occasions when Iraq failed, despite repeated requests, to provide credible evidence to substantiate claims

- Some 17 separate instances when UNSCOM/UNMOVIC uncovered information that directly contradicted the official Iraqi account

- 128 actions Iraq should now take to help resolve the outstanding issues

Dr Blix, 14 January. "Although I can understand that it may not be easy for Iraq in all cases to provide the evidence needed, it is not the task of the inspectors to find it. Iraq itself must squarely tackle this task and avoid belittling the questions."

- *Dr Blix 27 January* "It is not enough to open doors. Inspection is not a game of 'catch as catch can'"

- *UNMOVIC written report, 28 February.* "During the period of time covered by the present report, Iraq could have made greater efforts to find any remaining proscribed items or provide credible evidence showing the absence of such items. The results in terms of disarmament have been very limited so far"

- *Dr Blix, 7 March.* "With such detailed information regarding those who took part in the unilateral destruction, surely there must also remain records regarding the quantities and other data concerning the various items destroyed"

- *Dr El-Baradei, 27 January.* "Iraq's co-operation with the IAEA should be full and active, as required by the relevant Security Council resolutions."

There are a number of examples of Iraqi gestures which have been a pretence of co-operation.

Of papers handed over by the Iraqis in early February:

- *Dr Blix:* "No new evidence was provided in the papers and no open issues were closed"

- *Dr El-Baradei:* "Iraq has provided documents on the concerns outstanding since 1998, but no new information was contained"

Of legislation on Weapons of Mass Destruction (WMD)

UNSCOM - and now UNMOVIC - requested that the Government of Iraq pass legislation prohibiting the manufacturing or importing of WMD and associated material. Draft legislation was provided. On 14 February - the day of Dr Blix's last update to the Security Council - Iraq announced that it had passed a Presidential Decree to this effect In fact, the decree is totally inadequate: its scope is very limited, and it does not even suggest any penalties for offenders.

- *UNMOVIC written report 28 February.* "The presidential decree, which was issued on 14 February and which prohibits private Iraqi citizens and mixed companies from engaging in work relating to weapons of mass destruction, standing alone, is not adequate to meet the United Nations requirements. UNMOVIC has enquired whether a comprehensive regulation is being prepared in line with several years of discussions between Iraq and UNSCOM/UNMOVIC"

Of Iraqi excavation of some R-400 bombs and bomb fragments

In February, Iraq notified UNMOVIC that it had uncovered some R-400 bombs (indigenously produced, filled with chemical or biological agent). However, Iraq's declarations on R-400 bombs have been inconsistent and contradictory, leaving UNMOVIC with little confidence in the numbers produced or types of agents filled". Photographic evidence contradicts Iraqi claims that all R-400A bombs (marked as filled with botulinum toxin and anthrax) were destroyed in July or August 2001. It is unlikely that the results of the ongoing Iraqi excavation will resolve this issue.

- "UNMOVIC cannot discount the possibility that some CW and BW filled R-400 bombs remain in Iraq" *(Unresolved Disarmament Issues, 6 March)*

Printed in the UK by The Stationery Office Limited
on behalf of the Controller of Her Majesty's Stationery Office
Id 171429   07/2004   019585   988359